EVOLUTION, CREATIONISM, AND THE BATTLE TO CONTROL AMERICA'S CLASSROOMS

Who should decide what children are taught in school? This question lies at the heart of the evolution–creation wars that have become a regular feature of the U.S. political landscape. Michael Berkman and Eric Plutzer show that, since the 1925 *Scopes* "monkey trial," many have argued that the people should decide by majority rule and through political institutions; others variously point to the federal courts, educational experts, or scientists as the ideal arbiters. Berkman and Plutzer illuminate who *really* controls the nation's classrooms. Based on their innovative survey of 926 high school biology teachers, they show that the real power often lies with individual educators who make critical decisions in their own classrooms. Broad teacher discretion sometimes leads to excellent instruction in evolution. But the authors also find evidence of strong creationist tendencies in America's public high schools and, more generally, a systematic undermining of science and the scientific method in many classrooms.

Michael Berkman is Professor of Political Science at the Pennsylvania State University, where he also serves as the director of undergraduate studies and director of the minor in business and the liberal arts. He is the author (with Eric Plutzer) of *Ten Thousand Democracies: Politics and Public Opinion in America's School Districts* (2005) and many articles appearing in such journals as the *American Political Science Review*, *American Journal of Political Science*, *Public Opinion Quarterly*, *Political Research Quarterly*, and *PLoS Biology*. He currently serves on the editorial board of the *American Journal of Education*.

Eric Plutzer is Professor of Political Science at the Pennsylvania State University, where he also serves as the academic director of the Survey Research Center. He has traveled widely, including as a Senior Fulbright Lecturer at the University of Malaya and as a guest scholar at Humboldt University and the Wissenschaftszentrum Berlin für Sozialforschung (WZB). He is the author (with Michael Berkman) of *Ten Thousand Democracies: Politics and Public Opinion in America's School Districts* (2005) and many articles appearing in such journals as the *American Political Science Review*, *American Sociological Review*, *American Journal of Political Science*, *Public Opinion Quarterly*, *Political Geography*, and the *Journal of Politics*. He currently serves on the editorial boards of *Politics and Gender*, *American Politics Research*, *Social Science Quarterly*, and the *American Journal of Education*.

Evolution, Creationism, and the Battle to Control America's Classrooms

Michael Berkman

The Pennsylvania State University

Eric Plutzer

The Pennsylvania State University

CAMBRIDGE UNIVERSITY PRESS
Cambridge, New York, Melbourne, Madrid, Cape Town, Singapore,
São Paulo, Delhi, Dubai, Tokyo, Mexico City

Cambridge University Press
32 Avenue of the Americas, New York, NY 10013-2473, USA

www.cambridge.org
Information on this title: www.cambridge.org/9780521148863

First published 2010

Printed in the United States of America

A catalog record for this publication is available from the British Library.

Library of Congress Cataloging in Publication data

Berkman, Michael B., 1960–
Evolution, creationism, and the battle to control America's classrooms /
Michael Berkman, Eric Plutzer.
   p. cm.
Includes bibliographical references and index.
ISBN 978-0-521-19046-6 (hardback)
1. Human evolution – Study and teaching (Primary) 2. Creationism – Study
and teaching (Primary) 3. Intelligent design (Teleology) – Study and
teaching (Primary) I. Plutzer, Eric. II. Title.
GN281.4.B45 2010
379.2'80973 – dc22   2010006776

ISBN 978-0-521-19046-6 Hardback
ISBN 978-0-521-14886-3 Paperback

CONTENTS

FIGURES

TABLES

ACKNOWLEDGMENTS

This book could not have been written without contributions from many institutions and individuals, and we are particularly grateful to four institutions that provided financial resources. Very early in the project, we received a small amount of "seed money" from the Research and Graduate Studies Office of Penn State's College of the Liberal Arts. This allowed us to do some preliminary research that laid the groundwork for Chapters 2 and 3. At roughly the same time, we used funding from the National Science Foundation to field our national survey of high school biology teachers. This was the very first coast-to-coast scientific sample survey of teachers that focused on the teaching of evolution, and we could not have fielded this study without the early financial support of the NSF. As we moved into the analysis and writing stages, we benefited enormously from grants from the Spencer Foundation and the John F. Templeton Foundation. These two grants helped extend Plutzer's sabbatical from one semester to an entire year, provided additional time for Berkman to devote to the project, and supported international travel that permitted the authors to collaborate in person.

These foundations, along with the College of the Liberal Arts, also helped to support several undergraduate and graduate research assistants. We are especially indebted to the efforts of the undergraduates, all of whom had to draw much more from their high school biology classes than they might have expected to as political science majors. These research assistants included Siobhan O'Connor, Edward Torres, Tausif Kahn, Kristen Tunney, Kristen Dennison, and Michelle Falvey. We were also able to support several graduate students who assisted in data management and statistical analysis: Nicholas Stark, Claudiu Tufis, Julianna Sandell Pacheco, and Christopher Ojeda.

We are especially indebted to the nation's biology teachers. We began the survey portion of the project by meeting with six science teachers from the State College Area School District who provided *pro bono* advice to us. They read the initial draft of our survey questionnaire and provided dozens of useful suggestions and insights – ultimately improving the project immeasurably. And of course we are grateful to the more than 900 teachers who took time to not only answer our survey, but also to add additional comments and materials that became an important part of our data set. We appreciate the efforts as well of Sally Crandall, Teresa Crisafulli, Patty Nordstrom, and Patricia Wamboldt of the Penn State Survey Research Center for their exceptional work in fielding the survey and their patience in responding to our never-ending series of queries and modifications.

Much of Chapters 2 and 3 are based on data that were originally collected by others and then made freely (and unconditionally) available to us. Many of these data sets were originally collected for polls published by the *New York Times*; the ABC, CBS, NBC, and Fox television networks; and magazines such as *Time* and *Newsweek*. These organizations graciously deposited their data in the Roper Center Archive, a wonderful resource for scholars whose collections of polls span more than six decades. The Roper Center provides an invaluable service by archiving, preserving, and distributing these polls to scholars and writers such as ourselves. We also want to thank David Urban and the staff at Virginia Commonwealth University for making their 2005 Life Sciences Survey data available. We thank Scott Keeter of the Pew Research Center for providing us with their question randomization files and, more generally, for making their studies available to scholars through their own archive. Brian Starks wrote the Stata code to allow our coding of religious denominations, and we appreciate that he made it available to us. Dan Meehan of the Geographic Information Analysis unit at PSU helped us produce the maps that are both accurate and informative.

The actual analysis and writing of the book took place over more than two years, but we made exceptional progress during the winter and spring of 2008–2009. During this time, Plutzer was a guest scholar in residence at the Wissenschaftszentrum Berlin für Sozialforschung

(Social Science Center Berlin) in the unit on social inequality, directed by Professor Jens Alber. Plutzer thanks Jens and the research scientists in the unit for providing a wonderfully stimulating environment in which to think, write, and discuss ideas. In addition to Jens, we are sure that Uli Kohler, Tom Cusack, Jan Paul Heisig, and Chiara Saraceno will all see that the book reflects improvements resulting from their helpful suggestions and constructive criticisms.

In addition to the WZB group, we have received helpful comments and suggestions from many of our colleagues. Lael Keiser, Chris Mooney, Paul Peterson, Mark Rom, and Charles Barrilleaux provided helpful comments on conference papers and invited lectures that became the basis of several chapters. Frank Baumgartner offered valuable comments at different stages of the book as did the American/Comparative working group at Penn State. Joyce Banaszak (well exceeding any reasonable expectation as Plutzer's mother-in-law) and Christopher Ojeda read the entire manuscript and provided helpful editorial suggestions. We also received comments from many participants at the Darwin symposium at the University of Cincinnati, in particular from Glenn Branch, Robert Pennock, and Stephen Mockabee. Special thanks go to George Bishop for organizing the symposium and his ongoing interest in our work.

We also give special thanks to our extended families. Our parents (and even our in-laws) not only cultivated within each of us a deep curiosity about science and the natural world, but also showed a keen interest in this particular book – offering frequent questions and encouragement. The natural curiosity shown by our children – Clara Plutzer, Isaac Plutzer, and Benjamin Berkman – continually inspired and motivated us. Eric thanks Lee Ann Banaszak in particular for her support during this project.

Last but not least, we thank Ed Parsons (formerly) of Cambridge University Press. Ed not only showed interest in this book when it was little more than an outline, but recruited three exceptional anonymous manuscript reviewers. Each of the reviewers was helpful and pushed us to improve the manuscript; however, we want to single out Reviewer #2, whose 12-page, single-spaced report went well beyond the call of duty. Any errors remaining after that review and the many suggestions we have received are truly our own.

Introduction

FOR THE LAST SEVERAL YEARS, we have been conducting research and writing about the teaching of evolution – and the teaching of creationism – in America's public schools. From time to time, we talk to biologists, paleontologists, and other scientists, and they inevitably tell us that they simply do not understand the United States today. They do not understand why so many ordinary citizens do not accept that evolution occurred, and they are shocked that three serious candidates for the presidency stated that they did not believe in evolution.

Scientists are at a loss to understand how so many educated Americans believe that creationism should be accorded "equal time" in science education. And they cannot comprehend why evolution occupies such a marginal place in the high school biology curriculum and why it continues to be controversial today. How is it possible that we are still in a "war" over evolution?

Regardless of your personal beliefs and opinions, it is useful to understand why scientists are so puzzled by the way things are today. And to do that, we need to take a scientist's perspective, which goes something like this.

When Darwin returned from his voyage on the *Beagle*, he speculated that natural selection could transform species and that currently living species and extinct species might share common ancestors. In 1837, he sketched the now famous "tree of life" in his notebook and wrote, in the upper margin, "I think."

For the next 22 years, Darwin investigated hundreds of kinds of evidence bearing on his initial hunch; this he reported 150 years ago in *The Origin of Species*. At the time, many scientists were skeptical – the ideas were new, after all. Yet, the evidence was so voluminous and carefully documented that the notion of common ancestry would become quickly and widely accepted. As for the mechanism Darwin proposed – natural selection – *The Origin* fell short of absolute proof, and scientists debated this idea for many decades.

But over the next 60 years, scientists were won over by an accumulation of evidence, all of which pointed to the same basic conclusions – that the earth was extremely old (far older than was understood in Darwin's day), that the progression of fossils in the geological record suggested descent with modification, and that these fossils and the findings from comparative anatomy suggested that species living in the 1920s – apes and humans, for example – had common ancestors.

Indeed, by the 1920s, skepticism concerning the fact of common ancestry was essentially absent from the scientific community. The American Association for the Advancement of Science passed a resolution in 1922 trying to set the record straight. Amazingly, this reads as if it could have been issued by the same organization today – nearly 90 years later.

1. The Council of the Association affirms that, so far as the scientific evidences of evolution of plants and animals and man are concerned, there is no ground whatever for the assertion that these evidences constitute a "mere guess." No scientific generalization is more strongly supported by thoroughly tested evidences than is that of organic evolution.
2. The Council of the Association affirms that the evidence in favor of the evolution of man are sufficient to convince every scientist of note in the world, and that these evidences are increasing in number and importance every year (Council of the American Association for the Advancement of Science, December 26, 1922).

By 1925, in testimony to those attending the *Scopes* "monkey trial" on July 15, 1925, biologist Maynard Metcalf reported, "I am somewhat acquainted personally with nearly all the zoologists in America . . . Of all these hundreds of men, not one fails to believe as a matter of course, in view of the evidence, that evolution has occurred" (quoted in Gieryn, Bevins, and Zehr 1985, 397; see also Moore 2002a, 38, 377).

When Metcalf testified, Mendel's model of genetic inheritance was universally accepted and widely applied. By the 1940s, findings from genetics, ecology, and paleontology were independently confirming the same hypotheses.

In the 1960s, the National Science Foundation (NSF) led an effort to rewrite high school biology textbooks so that they reflected the scientific consensus at the time. The NSF-sponsored textbooks all forthrightly argued that evolution was a fact and that natural selection and descent with modification were essential to understand modern biology. By 1963, the evolution war had seemingly been won.

Today, scientists ask this: How is it, then, 150 years after *The Origin of Species*, 100 years after the birth of modern genetics, and 50 years after scientists made a major effort to rework textbooks to their liking, that teaching evolution in public schools remains a controversial subject?

The most obvious way to answer this question is to view evolution controversies as rooted in a still simmering *battle of ideas*, one that is inextricably linked to conservative Protestant theology, to an ongoing tension between traditionalism and modernity, and even between science and religion generally. We agree, and we have something to contribute to this particular explanation. But a disagreement about ideas is not sufficient to account for the amazing durability of this conflict on the American scene. A more complete explanation for why the conflict continues to exist must account for *politics*. And not just any kind of politics, but a politics concerning the very meaning of democracy in America. This is why we believe that two political scientists can contribute something to our understanding of the history of the evolution conflict and help us see more clearly the dimensions of the conflict today.

As political scientists, we highlight a key normative question: Who *should* govern the nation's public schools and determine what students should learn? Much of the debate concerning evolution and creationism in the United States, we will show, is fundamentally a debate about who should decide what students are taught: Should decisions be made by state officials representing voters and taxpayers? By federal courts looking out for individuals' civil liberties? By scientists who claim unique expertise concerning the content and nature of science? By educational policy makers and bureaucrats with expertise in pedagogy, assessment, and effectiveness? Or should the final decision lie with individual classroom teachers, guided by their training, experience, personal values, and strong professional norms?

In light of this normative question of who should govern our nation's classrooms, we explore two broad empirical questions:

- How is education policy made in each of the fifty states?
- How is policy actually implemented in each of the thousands of individual classrooms throughout the nation?

To answer these questions, we rely on the best practices of political science, which implies a disinterested search for evidence-based answers to our questions. Disinterested, in this sense, does not mean that we do not care about our findings; quite the contrary. We each have school-age children and care deeply about science education in our nation's public schools. But we have done our best to follow the evidence and report it objectively, even when that evidence has proven to be disturbing or has not confirmed our initial hypotheses. We have sought multiple and independent sources of evidence whenever possible, reporting our conclusions with confidence only when they converge. For example, in Chapter 3 we use polling data from the conservative Fox News, from the liberal People for the American Way, and from several university-based surveys that all lead to the same conclusion. The grants that supported much of our research were awarded after rigorous peer review, and some of the preliminary research findings also passed the muster of peer review before being published in scientific journals. Even at the risk of seeming too technical at times (readers can skip some of this material, of course), we have reported our methods and procedures in sufficient detail so that other researchers can independently replicate and verify our findings. And we provide our original data freely to all scholars who request it. Thus, we hope that all readers will have confidence in our empirical conclusions even though they may not share our political values. From time to time, we will express our opinions. But readers should have no difficulty in noting where the scientific evidence ends and our own values begin.

1 Who Should Decide What Children Are Taught?

Teachers in public schools must teach what the taxpayers desire taught.

William Jennings Bryan (1924)[1]

The people have spoken on this subject and have shown by an overwhelming vote that they do not want their children taught the theory of evolution in the public schools.

Bruce Bennett, prosecutor in *Epperson v. Arkansas* (1968). Susan Epperson sought to teach evolution in Little Rock in violation of Arkansas state law.

The people of Louisiana . . . are quite entitled . . . to have whatever scientific evidence there may be against evolution presented in their schools . . .

Antonin Scalia in dissent in *Edwards v. Aguillard* (1987). Don Aguillard was a high school teacher who challenged a Louisiana law that required the teaching of Creation Science along with evolution.

To refer the students to "*Of Pandas and People*" as if it is a scientific resource breaches my ethical obligation to provide them with scientific knowledge that is supported by recognized scientific proof or theory.

High school science teachers in Dover, PA, in response to a district requirement that they read a statement promoting an Intelligent Design textbook as an alternative to Evolution (2005).

JOHN THOMAS SCOPES, a twenty-four-year-old football coach and general science teacher in Dayton, Tennessee, is the often

---

[1] Sources of epigraphs: Bryan (1924, 154). Bennett quoted in Moore (2002a, 52–53). Teachers' statement cited in *Kitzmiller v. Dover* (2005, 127).

forgotten figure in the 1925 *Scopes* "monkey trial," dominated as it was by the expansive personalities of William Jennings Bryan, Clarence Darrow, and H. L. Mencken.[2] Recruited by local business-men interested in generating attention for Dayton, Scopes acknowl-edged using a text – one used by most science teachers in Tennessee – that taught human evolution in contradiction to the biblical account in Genesis, a violation of Tennessee's recently passed Butler Act.[3] Scopes soon found himself in the middle of one of the most closely watched trials in U.S. history. Radio station WGN of Chicago broad-cast the trial live each day, and all of the nation's major newspapers sent reporters to Dayton, with many printing verbatim transcripts of the trial. Syndicated columnist H. L. Mencken made daily reports that were published in scores of newspapers.

Scopes' jury trial in Dayton and his appeal to the Tennessee Supreme Court were dominated by three different debates: one sub-stantive, one procedural, and one concerning the autonomy of teach-ers in their classrooms. The substantive debate is one familiar to Americans today: How compelling is the scientific evidence for a very old earth, evolution in general, and the evolution of human beings in particular? In addition, if the evidence for evolution were strong, would this contradict the teachings of the Bible? These questions came to the fore when William Jennings Bryan took the stand for four hours and debated questions of biblical interpretation and human origins with defense attorney Clarence Darrow.

The procedural theme in *Scopes* concerned democracy: Should ordi-nary citizens – acting through their elected representatives – be able to set curricular policies for public schools? Scopes' legal team, sup-ported by funds from the American Civil Liberties Union (ACLU), argued that Tennessee's Butler Act was unconstitutional. Their tactics at the trial were intended to make it possible to appeal the case to the U.S. Supreme Court in the hope that the Court would invalidate the

---

[2] As Scopes himself described it, "So I sat speechless, a ringside observer at my own trial, until the end of the circus" (quoted in Larson 1997, 173).

[3] The Butler Act (officially titled *An Act Prohibiting the Teaching of Evolution in all the Universities, Normals and all other public schools of Tennessee*) read that it was in violation of the law to "teach any theory that denies the story of the Divine Cre-ation of man as taught in the Bible, and to teach instead that man is descended from a lower order of animals." (See the full text of the Act at http://www.law.umkc. edu/faculty/projects/ftrials/scopes/tennstat.htm; last accessed July 1, 2009).

democratically enacted law. In opposition, the prosecution insisted that the Tennessee legislature, acting on behalf of the state's citizens, had the right to dictate what teachers – as public employees – taught to their students.

The final theme concerns the academic freedom of public school teachers. Academic freedom is a right we often associate with university professors, but it was championed by proponents of teaching evolution early in the twentieth century. Indeed, in describing the strategy of the *Scopes* trial's defense teams, the *New York Times* reported, "State Will Denounce Scientific Theory, Teacher Will Defend Academic Freedom."[4] Somewhat ironically, the principle of academic freedom is currently advocated by supporters of creationism and intelligent design.

The Criminal Court of Rhea County ignored the substantive questions. Indeed, Judge John Raulston excluded expert testimony from scientists and clergy that might have addressed these questions. Although he permitted Bryan to take the stand as an expert on the Bible, for the majority of the trial, his procedural rulings steered the case narrowly toward the question of academic freedom and the facts of the case: Do teachers have the freedom to ignore a state prohibition of what can be taught, and if not, did Scopes really teach evolution? Upon appeal, the Supreme Court of Tennessee ignored the substantive debate entirely and instead focused on questions of democratic practice. Writing for the majority, Chief Justice Grafton Green wrote:

> If the legislature thinks that, by reason of popular prejudice, the cause of education and the study of Science generally, will be promoted by forbidding the teaching of evolution in the schools of the State, we can think of no grounds to justify the court's interference.[5]

As to Scopes himself, the Tennessee Supreme Court concluded that, as a public employee, it was his responsibility to teach whatever the state said he should teach.

The *Scopes* monkey trial retains its relevance because these same three themes characterize the evolution wars today. The substantive debate concerning human origins, evolutionary biology, and

---

[4] "Evolution Trial Raises Two Sharp Issues." *New York Times*, May 31, 1925, XX4.
[5] Quoted in Moore (2002a, 292).

alternative explanations has been subject to an enormous amount of scholarly writing. We will have quite a bit to say about this, particularly from the perspective of U.S. public opinion, state curricular policies, and teachers' approaches to human origins in the classroom. However, this book is also concerned with who decides in a democracy. What is the proper role of *the people* and their elected representatives, the courts, and scientific and educational experts? Most especially, what is the role of teachers who, like John Thomas Scopes, are asked to implement public policy every day in their classrooms and can sometimes find that their classrooms have become ground zero in the evolution wars?

SCHOOL GOVERNANCE AND DEMOCRACY IN THE UNITED STATES

School governance in the United States is established under strong principles of local control and democratic responsiveness. Public school districts, as we termed them in an earlier work, are America's *Ten Thousand Democracies* (Berkman and Plutzer 2005). Other scholars have argued that the expression of America's "democratic wish" is often projected most emphatically on the nation's public schools (Iannaccone and Lutz 1995; McDermott 1999, 13; Wong 1995, 24). The argument put forward in this chapter's epigraphs by William Jennings Bryan and Justice Antonin Scalia is a compelling one that is deeply rooted in American political culture: In a democratic system, *the people* should decide what shall be taught in publicly funded schools. And polls have consistently shown that *the people* have been and remain firmly in favor of teaching alternatives to evolution and perhaps excluding evolution from the classroom altogether (Plutzer and Berkman 2008).

It is no accident that the most visible anti-evolutionist in the early twentieth century was William Jennings Bryan. A three-time Democratic nominee for President, Bryan is perhaps best known today as the prominent and flamboyant prosecutor in the 1925 "Monkey Trial." Bryan's portrayal by two-time Oscar winner Fredric March in the Hollywood film *Inherit the Wind* has fixed in many people's minds the image of Bryan as a fundamentalist bigot. Yet, the real Bryan was a much more complex figure than his depiction on stage and screen. Although he did believe that Darwinism contradicted the biblical account of creation and that the teaching of evolution undermined

Christian faith and gave rise to atheism, he did not, like many of his supporters, endorse a literal reading of Genesis or believe in a "young earth" (Ginger 1958; Numbers 1992).

At the same time, throughout his career, Bryan was a passionate supporter of majoritarian democracy who placed considerable faith in the wisdom of the mass of ordinary citizens. As Walter Lippmann described him, Bryan

> had always argued that a majority had the right to decide. He had insisted on their right to decide war and peace, on their right to regulate morals, on their right to make and unmake laws and lawmakers and executives and judges. He had fought to extend the suffrage so that the largest possible majority might help decide; he had fought for the direct election of senators, for the initiative and referendum and direct primary, and for every other device that would permit the people to rule (Lippmann 1927, 46).

Knowing that public opinion was on his side, Bryan argued – a year before the *Scopes* trial – that taxpayers should determine whether or not to teach evolution. Indeed, the entire *Scopes* trial can be seen as a vindication of majoritarian democracy. The Butler Bill that banned the teaching of human evolution was passed by many ambivalent legislators who were understandably concerned that a vote against the bill would have electoral consequences; a less than enthusiastic Governor Austin Peay similarly felt pressured into being a supporter (Ginger 1958; Larson 1989). Judge John T. Raulston, who presided over the original *Scopes* trial, consistently made procedural rulings that favored the prosecution, and it is reasonable to infer that his conduct in the case was intended to aid his chances for re-election in the following year.[6]

This notion of popular sovereignty is a core question for political philosophers and political scientists. Democratic theorists disagree about many particulars but agree that "democracy" must involve processes that permit the results of governance to reflect (sometimes only roughly) the will of ordinary citizens. The will of citizens would, ideally, result from considerable deliberation (e.g., Barber 1984; Dryzek 1990; Habermas 1994) in an environment in which citizens have

---

[6] In many respects, Raulston behaved like a judge running for re-election – which he was. For example, Raulston frequently interrupted or delayed the trial to afford photo opportunities with the visiting press (Ginger 1958).

access to many sources of information and where they feel free to express their opinions, whatever these might be (Dahl 1989). Ordinary citizens would know the various policy options and have the capacity to understand the arguments made on behalf of competing proposals. Citizens would also act on behalf of the general good and avoid violating the fundamental rights of others, rather than acting only on the basis of their personal or parochial interests. And ideally, the public would have the means to communicate their views to government officials and to remain active participants in all stages of the policy-making process. We will return to some of these subtleties in Chapter 2, where we try to understand the beliefs and policy preferences of ordinary American citizens. But there can be no doubt that the majoritarian principal is a compelling one that lies at the heart of any definition of democracy.

ALTERNATIVES TO MAJORITARIAN DEMOCRACY

The participatory ideal stands in contrast to the arguments of Plato who believed that rule by benevolent *guardians* was the best form of governance. In Plato's ideal state, guardians would be interested only in the well being of the *polis*, and they would be trained in the arts of governance. In the contemporary United States, the notion of rule by guardians, philosopher kings, or any other benevolent ruler is an alien concept in principal. And yet guardianship, or what Dahl (1989) has labeled *quasi-guardianship*, occurs in a number of guises. We will consider three different forms of quasi-guardianship – each with its own argument against the majoritarian principal and each providing its own answer to who should decide what students learn.

The first argument is that the protection of civil liberties must always trump the majority. Today, state and local educational policies that infringe on freedom of speech, freedom of religion, or rights of due process will be voided by U.S. Courts even if they represent the will of the majority. Anti-evolutionism is firmly rooted in American Protestant fundamentalism and developed into a potent political force from this theological and organizational base. And alternatives to evolution, whether termed creationism, creation-science, or intelligent design, are themselves rooted in the Genesis creation story. Federal courts have therefore consistently held that laws and policies about evolution and its alternatives – even if democratically reached by school boards or state legislatures – often violate constitutionally guaranteed rights, in particular First Amendment protection against the government establishment of religion.

A second form of guardianship is the delegation of technical policy making to experts. Science is complex and often eludes lay understanding. For some public policies, there is a compelling case for giving experts substantial powers: Should a particular prescription drug be approved for the market? What is the best way to clean up a toxic waste site? To deter nuclear proliferation? Walter Lippmann's analysis of the *Scopes* trial led him to take an extreme position in this regard:

> The votes of the majority [should] have no intrinsic bearing on the conduct of a school . . . Guidance for a school can only come from educators, and the question of what shall be taught as biology can be determined only by biologists. The votes of a majority do not settle anything here and they are entitled to no respect whatsoever (1927, 59).

For technical issues generally, where ordinary citizens have little chance of studying and learning the specialized and scientific underpinnings of each policy option, we have institutionalized quasi-guardianship in the form of various commissions, regulatory agencies, and bureaucracies. Originally intended to use technical expertise to identify the best *means* to implement goals that have been determined through democratic processes, most expert bodies formulate goals for the community as well (Barber 1984; Dahl 1985, 1989; DeLeon 1997; Douglas 2005; Fischer 1993).

The justification for this form of quasi-guardianship lies in the limited capacity of ordinary citizens to make informed choices. The evidence in favor of evolution may be partially understood by lay citizens who visit museums and watch documentaries on television. But scientists can point to thousands of published scientific papers whose understanding may require knowledge of radio-isotope dating, fish morphology, or the mathematical basis for inferring rates of genetic changes in mitochondrial DNA. Scientists argue that the validity of these methods can only be established by peer review, a process in which scientists critically assess the lab procedures, field work, and inferences of their scientific peers.

According to this view, therefore, only the scientific community can identify weakness or "gaps" in evolutionary theory, or whether, for example, creation science or intelligent design is science at all (Gieryn, Bevins, and Zehr 1985). Neither the public nor its elected representatives should, from this perspective, be permitted to make policies concerning equal treatment of alternatives to evolutionary theory or draft disclaimers of the type that led to *Kitzmiller v. Dover*. In curricular policy making, generally, one may argue that it makes sense for *the people* to cede decision-making power to experts in pedagogy and experts in a particular subject matter. Further, some suggest that elected bodies stay out of these decisions entirely. In reaction to recent debates in Texas concerning whether official policy would urge teachers to emphasize strengths and weaknesses in evolutionary theory, an editorial in the *New York Times* ("Texas Two Step" 2009) argued that "scientifically illiterate boards of education should leave the curriculum to educators and scientists who know what constitutes a sound education."

Thus, with respect to evolution, a second argument against popular sovereignty is that expertise should replace public preferences and the political process whenever policies involve highly technical arguments. Edward Larson tells the story of legal controversies over evolution in terms of this tension between majoritarianism and expertise, concluding that litigants use the legal system "to redress the relationship of science and society" (2003, 4). This tension may be more salient with evolution than other technical issues because many of the findings of evolutionary biology and paleontology clash with deeply held religious beliefs, beliefs that often drive majoritarian outcomes.

The third argument, expressed at the beginning of this chapter by the science teachers in Dover, Pennsylvania, is that educators are professionals and, as such, are entitled to exercise their professional judgment in conducting their classes. Like other public employees, teachers are selected to carry out responsibilities "in the interests of all the people" (Mosher 1982, 5). Their judgments are expected to be motivated by the best interests of the students and guided by their subject knowledge, their pedagogical expertise, and the strong norms of conduct typical of the profession. This argument suggests that high school teachers ought to enjoy a substantial degree of *academic freedom*, an argument accepted as legitimate by Arkansas's Chancery Court in its opinion in *Epperson v. Arkansas*.[7]

For advocates of academic freedom, the public may properly determine whether excellent science education is a priority, and their elected representatives may properly act to set the level of resources that schools receive for science education. Neither *the people* nor the government, however, should micromanage individual classrooms. Instead, teachers should be given wide latitude to implement public policy. More broadly, advocates of academic freedom argue that delegating substantial discretion to teachers and other professionals is not inconsistent with democracy (e.g., Dahl 1989; Mosher 1982). Interestingly, the academic freedom argument – long associated with teachers defying anti-evolution legislation – is now being voiced by those who object to teachers being sanctioned for endorsing creationism or intelligent design in their science classes.

These three different arguments have one thing in common: Federal judges, scientists, education policy makers, and teachers have all argued that crucial decisions about what students should learn should be *left to them* to decide. And they argue further that, in making those decisions, they need not give consideration to public opinion. Thus, there are arguments both for and against majoritarian democracy as the ideal method for setting curricular policy in the United States, and these arguments have been made explicitly and continuously during the ninety years of evolution–creation battles in the United States. As we will see in the pages to follow, *who actually does decide* has important implications for what students are taught in the classroom.

THE EVOLUTION CONFLICT TODAY AND HOW WE GOT HERE

The controversy over evolution in the classroom has been a hot war during the opening decade of the twenty-first century. Conflicts at the level of state government in Kansas and Florida were front page

---

[7] The U.S. Supreme Court would invalidate the law not on concerns about academic freedom but based on violation of the Establishment Clause; see *Epperson v. Arkansas* (1968).

stories in newspapers throughout the nation. *Time* magazine made evolution politics its cover story on August 15, 2005. A trial concerning the teaching of intelligent design as science in the small town of Dover, Pennsylvania attracted national and international attention and was the subject of a documentary in the Public Broadcasting Service's *NOVA* science series. Candidates for nearly every office in the nation, including the presidency, are asked where they stand on evolution.

Larson reports that, after the critical pro-evolution ruling in *Aguillard* (1987) "squashed efforts to introduce" creationism into public schools, "biblical creationists turned inward to entrench their views within America's vibrant Christian subculture" (Larson 2003, 190). This allowed them to consolidate and be prepared for more active political involvement today. Activists on both sides have substantially stepped up their activities in the last decade or so. Among young earth creationists, the opening of the Creation Museum in Kentucky and the launch of the syndicated television show *Creation Hour* are just the most recent efforts to widely promote "creation science"[8] and criticize evolutionary biology. The Institute for Creation Research makes educational materials widely available to those who are sympathetic, and books about intelligent design have sold well. The nationwide release of the anti-evolution film *Expelled* in 2008 is only the most widely publicized of many recent efforts.

At the same time, leading scientific organizations have redoubled their efforts to both influence public opinion and support educators. The National Academy of Sciences (NAS) issued a press release entitled "Scientific Evidence Supporting Evolution Continues to Grow." The release announced publication of

---

[8] *Creation science* is an effort to develop scientific explanations of natural phenomena, like fossils, that is consistent with the Old Testament accounts of creation. According to Eugenie Scott (2009), creation science was "born" with the publication of Henry M. Morris and John Whitcomb Jr.'s *The Genesis Flood*, which argues that the "earth's geological features could be explained by catastrophic events described in the Bible, especially Noah's Flood. But rather than merely positing theological reasons for believing this, Whitcomb and Morris claimed that scientific theory and evidence supported these ideas" (Scott 2009, 373). Creation science comes in two forms: in *biblical creation science*, evidence from both science and the Bible are used, whereas the *scientific creationism* proposed by some to be taught in schools uses only scientific evidence. Whereas early versions of creation science focused on fossils and the geological record, the newer *intelligent design* has focused on biology and biochemistry.

Science, Evolution, and Creationism, a book designed to give the public a comprehensive and up-to-date picture of the current scientific understanding of evolution and its importance in the science classroom. Recent advances in science and medicine, along with an abundance of observations and experiments over the past 150 years, have reinforced evolution's role as the central organizing principle of modern biology (National Academy of Sciences 2008b).

This is just one of many publications by the NAS (e.g., 1998, 1999, 2008a) that supports the teaching of evolution and complements efforts by the National Research Council (1996), American Association for the Advancement of Science (1993), and educational groups such as the National Science Teachers Association (2003). In short, efforts of public persuasion have increased dramatically in the last fifteen years; they have come from many different sources and represent a wide range of positions in the debate.

How did we get from the trial of John Thomas Scopes to the present set of controversies? The history of the evolution wars in the United States has been told many times, from many perspectives. The intellectual progression of anti-evolutionism has been examined from the perspective of the history of ideas by Michael Ruse (2005) and from the perspective of the most influential creationist personalities by Ronald Numbers (1992, 2006). Michael Lienesch's (2007) excellent book tells the same story by viewing anti-evolutionism as a modern social movement (a perspective also adopted by Eve and Harrold, 1991). Randy Moore has assembled a terrific documentary history, *Evolution in the Courtroom* (2002a), to tell the story from the legal perspective, and Edward Larson's (1989, 1997, 2003) incisive analyses of the major legal battles show the importance of politics and public opinion on legislators, science, and the courts. But, for this book, we have a particular purpose – we want the readers to understand enough of the historical background so that they can make sense of the current state of evolution politics. This leads us to focus on several key historical events and legal cases that have had the effect of narrowing the political arena for today's activists on both sides and that have implications for teachers who often find themselves caught in the crossfire. For it is in focusing on teachers, on their experiences and perspective, on their unique position in carrying out policy directions from the state as well as their local board and community, and in our extensive treatment of public opinion that we bring an original perspective to the scholarship of the evolution–creation wars. Here, then, are some highlights that help to explain the legal, political, and cultural aspects of the conflict as we experience it today.

Tennessee v. Scopes and the First Wave of the Anti-evolution Movement

Although Scopes' one-hundred-dollar fine would not stand up to appeal, the Butler Act was affirmed by the Tennessee Supreme Court and the case never made it to the U.S. Supreme Court. As it turned out, the Butler Act was the leading edge of a wave of anti-evolution activity that would have a dramatic impact on how biology was taught throughout the nation. Throughout the 1920s, anti-evolution legislation was introduced in many states; anti-evolution bills of different sorts became law not only in Tennessee but Arkansas, Louisiana, Mississippi, and Oklahoma as well (Lienesch 2007, 115). After the trial, "antievolution activity would not only continue but also come to a climax" (Lienesch 2007, 171).

Even though the passage of laws banning evolution was restricted to southern states, the introduction of anti-evolution legislation and mobilization of anti-evolution groups was a national phenomenon. William Jennings Bryan and others in the anti-evolution movement spoke at hundreds of venues during the 1920s in the north as well as the south, in cities as well as the countryside, on college campuses as well as in churches. Individual events at Chicago's Moody Church and New York's Carnegie Hall and Hippodrome each attracted several thousand participants (Lienesch 2007). By the late 1920s, the anti-evolution movement was mobilized, motivated, and visible throughout the nation.

With the onset of the Great Depression, legal activity by both sides slowed considerably to what Larson calls a "thirty-year truce" (1989, 81). But the creationist efforts of the 1920s produced a long-lasting success during this period. Evolution – and not just human evolution as specified in Tennessee's Butler Act – disappeared from American science textbooks (Larson 1985; Skoog 1979). The most widely used high school biology text, *A Civic Biology*, was changed in response to creationist objections; by 1927, the word "evolution" was even eliminated from the renamed *New Civic Biology*. As the early creationist George McCready Price observed in 1929, "Virtually all textbooks on the market have been revised to meet the needs of fundamentalists."[9]

The Cold War and the Re-awakening of Anti-evolutionism

With evolution absent from textbooks, public schools would not be a major venue of the evolution–creation wars again until the Cold War, when the Soviet Union's successful launch of its Sputnik satellite awakened many Americans to the need for better science education. One consequence of Sputnik was a 1958 National Science Foundation-sponsored review of the American biology curriculum. This led to the distribution of new teaching materials and the 1961 publication of new textbooks written by the nation's leading scientists under the auspices of the Biological Science Curriculum Study (BSCS). The three BSCS textbooks were widely adopted and quickly captured half the textbook market (Larson 2003).

The new BSCS textbooks gave evolution a prominent place in the biology curriculum and re-ignited controversy in two ways. First, conservative Christian parents and leaders reacted to the introduction of evolution in their local public schools. As Lienesch concludes, "almost as soon as the BSCS curriculum appeared in the schools, parents began to protest" (2007, 206). Anti-evolution sentiment had lain dormant through the Depression, World War II, and the Korean Conflict. But it re-emerged rapidly as parents objected to their children being exposed to ideas that, they argued, were offensive to and undermined their faith. Elected and appointed officials in many states reacted to the textbooks by canceling orders, requesting modification of content, and pasting "evolution is simply a *theory*" disclaimers to the textbooks (Lienesch 2007; Nelkin 1982; Skoog 1979).

This second wave of the evolution controversy might have ended much like the first wave in the 1920s – with acquiescence to the anti-evolution movement[10] – had teachers not entered the fray. The

---

[9] Quoted in Moore (2002a, 792).
[10] Although BSCS author and biologist John Moore contended that BSCS "carried sufficient clout to insist that evolution be included in its texts even though sales would suffer"

widespread adoption of the new textbooks provided teachers with a rationale and resource for teaching evolution and natural selection; advances in evolutionary biology and the support of the new textbooks by the scientific establishment gave them confidence to speak out. These texts were welcomed by science teachers throughout the nation. Most notably, biology teachers in Little Rock, Arkansas recommended the use of a BSCS textbook, and the administration of Little Rock's Central High School adopted the text for the 1965–1966 school year.

Susan Epperson was then a second year teacher of tenth grade biology. Holding a master's degree in zoology, she welcomed a textbook with a chapter devoted to evolution. However, as Supreme Court Justice Abe Fortas would later describe it, Epperson faced a "dilemma because she was supposed to use the new textbook for classroom instruction, and presumably to teach the statutorily condemned chapter; but to do so would be a criminal offense, and subject her to dismissal" (*Epperson v. Arkansas* 1968, 100). This is because a 1928 Arkansas law remained in force that made it illegal for any teacher at a public school or university to teach that humans "descended or ascended from a lower order of animals."

Epperson was victorious in Arkansas's Chancery Court, which held that the law violated the First Amendment because it "tends to hinder the quest for knowledge, restrict the freedom to learn, and restrain the freedom to teach" (quoted in *Epperson v. Arkansas*, 100). This opinion is notable because it legitimizes the notion of *academic freedom* as a factor that may outweigh majoritarian democracy in the setting of educational policy. The Arkansas State Supreme Court rejected this argument upon appeal. Banning evolution, the court ruled, "is a valid exercise of the state's power to specify the curriculum in its public schools" (quoted in *Epperson v. Arkansas*, 1968, fn. 7). The majoritarian position is especially compelling in this case because, unlike other anti-evolution statutes, the law in Arkansas was passed by the initiative – a law proposed by citizens and subject to approval by a majority of voters in a general election. The Arkansas anti-evolution statute was approved by 63% of voters (Gray 1979).

(quoted in Larson 2003, 96), the second and third editions of these textbooks retreated from the bold endorsement of evolution present in the first editions (Lienesch 2007, 206; Skoog 1979).

U.S. Federal Courts and the Narrowing of the Democratic Space

Epperson appealed her setback to the U.S. Supreme Court, which voted 9–0 in her favor. In the majority opinion, the Court ignored the academic freedom argument but instead focused on the First Amendment's establishment clause. Writing for the majority, Abe Fortas noted, "there can be no doubt that Arkansas has sought to prevent its teachers from discussing the theory of evolution because it is contrary to the belief of some that the Book of Genesis must be the exclusive source of doctrine as to the origin of man" (*Epperson v. Arkansas* 1968, 107). In effect, the Court said that state governments are free to determine their science curricula and select their own textbooks, as long as they do not favor a particular religious viewpoint when they do so. Further, the majority concluded that efforts to ban evolution entirely necessarily stemmed from just such a particular religious viewpoint. This was a major defeat for those opposed to evolution in the public schools. Just as evolution was spreading through the adoption of new textbooks, the Supreme Court invalidated laws that would ban evolution entirely.

As is typical of many such judicial opinions, the result was new legislative activity. Anti-evolution forces sought to develop laws and policies that reflected their values but could also pass constitutional muster. California revised its curriculum standards to include mention of "several theories" to explain origins of life, and Texas mandated that all texts used in the state must identify evolution "as only a theory" (Larson 2003, 128–129). Much of the debate became focused on "equal time" proposals. These policies – sometimes introduced as bills and sometimes as policy rules made by state boards of education – essentially said that, if teachers covered evolutionary biology, they must also teach alternatives. Knowing that explicitly religious alternatives would be impermissible, some bills specifically outlawed religious perspectives. Arkansas's 1981 legislation, known as Bill 590, included Section 2 for the purpose of inoculating the law from First Amendment challenges:

> BE IT ENACTED BY THE GENERAL ASSEMBLY OF THE STATE OF ARKANSAS:
> SECTION 1. Requirement for Balanced Treatment. Public schools within this State shall give balanced treatment to creation-science

and to evolution-science. Balanced treatment to these two models shall be given in classroom lectures taken as a whole for each course, in textbook materials taken as a whole for each course, in library materials taken as a whole for the sciences and taken as a whole for the humanities, and in other educational programs in public schools, to the extent that such lectures, textbooks, library materials, or educational programs deal in any way with the subject of the origin of man, life, the earth, or the universe.

SECTION 2. Prohibition against Religious Instruction. Treatment of either evolution-science or creation-science shall be limited to scientific evidences for each model and inferences from those scientific evidences, and must not include any religious instruction or references to religious writings.

This strategy was wholly ineffective. The Arkansas statute was declared unconstitutional by Federal District Court Judge William Overton in *McLean v. Arkansas* (1982). Overton concluded that, despite the strong wording of Section 2, the law "was simply and purely an effort to introduce the biblical version of creation into the public school curricula" (*McLean v. Arkansas*, 1982, 1264).

Although federal district courts have jurisdiction only for their small region of the country (typically a state or part of a state), this invalidation of balanced treatment laws would be extended to the entire nation when the Supreme Court examined a Louisiana law that mandated equal time for "creation science" if evolution were to be taught in public schools. Again, it was a young science teacher – Don Aguillard – who challenged the constitutionality of the law. Although Justice Antonin Scalia and Chief Justice Rehnquist disagreed, the Court's majority concluded that Louisiana's equal treatment law had a religious purpose, rendering it unconstitutional.

The cumulative impact of the *Epperson* and *Aguillard* cases was to eliminate from consideration a wide range of public policies that might be favored by the majority of citizens in most states. State governments – their legislatures, state boards of education, textbook commissions, and local school boards – could not endorse the biblical story of creation, could not endorse "creation science," and could not ban evolution entirely.

It was in this legal environment that the perspective of "intelligent design" received considerable attention. Contemporary intelligent design essentially is based on two key arguments (see, e.g., Behe 1998; Behe, Dembski, and Meyer 2000). First, it appeals to common sense – building on language used by many evolutionary biologists, they observe that many biological systems appear to be *designed* for specific purposes and designed both narrowly and ingeniously. This appearance of "design," long associated with William Paley's discussion of the Watchmaker in the early 1800s, therefore implies an intelligent designer (see Paley 1986 [1809]). Second, intelligent design writers document instances of biological systems that they claim cannot be explained by the processes of natural selection and descent with modification. In particular, intelligent design proponents point to organs and systems that feature "irreducible complexity" – complicated systems that will not operate unless all components evolved simultaneously. Proponents pushed intelligent design as a nonreligious alternative to Darwinian evolution, and its supporters in the Discovery Institute and elsewhere tried hard to give it a scientific veneer.

When the school board of Dover, Pennsylvania injected intelligent design into their local curriculum through a mandated disclaimer to be read by teachers, it was immediately challenged by a group of science teachers and several parents. The trial was widely reported, in part because federal Judge John E. Jones III permitted both sides to offer evidence and expert testimony on the scientific validity of intelligent design. Ruling in favor of the teachers, Jones addressed the question of whether intelligent design is science: "We have concluded that it is not, and moreover that Intelligent Design cannot uncouple itself from its creationist, and thus religious, antecedents." Although Jones's opinion technically only applies to the middle-Pennsylvania judicial district, it has likely served to discourage others who may wish to introduce intelligent design into their state or local curricula.

The Standards and Assessment Movement

Efforts to advance the cause of intelligent design as well as a new anti-evolution emphasis on "equal time" measures were further propelled by important shifts in the American educational regime. In 1989, President George H. W. Bush and the then-head of the National Governors' Association, Arkansas Governor Bill Clinton, both promoted a stronger role for the national government in determining what states will teach. These reform efforts placed a focus on the review and revision of state content standards. Although the first President Bush's *America 2000 Act* was never enacted, President Bill Clinton's *Goals 2000: The Educate America Act* would, for a short time, tie federal funds to state educational standards, leading states to engage model national standards while writing their own across the entire curriculum. This process provided openings for intelligent design supporters and other opponents of evolution. However, as we show in Chapters 4 and 6, the standards reform process ultimately solidified the place of evolution in the science curriculums promoted by many states.

Goals 2000 would not survive the culture wars of the early 1990s. Conservative activists successfully attacked what they and some historians perceived as an excessive orientation toward multiculturalism in still unreleased national history standards.[11] But, for the forces on both sides of the evolution question, the process of writing state standards created new venues to influence the content of classroom instruction. *Goals 2000* also led, in 1994, to the release of proposed national science education standards by the National Research Council (NRC), the policy recommendation arm of the National Academy of Sciences. "Long a champion of rigorous instruction in evolution" (Larson 2003, 197), the NRC was unambiguous in identifying a central role for evolution throughout the science curriculum as well as in distinguishing scientific inquiry from nonscientific alternatives. Even though the federal mandates were dropped in reaction to the 1994 congressional elections, the NRC was influential upon the states where "the state standards setting process proved an effective means to promote evolution teaching in American public schools" (Larson 2003, 205). This state-centered standards writing process also gave focus to anti-evolution forces and became the flashpoint for many evolution controversies throughout the 1990s because *Goals 2000* stimulated

---

[11] The pivotal moment for *Goals 2000* was probably an op-ed written in the *Wall Street Journal* by Lynne Cheney, former chair of the National Endowment for the Humanities. Conservative candidates for Congress followed up with attacks on the Act during the 1994 elections, which would bring in a Republican majority (Ravitch 1996).

a process of regular review of state education standards. By 2000, forty-nine states had adopted some form of standards, and Lienesch (2007) reports that intelligent design was prominent in many of these debates and raised as a legislative issue in as many as a dozen states in the 1990s.

There continues to be legislative action that seeks to sidestep current legal precedents. Most notably, legislators in at least nine states have sought to create room for anti-evolution teaching under the guise of "academic freedom" proposals.[12] Although couched in general language, the intent of these proposed laws is to protect creationist teachers from sanctions if they teach creationism or intelligent design and their teaching is based on their professional judgments (Branch and Scott 2009). Much of this activity was spurred by the U.S. Senate's adoption in 2001 of a Sense of the Senate Amendment sponsored by Pennsylvania Senator Rick Santorum as an amendment to the *No Child Left Behind* bill, the last major piece of national education legislation. Even though Santorum's amendment would eventually be dropped in conference, the inclusion of minor language in literature accompanying the act gave anti-evolutionists reason to argue that *No Child Left Behind* promoted equal time for nonscientific approaches.[13] In 2008, Louisiana passed the *Science Education Act* to protect teachers from being disciplined if they teach perspectives critical of evolution, whereas a bill was introduced in the South Carolina legislature that borrowed the language of the original Santorum amendment.

The standards writing process continues to provide activists an opportunity to either support or oppose evolution. Between 2000 and 2008, a quarter of the states changed their standards concerning

---

[12] "Academic Freedom" laws have also been introduced in Alabama, Florida, Iowa, Louisiana, Maryland, Michigan, Missouri, New Mexico, Oklahoma, South Carolina, and Texas (http://ncseweb.org/creationism/general/academic-freedom-bills-by-state-year; last accessed December 21, 2009).

[13] With final passage of *No Child Left Behind*, the Santorum amendment appeared only in the "Joint Explanatory Statement of the Committee of Conference" in this form: "The conferees recognize that a quality science education should prepare students to distinguish the data and testable theories of science from religious or philosophical claims that are made in the name of science. Where topics are taught that may generate controversy (such as biological evolution), the curriculum should help students to understand the full range of scientific views that exist, why such topics may generate controversy, and how scientific discoveries can profoundly affect society."

evolution enough to be noticed by the National Center for Science Education, a pro-evolution organization.[14] These *content standards* stand as official policies concerning what students should learn in their public school biology classes. In some states, these standards are coupled with assessment tests or linked to textbook selection, in effect strengthening their potential to direct classroom instruction. Recent controversies over these content standards in Kansas, Ohio, Florida, and Texas represent the most visible conflicts in the last decade. However, the enacting of standards in all fifty states is a *political* process, and one that is important to understand.

PUBLIC CONTROL OF THE SCIENCE CLASSROOM

As historian Edward Larson has noted, "late 20th century legal developments boxed in early 21st century creationists" (2003, 205). There have not yet been any cases in federal courts that directly address the academic freedom claims used by some teachers and states to introduce anti-evolutionary instruction into the classroom, although a 2001 case in the Minnesota Court of Appeals soundly rejected the argument (*LeVake v. Independent School District*). Nonetheless, at least at the state level, "as matters stand in most states, evolution is included in the science curriculum by the state's education standards, while creation science is excluded from it by Supreme Court decree" (Larson 2003, 205).

Indeed, acting as quasi-guardians protecting rights enshrined in the First Amendment, U.S. federal courts have substantially narrowed the policy space. We can see this in Figure 1.1. The lower part of the panel shows the range of policies that have been declared unconstitutional by federal courts, starting with the earliest cases at the bottom and the more recent ones closest to the "bright line" between permissible and impermissible policies. States cannot mandate in their standards, nor can instructors teach in their classrooms, perspectives that reflect particular religious perspectives on creation. The courts have thus *limited* the legal space within which school districts, states, and teachers can

---

[14] Based on a state-by-state review of the National Center for Science Education's news archives for 2000–2008 (http://ncseweb.org/news; last accessed June 22, 2009). Our count includes states that strengthened or weakened their state standards through the legislature, state board of education, or state school board.

Constitutional Policies and Practices

Extensive discussion of evidence and the use of evolution as a unifying theme for the general biology course.

Cursory, but neutral, mention of evolution.

Use of "theory" in the colloquial sense, mention of "gaps," or other language incorrectly undermining findings of evolutionary biology

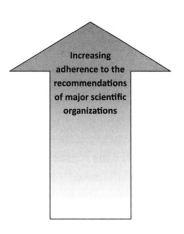

Constitutional Boundary

Unconstitutional Policies and Practices

Endorse Intelligent Design (*Kitzmiller v. Dover 2005*)

Require equal time (*Daniel v. Waters 1975, McLean v. Arkansas* 1982, *Edwards v. Aguillard 1987*)

Endorse "creation science" (*McLean v. Arkansas* 1982, *Edwards v. Aguillard 1987*)

Ban instruction in evolution (*Epperson v. Arkansas*, 1968)

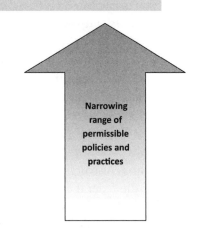

Figure 1.1. Constitutional and unconstitutional policies toward instruction in evolution.

decide what to teach. But this narrowed space still provides significant room for them to make their own decisions.

The upper part of the panel illustrates the range of policies permissible under the current legal precedents. Although more limited than it was in the past, the possibilities remain diverse enough to promote intense controversy. For example, at one extreme, states, school districts, and teachers can decide to follow the recommendations of the NRC and other national scientific organizations. This would entail endorsing a rigorous treatment of evolutionary biology, supplemented by supporting evidence from paleontology, geology, and genetics. Or, they could choose to teach the basics of evolution but (as a strictly political strategy) omit specific mention of human origins. This would promote the rigorous teaching of the basic principles of evolutionary biology without eliciting protest from those who find the idea of common ancestry among primates especially offensive and objectionable. Or states, through their standards, could also take a minimalist position by endorsing a cursory mention of species diversity and acknowledging that there has been change in the kinds of species populating the earth, without discussing concepts such as natural selection and without emphasizing estimates of the age of fossils and the geologic strata in which they were discovered. And, finally, states can characterize evolutionary theory in ways that might minimize its status and credibility – for example, by emphasizing "gaps" in the theory or fossil record and using the word "theory" in the colloquial sense of a hunch rather than its scientific meaning.

Within the range of permitted policies and practices, who *should* decide what students should learn? And who really does decide? These are two distinct questions. William Jennings Bryan in the *Scopes* trial and Supreme Court Justice Antonin Scalia in *Edwards v. Aguillard* both clearly took the position that the public should control public school instruction. This view, however, has not been the dominant one of the federal courts. By declaring laws banning evolution and those endorsing creationism, creation science, or intelligent design unconstitutional, federal courts essentially have declared that the democratic process produced outcomes anathema to the Bill of Rights. It did not matter that these laws had been passed through democratic processes and presumably represented the majoritarian preferences in their states. A gap between what the public may want and the policies it eventually gets is not problematic because protecting civil liberties from majority opinion is an essential part of democracy, albeit one that produces constant tensions. Indeed, the frequent probing of the constitutional boundary by anti-evolution groups seems undeterred by previous defeats. Anti-evolution activists continually propose new approaches to limit the influence of evolution and its related ideas in their local schools.

The power of courts to invalidate laws deemed unconstitutional creates the potential for a gap between public preferences and public policy, and the magnitude of such a gap is an empirical question. Indeed, we will argue that there is not a single state in which the official state policy, as reflected in state science standards, fully reflects the wishes of the majority of citizens. To come to this conclusion, we need to determine both public policy (what do people get from their government?) and public opinion (what do people want?) To do this we must first ask if it is even possible to speak of "public opinion" concerning evolution in the classroom. Although we have scores of public opinion polls on the topic, it is not clear that we can say that the public has had sufficient opportunity to deliberate and form opinions that reflect the best interests of their communities. Perhaps the public is so scientifically illiterate, and citizens' opportunities for deliberation so severely restricted, that we can dismiss their answers to public opinion researchers as irrational, ignorant, or capricious. Perhaps public opinion as recorded in public opinion polls is simply an illusion (Bishop 2004) that is manufactured by media pollsters to create interesting stories that will sell newspapers and drive up television ratings (Moore 2008).

We address this key question about the nature of public opinion in the next chapter. We examine more than a quarter century of public opinion polls and academic social surveys to understand Americans' expressed preferences concerning evolution in the classroom. We look at public opinion polls that seem to show strong support for equal treatments of evolutionary biology and Bible-based alternatives. We ask whether the opinions expressed by ordinary Americans are capricious or random and whether the apparent support for creationism is an artifact of question wording or other features of polls that bias results in a particular direction. We also look to see if Americans' policy preferences are rooted in broader belief systems that provide a logical basis for those opinions. And we consider whether ordinary Americans are well enough informed to produce opinions that merit respect and consideration in the policy process.

We conclude Chapter 2 by arguing that, when one considers all the evidence, public opinion polls should be afforded legitimacy. These polls consistently show that a majority of Americans express support for teaching some form of creationism in addition to instruction in evolutionary biology. In Chapter 3, we show how opinions regarding evolution are structured by religious ideas and worldviews by exploring how religion, education, and geography structure opinion. This allows us, by the end of Chapter 3, to generate estimates of public opinion for each of the fifty states.

Having established the legitimacy of public opinion and having described its psychological, religious, and geographic sources, we can then ask: Who *does* decide? To what extent does instruction in evolution reflect the values and preferences of the public? If the will of the people is not being realized and implemented in public policy, whose is? This requires analysis at two distinct levels: (1) in the states, where standards and examinations developed in departments of education and state school boards set expectations for teachers throughout the state, and (2) in the classrooms, where these standards are, or are not, actually implemented.

We begin this empirical investigation in Chapter 4, where we assess whether public opinion really matters in state policy making of standards or whether scientists and educational bureaucrats have been successful in shielding the policy-making process from majoritarian opinion. We will show that, within the space provided by the federal courts, state policies were modestly responsive to public opinion a decade ago, but there is evidence that, under certain conditions, scientists can have their way.

Having examined how states make curricular policy, we then move to the classroom level to see how policies are actually implemented. Throughout the extensive body of research on the evolution–creationism politics in the United States, teachers remain relatively minor figures. John Thomas Scopes, Susan Epperson, Don Aguillard – the teachers whose names are associated with landmark legal decisions on evolution – were typically recruited by others who needed a teacher with the legal standing to challenge the law. Their names remain associated with the landmark trials of the evolution–creationism wars, but we know little about them as everyday classroom teachers. Beyond these litigants, however, are tens of thousands of other classroom teachers, and they have gone virtually unstudied in the major historical accounts of the evolution controversy.

Do enthusiastic supporters of evolution – teachers like Susan Epperson or Don Aguillard – go well beyond what states expect them to teach? How many teachers are there like Minnesotan Rodney LeVake, who refused to teach evolution because he does not accept it and finds it contradictory to his religious beliefs?[15] During the oral arguments in *Edwards v. Aguillard*, Supreme Court Justice Lewis Powell predicted, "once you get into the classroom ... the teacher is going [to] teach whatever she or he really thinks."[16] To what extent is this true?

We show in Chapters 5–8 that teachers find themselves on the front lines of the evolution/creation controversy. Moreover, how they navigate that precarious position has important implications for democracy in education policy making. We do this by presenting results of our national survey of 926 public high school biology teachers. This is the first nationwide survey that focuses on the teaching of evolution, and it allows us to see how teachers in different states, operating under different standards and testing regimes, actually teach evolution and its alternatives in American public schools. This survey allows us to not only provide a national portrait of how evolution is actually taught, but also to trace the policy process all the way to implementation in individual classrooms.

This exploration of how teachers teach evolution sheds new light on how public policy can be brought closer in line with local sentiment at the implementation stage. We argue in Chapter 5 that teachers are *street-level bureaucrats*, a term first coined by Michael Lipsky (1980) to capture the importance of a range of public employees charged with implementing policies but who are granted significant discretion when doing so. We show that there is important variation in how teachers choose to teach evolution. Some teachers actually fall below the line

[15] Rodney LeVake was assigned to teach biology in a tenth grade Minnesota classroom. Although Minnesota state standards at the time did not explicitly mention evolution, it was required by the district curriculum. LeVake essentially refused to teach the evolution sections and raised many doubts about it. Reassigned to another class, LeVake brought suit. The Court of Appeals in Minnesota rejected the appeal on multiple grounds, including the claim that this violated LeVake's free speech and academic freedom, holding that "the established curriculum and LeVake's responsibility as a public school teacher to teach evolution in the manner prescribed by the curriculum overrides his First Amendment rights as a private citizen" (*LeVake v. Independent School District* 2001, 8).

[16] *Edwards v. Aguillard* (1987). Transcripts of oral arguments are available at http://www.oyez.org/cases/1980-1989/1986/1986_85_1513/ (last accessed September 29, 2008).

drawn in Figure 1.1, separating constitutional from unconstitutional policies; more widespread, however, are significant differences in how they present evolution across the broad spectrum of constitutionally permitted policies and practices.

In Chapter 6, we look at whether these classroom practices are guided by state standards. This analysis demonstrates both the significant discretion teachers have to teach what they want and the way standards can, in some cases, impact classroom behavior. In exercising their discretion, teachers may be pulled either close to what the public within their local districts wants or further from it; in any case, we know that, when they let standards influence their behavior, the state is deciding what students should learn, and in cases when standards are not influencing their behavior, the teachers themselves are making these decisions.

Critical to these decisions are the values and training of public employees (Mosher 1982). In Chapter 7, we show how each of these shape teachers' classroom behavior. But as we move deeper into our data in Chapter 8, we demonstrate two ways that this policy discretion may actually bring policy *closer* in line to the preferences of their local school district residents. One is by bending to local pressure to either emphasize or de-emphasize evolution or by anticipating pressures they might experience if they stray too far from local preferences. The other is through a sorting process where teachers end up in districts much like themselves. Many teachers may be able to locate where they want, accepting jobs in districts in which they will feel most comfortable. What we find is that many teachers' individual values match up well with those of the district in which they teach. This yields public schools that are representative of the communities they serve. These teachers implement policy in ways that appear highly responsive to public opinion, although this responsiveness is a consequence of shared values rather than through a deliberate effort to meet community demands.

SUMMARY

The great works on the evolution–creation controversy have highlighted the conflict's underlying battle of ideas. Yet, the battle between evolution and creationism is not simply one of ideas, where each side aims to convince a majority of the public that their view of the origin and development of species is the correct one. Rather, it is a political struggle over who decides, a question central to democratic politics. Experts seek influence in the political battle to write state level standards. Schools are public entities, enmeshed in a culture and history of local control, created and increasingly controlled by their states. They are also staffed by public employees, charged with implementing state and district policies but with professional training and values of their own. The question of who decides is both normative and empirical, and we show in the chapters to come that who decides is critically important to what students learn.

2 The Public Speaks: "Teach Both"

The people, as a rule, do not believe in the ape theory.

> William Jennings Bryan (1924)[1]

Understanding how the Gallup poll induced such opinions about the creationism issue in this case provides an object lesson as to how an illusion of public opinion can be generated in public opinion surveys generally.

> George Bishop (2005)

But we decide which is right.
And which is an illusion?

> The Moody Blues (1967)

OPPONENTS OF EVOLUTION have claimed for nearly a century that public opinion is on their side. The proponents of the nation's first anti-evolution laws in the 1920s were confident that these laws would be popular with voters and reflected majority sentiment. In the latter half of the twentieth century, state legislators and school board members could also claim citizen support for policies that mandated "balanced treatment" for evolution and creationism and, later, that mandated the teaching of intelligent design or curricula that emphasized "gaps" in the theory of evolution. As we noted in Chapter 1, both populists like Bryan and strict constructivists like Scalia have made strong normative cases for following the wishes of the majority,

---

[1] Bryan is quoted in Larson (2003, 46); the second quotation is from Bishop (2004, 158), and the Moody Blues lyrics come from their album *Days of Future Past* (1967).

even against the strong objections of scientific or pedagogical experts. Thus, it is essential to understand the policy preferences of ordinary citizens.

In this chapter, we marshal evidence from more than a quarter century of surveys of the American public concerning evolution. We will begin with the public's *policy preferences* – what Americans say that they want taught in public schools. This review will show that the majority of Americans favor teaching students a biblical perspective on the origins of life on earth. For most, creationism should be taught *alongside* evolutionary biology – what many refer to as "balanced treatment." However, a fairly sizable minority say they want biblical perspectives to *supplant* scientific treatments of the origin of species.

But can we dignify the results of these polls with the term "public opinion"? *Public opinion* connotes a collective judgment that merits respect in the democratic process. It is entirely possible that what appears to be strong support for teaching creationism is an artifact of the polling process itself. We must ask whether polls showing substantial support for teaching creationism meet the standards of public opinion as an informed collective judgment that policy makers can discern and which they should consider.

To answer this question, we must devote considerable attention to understanding *why* Americans give particular answers to these polls. Could the answers be methodological artifacts created by the pollsters themselves? More specifically, might apparent support for creationism be a result of biased questionnaires and biased question wording? Or might citizens' answers be capricious, thoughtless, and essentially random? Alternatively, can we see a logic and rationale underlying the answers so that we can say – to borrow Page and Shapiro's (1992) term – the public is rational? We will address all of these questions. But first we must see what the public says when asked about evolution and creationism in public schools.

POLICY PREFERENCES

What should children be taught in high school biology classes? That is the policy question that serves as the flash point of the evolution controversy in the United States. A good place to begin is with two surveys conducted in the summer of 2005. The first was a survey conducted by the Survey and Research Evaluation Laboratory at Virginia Commonwealth University (VCU). Every year since 2001, VCU has conducted a survey devoted to science, science policy, and science ethics (including medical ethics). About midway through the 2005 survey (the 24th question), respondents were asked about their beliefs regarding the origins of biological life and then were asked,

Regardless of what you may personally believe about the origin of biological life, which of the following do you believe should be taught in public schools?

☐ Evolution only – evolution says that biological life developed over time from simple substances.

☐ Creationism only – creationism says that biological life was directly created by God in its present form at one point in time.

☐ Intelligent design only – intelligent design says that biological life is so complex that it required a powerful force or intelligent being to help create it.

☐ Or some combination of these?

A few months earlier, the commercial firm Harris Interactive conducted a telephone poll in which the first five questions concerned beliefs about *human* origins (e.g., did human beings develop from earlier species, whether apes and man have a common ancestry). For the sixth question, citizens were then asked,

Regardless of what you may personally believe, which of these do you believe should be taught in public schools? Evolution only, creationism only, intelligent design only, or all three.

The results of these two recent surveys are reported in the first two columns of Table 2.1. The results are remarkably similar despite differences in the survey organizations, the length of the survey, the context of previous questions, and the fact that the VCU survey never mentions *human* evolution explicitly. In both surveys, roughly half of the public endorses teaching *a combination* of approaches to human and biological origins. In both surveys, more than 25% of the public would prefer to teach either biblical creationism or intelligent design exclusively. And in both surveys, only 12–15% endorse teaching evolution only. Because teaching *evolution only* was the official policy in all fifty states in 2005, we have strong evidence of a large gap

Table 2.1. Public preferences for teaching evolution and creationism, single-question format, 1981–2005

	Recent polls		Older polls	
	VCU 2005 (%)	Harris 2005 (%)	CCD 1987 (%)	NBC 1981 (%)
Teach creationism only	21	23	11	10
Teach intelligent design only	5	4	–	–
Teach creationism and intelligent design	4	–	–	–
Teach a combination including evolution	43	55	68	76
Teach evolution only	15	12	11	8
Don't know or no answer	12	6	10	6
Total	100%	100%	100%	100%
(N)	(1,002)	(1,000)	(1,708)	(1,598)

Sources: See Appendix 2.

between public opinion and public policy. We will have much more to say about sources of this gap in the next chapter, but we can say that the Supreme Court's judgment that balanced-treatment laws violate the First Amendment is the major factor preventing policy from conforming to opinion.[2]

Table 2.1 also shows the results of similar, but not identical, questions asked in two polls in the 1980s (source information and original question wording for all tables in this chapter can be found in Appendix 2). Taken as a whole, the trend data suggest that most Americans would like public schools to "teach the controversy" by providing both sides of the argument. However, the percentage of Americans endorsing this centrist position appears to have fallen sharply as the percentage supporting evolution-only has increased at least 50%, whereas the percentage supporting alternatives has more than doubled. We cannot rule out the possibility that the trends are an

---

[2] Some table entries in this chapter may differ slightly from data we previously reported (Plutzer and Berkman 2008) in our comprehensive review of evolution polls. The differences stem from our reliance on published results in the former article. In this chapter, we have based all tables on our own analyses of the original data, which have been generously placed in the public domain by the major polling organizations. Slight differences in the way that sample weights and missing values are handled account for these small differences. All tables in this chapter are based on data that have been weighted to match the population on characteristics such as race, age, and sex. Unweighted analyses are very similar, however, rarely differing by more than a percentage point or two.

Table 2.2. Percentage favoring the teaching of creationism instead of evolution, 1999–2005

Would you generally favor or oppose teaching creation INSTEAD OF evolution in public schools?

Survey (date)	Favor (%)	Oppose (%)	Don't know (%)	Total	N
Gallup (1999)	44	50	5	100%	1,016
CBS/NYT (2004)	37	51	12	100%	885
Newsweek (2004)	40	44	16	100%	1,009
Pew (2005)	33	54	13	100%	1,090
Pew (2005)	38	49	13	100%	2,000

Sources: See Appendix 2.

artifact of different question wording or survey design, but these data suggest a substantial increase in polarization as the issue has remained in the public eye. The apparent increase in polarization would be consistent with the stepped up mobilization and education efforts on both sides of the issue during the last twenty years and with polarization on other social issues in the United States (e.g., Layman and Carsey 2002).

Before we accept the conclusion of a massive disconnect between what the public says it wants and the policies it receives, however, we need to pursue public opinion in much greater depth. We will show that the apparent size of the evolution-only constituency depends somewhat on how pollsters ask the questions. After demonstrating this and considering the implications, we offer an extended discussion of whether public opinion concerning evolution and creationism is sufficiently "rational" so as to merit respect in the policy-making process.

Another Way to Ask About Evolution in the Schools

Since 1999, a number of respected polling organizations have asked citizens whether they would *"generally favor or oppose teaching creation instead of evolution in public schools?"* Results from five different surveys are reported in Table 2.2. This question elicits a much larger percentage of Americans in the *creationism-only* camp than we see in the Harris and VCU surveys. On average, about 38% of Americans seem prepared to *replace* scientific discussions of human origins with biblically inspired alternatives.

Table 2.3. Percentage favoring the teaching of creationism along with evolution, 1998–2006

Would you generally favor or oppose teaching creation ALONG WITH evolution in public schools?

Survey (date)	Favor (%)	Oppose (%)	Don't know (%)	Total	N
University of North Carolina (1998)	59.5	33.7	6.7	100%	1,257
Gallup (1999)	68.1	29.0	3.0	100%	1,016
CBS/NYT (2004)	65.3	28.8	5.9	100%	885
Newsweek (2004)	60.2	28.0	11.8	100%	1,009
Pew (2005)	56.9	32.6	10.5	100%	1,090
Pew (2005)	63.6	26.1	10.3	100%	2,000
Pew (2006)	58.2	35.0	6.8	100%	996
Average of seven polls	61.7	30.5	7.9	100%	

Sources: See Appendix 2.

One reason that the percentage of anti-evolutionists is so much higher here may be the limited alternatives. Those uncomfortable with evolution are not given a choice that might reflect a middle ground and may select "instead of" in order to register their ambivalence toward evolution. This would be a reasonable response if the question were asked before other questions about the teaching of evolution.

For this reason, this survey question is usually paired with a second question that asks, "*Would you generally favor or oppose teaching creation along with evolution in public schools?*" The results of this question across several different polls and polling organizations are shown in Table 2.3. This time series shows that roughly two-thirds of Americans endorse equal treatment. As we noted earlier, public opinion pollsters typically pair these questions, and, in most recent polls, the questions are presented in random order, with half of the respondents first being asked about replacing evolution before being asked about teaching creationism along with evolution.[3]

One way to glean some additional information from these questions is to combine them into a single summary. For surveys that

---

[3] A close inspection of the effects of randomization shows that if the "instead of" question is asked first, support is about 6.5 percentage points higher than if it is asked second (39.1% vs. 32.5% in the 2005 Pew Center Religion and Public Life Poll). We are grateful to Scott Keeter and the Pew Center for providing the randomization file that allowed us to see the effects of question order.

Table 2.4. Public preferences for teaching evolution and creationism based on two-question format, 1999–2005

	Gallup 1999 (%)	CBS 2004 (%)	Newsweek 2004 (%)	Pew 2005 (%)	Pew 2005 (%)
1. Teach creationism or ID* only	41	37	40	34	38
2. Teach creationism for sure (DK "instead")	2	6	7	4	5
3. Teach a combination	34	31	24	30	31
4. Teach evolution for sure (DK "along with")	0	1	1	1	1
5. Teach evolution only	21	19	19	22	17
Don't know or ambiguous response	2	5	9	9	9
Total	100%	100%	100%	100%	100%
(N)	(1,016)	(885)	(1,009)	(1,090)	(2,000)

* ID refers to intelligent design; DK refers to "Don't know."
Sources: See Appendix 2.

asked both questions, and for which the original raw data are available, we have created a summary classification with scores ranging from 1 to 5. Respondents who expressed a preference for teaching creationism instead of evolution (regardless of how they answered the other question) are scored a 1, and respondents who support teaching evolution only (answering "oppose" in both questions) are scored a 5. Respondents classified as "teach both" are scored a "3" if they endorsed creationism along with evolution and did not endorse the proposal to replace evolution. Two small categories of citizens who are unsure about one proposal or the other get intermediate scores ("DK" connotes "Don't know" in the table; see the appendix to this chapter, section A2.3, for an extended explanation of this coding scheme). The summary scores are reported in Table 2.4. As in the case of the Harris and VCU surveys, we again find that less than 25% of the public endorses current public policy and that, if forced to choose, many more would endorse creationism than evolution.

To assess the potential impact of question format, Table 2.5 averages the results of polls using each polling approach and reports them in a comparable way. The results show that the way the question is asked can alter the percentages substantially. In particular, the single-item question used by VCU and Harris may be biased somewhat toward the intermediate position of teaching both approaches – in

Table 2.5. Comparing support for evolution and creationism in the classroom elicited by two different question formats

	Single-question format, 2005 (adapted from Table 2.1)	Two-question format, 1999–2005 (adapted from Table 2.4)
	2 Poll Avg	5 Poll Avg
1. Teach creationism or ID only	27	38
2. Teach creationism for sure (DK "instead")		5
3. Teach a combination	51	30
4. Teach evolution for sure (DK "along with")		1
5. Teach evolution only	14	20
Don't know or ambiguous response	9	7
Total	100%	100%

Sources: See Appendix 2.

part because of recency effects (the option of teaching "a combination" or "all three" is offered last) and in part because reciprocity norms (the willingness to accommodate an opposing view) may be stronger when multiple options are presented at the same time.

However, just because we have evidence of question-format effects does not make the results invalid. In fact, three important conclusions are *strengthened* by examining both sets of polls. During the 1999–2005 period:

1. Over two-thirds of the public endorse teaching creationism (either along with or instead of evolution). Thus, a supermajority expresses opposition to Supreme Court decisions banning this practice.
2. *Every survey* shows that anti-evolutionists outnumber pro-evolutionists.
3. The highest recorded support for teaching evolution and only evolution is 35%, very far from a majority. Most polls show even lower support. We will show in Chapters 4 and 6 that all state standards endorse evolution, although with varying degrees of comprehensiveness and rigor. Therefore, no more than one-third of U.S. citizens endorse the policy that is actually in place in all fifty states.

These three conclusions are critical to understanding evolution politics and policy in the United States. More fundamentally, they describe a situation in which *the people* appear at first glance to be largely irrelevant to the policy-making process. Across the whole country, we see a mismatch between public opinion and policy. Of course, education is a state and local responsibility. As we move on we will disaggregate public opinion to look at the congruence between opinion and policy in these venues. But first, in the remainder of this chapter, we must subject these three conclusions to additional methodological challenges and place them in broader social and political contexts.

A POLICY-OPINION GAP? OR AN ILLUSION OF PUBLIC OPINION?

If we take the most recent surveys at face value, it appears that only 15–20% of the public endorses the policy of teaching evolutionary biology and excluding both creationism and intelligent design from high school biology classes. But there are two key arguments that suggest we should not take these polls as serious expressions of public preference. First, it might be argued that all of these polls are subject to bias stemming from the way the questions were worded or from other cues provided in the survey interview. Second, it is possible that the public is so poorly informed about the topic that most individuals are answering the question in a thoughtless manner that makes the results something less than "public opinion." Both of these arguments are advanced by George Bishop in his *Illusion of Public Opinion* (2004), and the latter argument is made by David W. Moore in *The Opinion Makers* (2008). We think these two analyses are sufficiently important that we need to address each point.

Is High Support for Creationism a Methodological Artifact?

The first possibility is that the "real" support for teaching evolutionary biology is actually higher but the survey questionnaires used by polling organizations introduce bias that induces people to give anti-evolution answers. Indeed, we have already provided evidence (in Table 2.5) that question format can alter apparent support for "teaching both" by about twenty percentage points. The impact on support for teaching evolution, however, appears to be no more than five percentage points.

At the most general level, the dominant theme of a survey and the content of questions asked early in the interview can lead to biased results. We know that answers to questions are probabilistic in that individuals quickly recall various *considerations* that bear on the question. But the considerations that come to mind during a particular interview can reflect recent stimuli (Zaller 1992; Zaller and Feldman 1992). If, for example, large parts of a survey are devoted to religious themes, then religious considerations may be invoked more often than in a survey dominated by themes related to science, to civil liberties, or to the upcoming election. Indeed, several of the polls we have reported focus heavily on religion: the Pew Center's "Religion and Public Life Surveys" of 2005 and 2006, the 2004 *Newsweek* "Christmas poll," and a 1987 survey conducted on behalf of the Williamsburg Charter Foundation.

In contrast, the 2005 Harris poll asked its teaching question as the sixth in a series of questions about evolution, and respondents to the VCU survey had first been asked a series of questions about *science, science policy*, and *science and ethics*. In the 1981 NBC poll, the question about evolution in the classroom was the 42nd question in a poll about foreign policy, environmental protection, and education policy generally. And in the 2004 CBS poll, the evolution question was the 60th asked in a poll that touched on dozens of topics concerning politics and domestic and foreign policy. Among the polls reported in Table 2.4, those in the third and fifth columns contained extensive religious content preceding the questions about evolution in the classroom. And, in fact, we see support for teaching only creationism is three to four percentage points higher, and support for evolution as much as five points lower, in these polls than in others fielded in the same year; these are differences slightly larger than the margin of error (the 95% confidence interval for comparing two proportions is ±3.6% for "creationism only" and ±2.9% for "evolution only").

One especially useful pair of polls was conducted by the Pew Center in 2005, just four months apart. One was their annual "Religion and Public Life" survey that arguably contained precisely the type of cuing that can produce bias. The other poll, however, was the second part of a two-wave survey about topics in the news in which the evolution questions are introduced more or less "out of the blue" and are not preceded by any questions that might make one's religious commitments more salient. Comparing the results of these otherwise similar polls, we see that support for teaching only evolution was five points higher in the news topics survey than in the religion and public life survey (22% vs. 17%, as seen in the last two columns of Table 2.4). The fact that results could differ by 5% should not lead us to invalidate these results, of course, because the basic message is the same: only a small minority supports teaching evolution exclusively. But it suggests that our estimates of the size of that minority may depend on the frame of mind of the respondents when they were asked the question. These general framing effects are, however, substantively small and in no way challenge the three fundamental conclusions we have drawn from the data.

Is Bias Induced by Preambles or Question Wording?

If the overall theme of a survey is unlikely to account for the pattern of support for creationism in the classroom, perhaps bias is induced by the specific survey questions or the preambles that are used to introduce them. Bishop has roundly criticized a 1999 Gallup poll because its question about the teaching of evolution was preceded by an introduction that said, "*I'm going to read a variety of proposals concerning religion and public schools. For each one, please tell me whether you would generally favor or oppose it.*" Bishop has suggested that this preamble unduly framed the question as one not about evolutionary biology, creationism, or pedagogy but instead about religion in the public schools. The Gallup questions are, according to Bishop:

> ... fundamentally about whether religion should have any place in the public schools. Whether respondents knew much, if anything, about creationism, they knew it had something to do with *religion and public schools*, as they were informed in the preface to the sequence of questions. For many respondents, saying they favored "teaching creationism ALONG WITH evolution in the public schools" became just another way of expressing support for the idea of religion having a role to play in public education (Bishop 2005, 158–159).

In this particular Gallup poll, only 29% reject the idea of equal treatment, and perhaps the preamble accounts for this very low percentage. However, a quick glance at Table 2.3 suggests that the Gallup poll results are nearly identical to a University of North Carolina survey fielded a little more than a year earlier and similar to a number of polls conducted by CBS, *Newsweek*, and the Pew Center in later years. None of these other polls used the same preamble, and only three emphasized religion generally. On balance, the evidence suggests that polls that use this preamble *or* emphasize religion extensively in earlier questions inflate support for creationism by four to five percentage points.

It is possible, of course, that respondents in *every* survey – preamble or not – viewed this as a question about religion in public schools. But we fail to see why this should be a problem. After all, Supreme Court justices and many interest groups (on both sides of the issue) frame the conflict in precisely this way. For the ACLU, which supported the legal expenses of teachers John Scopes, Susan Epperson, and Don Aguillard, keeping religion out of public schools is *the* central issue. And although anti-evolutionists have increasingly framed their position as one about science (Lienesch 2007; Numbers 1992), the idea that teaching evolution undermines Christian faith has also been an enduring argument by political elites since the early 1920s. This was the principle argument in *Segraves v. California* (1981) in which a California Superior Court judge validated this view and prohibited California educators from teaching evolution "dogmatically." If large numbers of ordinary citizens think about the issue in this way, they would simply be reflecting one of the key arguments made by well-informed elites on both sides of the issue. Thinking about the issue as a specific instance of church–state politics would not impugn the public's ability to formulate policy preferences but should instead be viewed as evidence that ordinary citizens have a reasonable basis for the preferences they express.

"Split Ballot" Polls

One way to assess the possibility of bias induced by question wording is to examine questions that were *deliberately written to induce such bias.* The "split ballot" design of a 1982 Roper poll was intended to elicit question-wording effects. In one version of the question (administered randomly to half the respondents), the introduction was,

Here is a list of changes some people favor, but that others oppose. (Card shown respondent) Would you read down that list, and for each one tell me whether it is a change that you favor or oppose?

☐ Requiring that public schools teach the creation theory if they also teach Darwin's theory of evolution.

The other respondents had a different preamble, one that raises the salience of civil liberties:

Here is a list of changes some people favor on the grounds that they are needed for the good of our society, but that others oppose on the grounds that they violate various Constitutional guarantees, such as freedom of the press, separation of church and state, the right of privacy, etc. Would you read down that list, and for each one tell me whether it is a change that you favor or oppose?

☐ Requiring that public schools teach the creation theory if they also teach Darwin's theory of evolution.

Remarkably, the questions elicited nearly identical results. Fifty-five percent favored balanced treatment in the first formulation and 54% in the second.

Another useful survey was conducted on behalf of Fox News in 1998. This survey was interesting because it included a question whose preamble would seem to be strongly *biased in favor of evolution*. The question posed was,

Last year the National Academy of Sciences recommended that evolution be taught to all public school students as the most convincing theory for how human beings developed. Do you agree or disagree that evolution should be taught in all public schools?

Note that the question's introduction tells respondents that a prestigious scientific organization has endorsed the teaching of evolution. Note also that any potential yea-saying bias – the tendency to agree with statements rather than disagree – is in favor of evolution. In spite of this, 36% opposed the teaching of evolution altogether – a number that is nearly identical to those elicited by the "instead of" question reported in Table 2.2 (which is potentially biased in the opposite direction).

The same Fox News poll contained another question with a variation of an endorsement statement. This question explained,

The Kansas State Board of Education recently approved new standards for teaching science in public schools that remove the teaching of evolution from the mandatory curriculum. Do you agree or disagree with the Board's attempt to take the teaching of evolution out of the schools?

Despite the potential endorsement effect, the percentage suggesting that evolution should be removed entirely from the curriculum was 33% – a little higher than the multi-option questions posed by Harris and VCU (Table 2.1) and a little lower than the yes–no questions reported in Table 2.2.[4]

Support for Creationism is not a Result of Biased Polls

We believe we have identified and examined every poll or survey of the American public that has asked ordinary citizens whether creationism and/or evolution should be taught (see Plutzer and Berkman 2008 for a detailed chronology). Survey organizations have employed a number of different question wordings, and these have been embedded in surveys with many different themes. The survey organizations include think tanks such as the Pew Center, commercial firms such as Gallup and Harris, major media outlets such as CBS News and *Newsweek*, and academic survey research centers such as those at VCU and the

---

[4] A similar question on a 1999 poll commissioned by People for the American Way, a liberal advocacy group, showed only 28% support for the Kansas decision (PFAW 2000). We report results from this survey cautiously for several reasons. First, PFAW has been an active participant in the events we analyze, having filed briefs in several of the recent court cases. Second, although the poll was undertaken by a respected polling organization, the CEO of that firm, pollster Daniel Yankelovich, sits on the PFAW board. Third, unlike almost all the other polls we report, we do not have access to either the questionnaire or the original poll data from the PFAW survey. Staff from the David Yankelovich Group inform us that they no longer have the original data file (personal correspondence with Paul McIntire, 11/11/2008). We have repeatedly requested the data from PFAW, but without any response. Without the ability to independently analyze the data, we use it cautiously and infrequently in our analyses.

University of North Carolina. There is some evidence of question-wording effects and general framing effects, both on the order of 5% when considering support for evolution. At the same time, there is overwhelming evidence in support of our three core conclusions. No matter how the questions are asked, no matter the theme of the survey, no matter the sponsor of the survey, we see again and again evidence that large majorities of Americans want to see creationism taught in public schools.

A RATIONAL OR IRRATIONAL PUBLIC?

Carroll Glynn and her colleagues ask, "What sort of public opinion is worthy of becoming public policy?" (Glynn et al. 1999, 249). The question is spurred by the acknowledgment that ordinary citizens seem to have extraordinarily little knowledge of policy debates, have a meager understanding of the political process, and their answers to public opinion polls often provide evidence of random answering (Converse 1964; Delli Carpini and Keeter 1996).[5]

The Public Sees Important Distinctions among Alternative Policies

Perhaps a casual recognition of a few buzzwords – evolution, creation, public schools – leads people to answer randomly, without close attention to the meaning of the question. However, on this issue, we can show that this form of random answers bred of ignorance is not a major feature of the data. The two-question format also shows that respondents are not entirely responding to superficial symbolic words in the questions. The questions are identical in including "evolution," and "creationism." And both questions are set up to provide the same "yea-saying" bias by having the answer "favor" associated with the conservative response. If respondents were simply responding to the symbolic buzzwords, we would not expect to see differences of

[5] One possibility in any opinion poll is that a substantial number of respondents are guessing randomly. In his landmark essay on belief systems, Philip Converse (1964) argued that, on questions of major domestic policies, it appeared that roughly 80% of the public was answering randomly and only 20% had "real" opinions on the issues. If this were the case, then perhaps greater weight should be given to citizens with stable and reasoned opinions. We can essentially rule out this possibility in the present case and provide mathematical proof of this in Appendix section A2.7.

twenty to thirty points in the percentage favoring each proposal (compare Table 2.2 with Table 2.3). Clearly, the respondents are listening carefully enough to hear this distinction and give different answers when that difference coincides with their policy preferences.

On What Basis Do Citizens Answer Polling Questions?

If the great majority of citizens are not guessing randomly, that does not mean that they are expressing informed opinions. Bishop presents evidence of substantial ignorance among respondents. For example, in a 2000 poll conducted by the Daniel Yankelovich Group on behalf of the organization People for the American Way (PFAW 2000), 45% reported that they had never heard of the term "creationism," and only 41% of those who had heard of it claimed to be "very familiar" with the term. In Bishop's view, a majority of the public are typically induced by interviewers to express opinions on topics for which they are – by their own admission – poorly informed or wholly ignorant (2004, 158–159).

This raises some red flags. However, decades of research on political knowledge and policy attitudes have demonstrated that an inability to define technical terms or answer "quiz-like" poll questions does not mean that voters lack a reasonable basis for their expressed preferences. First, citizens may have a strong passive vocabulary and a weak active vocabulary. This means that, although they might not use words like "monetary policy," "superfund," or "most favored nation status" in their everyday conversations, citizens are capable of understanding news stories and debates about those topics. Similarly, although citizens might not be able to give details about "creationism," "creation science," "intelligent design," or "Darwin's theory of evolution," they nevertheless understand generally what these proposals mean and could follow a journalistic account that used these terms.

Second, innovative research by Milt Lodge and his colleagues about electoral campaigns demonstrates that citizens absorb very specific policy details advocated by candidates, incorporate those policy promises in their general evaluation of the candidate, and then forget the specifics. Nevertheless, their preference for the candidate reflects these details (Lodge, Steenbergen, and Brau 1995). This is not that much different from consumers who research different household appliances. At the beginning of the search, they consider many different brands, but as they do more and more research, they eliminate choices and gradually come to like a specific one. By then, they can't remember the details from the beginning of the search – details that placed the eventual "winner" in the lead among competitors. Thus, neither consumers nor voters can fully defend and explain their final choice, even though it was based on evidence and logic.

In the case of evolution, citizens are exposed to hundreds of stimuli relevant to the debate. These include details from their science education (and perhaps that of their children), snippets of documentaries on the Discovery Channel, stories of new fossil discoveries in the newspaper, discussions in church or on religious programming, and informational signs read at their local zoo or museum. Perhaps someone caught an episode of *Creation Hour* – the television show produced by the "young earth" organization, Answers in Genesis. He watched carefully and was impressed by the discussion showing limits to the use of radioisotope dating. He was paying attention when the show's host argued that these flaws lead scientists to incorrectly estimate the age of dinosaur fossils. Yet some weeks later, he only remembers that he found the argument persuasive and that it reaffirmed his confidence in the Genesis version of creation. When contacted by a pollster, he would use this memory in answering survey questions and express his feeling that creationism should be taught alongside evolution. But when pressed, he is not willing to claim he is "very familiar" with creationism or intelligent design. Lodge's research suggests that we cannot conclude that vote choices or policy preferences are irrational and mired in ignorance simply because respondents cannot recall specifics or seem unsure of the facts at the time of the survey.

The question is then not whether citizens can define specific terms on the spot or even if they feel confident that they could explain them. If Lodge's cognitive model applies to public opinion as well as campaign information, the real question is whether ordinary citizens have had the opportunity to see, read, or hear information relevant to the debate so that they may process it and update their "running tally" in favor of or in opposition to the teaching of creationism. The available data suggest that ordinary citizens do come across substantial relevant information over the course of their lives. In a typical year, for example, more than fifty million adults (22–26% of the adult population) visit a museum of natural history, staying an average of 2.9 hours (Griffiths and King 2008, Tables 1 and 45; Pew Internet Project 2006, 27). Science documentaries that provide basic facts about lines of descent and the age of fossils are watched by millions. According to a report by the Pew Internet Project (2006, 27), 43% say they "regularly" watch programming on the Discovery Channel. A single show, Discovery Channel's three-hour "Walking with Dinosaurs" special, was viewed by eight percent of all U.S. households with televisions (Higgins 2000). Major fossil discoveries are often featured as cover stories in magazines such as *Time* and *Newsweek*, and it is easy to come across *National Geographic* accounts of evolution at the dentist's office. In short, ordinary Americans are exposed to a great deal of information that can be the basis of a reasoned policy preference.

Yet having the possibility of a reasoned policy preference does not mean that every citizen made correct inferences at the time they were exposed to the information. Thus, ignorance and misunderstanding might still have a major impact on our estimates of public opinion. There can be no doubt that only a small portion of the public can be called scientifically literate. In the particular case of evolutionary biology, many members of the public seem unaware of the scientific consensus on evolution. For example, in a 2005 Pew Center poll, respondents were asked, "From what you've heard or read, is there general agreement among scientists that humans evolved over time, or not?" Only 54% said "yes," 13% were unsure, and 33% said "no." This shows clearly that the public education efforts of the scientific establishment have been ineffective. We will examine the notion of scientific literacy in greater detail in Chapter 3. However, our main concern at present is whether this ignorance of the scientific consensus can account for the large support for teaching creationism. And here the answer is both clear and perhaps surprising. If we restrict our attention to those citizens who acknowledge a scientific consensus concerning human evolution (the first column in Table 2.6), only 20% endorse the teaching of evolution alone. Even among this group of citizens, a large majority want to teach creationism and, once again, we find that teaching only creationism is more popular than teaching evolution exclusively. For evolution proponents who say, "if citizens only knew that scientists have long ago settled this issue, they wouldn't support such a policy," these data

Table 2.6. Preferences for teaching evolution and creationism, conditional on knowledge of the scientific consensus

	Yes, there is agreement among scientists that humans evolved (%)	No, there is not agreement among scientists that humans evolved (%)	Don't know or refused (%)	Total (%)
1. Teach creationism or ID only	32	49	31	38
2. Teach creationism for sure (DK "instead")	3	5	9	5
3. Teach a combination	39	25	14	31
4. Teach evolution for sure (DK "along with")	1	0	3	1
5. Teach evolution only	20	14	10	17
Don't know or ambiguous response	5	6	32	9
Total	100%	100%	100%	100%
(N)	(1,088)	(661)	(250)	(2,000)

Sources: Pew (2005), Religion and public life survey; see Appendix 2 for details.

suggest that there are enormous limits to the effectiveness of public science.

The only evidence we can find that suggests that ignorance is related to policy positions comes from the 1999 PFAW survey. As we mentioned before, we think that the sponsorship and lack of documentation for this survey requires some degree of caution (see footnote 4). Nevertheless, we do not want to ignore evidence that might weigh against our thesis. In the PFAW survey, only 21% of citizens who correctly stated that "evolution means that humans developed from less advanced forms of life" said they supported the Kansas School Board's decision; this is in contrast to 33% of those who incorrectly said that "evolution means that human beings developed from apes."

This twelve percentage point difference between those giving correct and incorrect answers is quite large (although not large enough to change any of our major conclusions). And it might be tempting to extrapolate and predict that hostility toward evolution would drop by about one-third if the public were better informed, learned the correct definition of evolution, and understood that paleontologists do not consider early *Homo* species to have evolved from "apes."

But this temptation should be resisted. If most citizens who do not accept evolution do so because of their religion, upbringing, or local culture, they may have fewer opportunities (and less motivation) to learn the details of evolutionary arguments. And what if they changed their understanding of evolution as a result of excellent public science efforts?

> ANTI: I can't accept that my great-great-great-great grandmother was a monkey.
>
> SCIENTIST: Evolution doesn't say that at all. It says that humans and apes have a common ancestor; that humans developed from earlier forms of animals. Let me explain...
>
> ANTI: Whatever. I can't accept that my great-great-great-great grandmother was an Australopithecus.

The absence of the original data file makes it impossible for us to account for factors (such as religious beliefs) that might render some or all of this correlation to be spurious. But the more important point is that correlation is not causation. We cannot conclude that ignorance of the scientific consensus accounts for the strong expressed support for creationism.

The most detailed analyses of the effects of scientific literacy have been carried out by Jon D. Miller and his colleagues. Based on a multivariate, structural equations analysis of U.S. data from 2005, Miller, Scott, and Okamoto found that the observed correlation (total effect) of a ten-item scale measuring "genetic scientific literacy" and belief in evolution was only 0.20. Moreover, after controlling for ideology and religious views, the effect of genetic literacy was not statistically significant (Miller, Scott, and Okamoto 2006, Table S1 and Figure S2). More generally, Miller finds that the United States ranks second in the world in overall science literacy (Miller 2006, Table 3) but ranks thirty-second in acceptance of human evolution among thirty-four nations studied (Miller et al. 2006, Figures 1 and S1). At the individual level, Miller also shows that, in the United States, correctly answering a question about human evolution is largely unrelated to the construct of general scientific knowledge (Miller 2006, Table 1).[6]

---

[6] In a factor analysis of 32 items on a scientific knowledge quiz, the question about whether humans evolved from earlier species of animals is the only question with a factor loading below 0.40.

Science illiteracy may play a small role in the distribution of policy preferences, and, over time, increased science literacy generally might shift the percentages supporting evolution and creationism in the classroom. Yet, the overall evidence suggests that the high support for creationism in the classroom cannot be attributed primarily, or even substantially, to overall scientific illiteracy in the United States. Rather, belief in special creation by God is high *in spite of* having one of the world's most educated and scientifically literate populations. The sources of this lie in cultural, and especially, religious features of the United States.

Finally, we should call attention to the impressive stability of public opinion on this issue. It is not simply the stability of particular survey items but the stability of the *differences between items*. Although there is a trend toward greater polarization, the public's preference for creationism over evolution has remained stable since at least 1981. Moreover, the apparent increase in polarization coincides with substantial "public science" activities on the part of both establishment organizations, such as the NAS, and by challengers, such as the Institute for Creation Science and the Discovery Institute. The small shifts that we see are consistent with patterns of change on other policy attitudes that Page and Shapiro take as evidence of a "rational public" (1992).

To summarize our conclusions thus far, we find no compelling reason to discredit the policy preferences that Americans have expressed for the last quarter century. Support for teaching evolution alone might be a few percentage points higher if we avoid polls with religious cues; and we cannot be sure of the degree of polarization because we get very different estimates of the size of the "middle group" depending on whether pollsters use a single question or the two-question format. But support for teaching creationism is high and it is not an illusion. The public may not know many of the details of contemporary evolutionary biology, but there is no evidence that they lack a reasonable basis for the opinions they express. To pursue this last idea more fully, however, we need to understand what social scientists call the "structure" of attitudes toward evolution and creationism. By this, we mean the extent to which people's policy preferences are influenced at the psychological level by their more general ideology and by other attitudes they hold. Central among these attitudes are those stemming from religion.

THE STRUCTURE OF PUBLIC OPINION

In his landmark essay on "Belief Systems in Mass Publics," Philip Converse (1964) suggested that the hallmark of political sophistication was holding a coherent "belief system." Coherence, for Converse, was encapsulated in the concept of *constraint* – the notion that attitudes cluster together such that changing opinion on one issue would likely lead to changes on another. For Converse, constraint was a psychological concept involving *idea elements*. Idea elements might include policy preferences, values, beliefs, and political ideology. The constraint among idea elements could result from several different sources.

At the cognitive level, citizens might perceive that some policy preferences follow *logically* from their beliefs, values, or other attitudes they hold. For example, a strong belief in the separation of church and state might logically lead a citizen to oppose prayer in schools, oppose tax support for parochial schools, and oppose the teaching of the biblical story of creation. Here, holding a more generally ideological position would create constraint (correlations) among three different policy attitudes. Peffley and Hurwitz (1985) have called this a *hierarchical* attitude structure because the general belief structures the more specific ones. Similarly, if one believes that the Bible is inerrant, then it may be perceived to be *illogical* to also believe that human beings walked the earth more than 100,000 years ago.

Also at the cognitive level, Converse suggested that some ideas may serve a common interest or function. Interests are tricky to discern in the realm of cultural politics. Nevertheless, it is clear that certain social groups have a lot riding on the outcome of the evolution/creation controversy. Major professional organizations – ranging from the NAS to the National Science Teachers Association – have all weighed in on the debate. On the other side, anti-evolutionism as a *social movement* was instrumental in the growth of fundamentalism in the United States (Lienesch 2007; Marsden 1982). To the extent that individuals perceive that the outcome of each court case and school board action reflects on the prestige of their key group (Gusfield 1963), then the attitudes held by individuals may reflect those group interests.

Converse also argued that individual citizens learn "what goes with what" from taking in debates by elites. Citizens do not get relevant facts piecemeal but already connected by the authors of sermons and textbooks, by teachers and guests on Sunday morning public affairs shows, by neighbors who canvas the neighborhood, and by officials running for public office. If advocates of teaching creationism explicitly want to return God to public schools, and if intelligent design's opponents focus as much on the First Amendment principles as they do on the scientific arguments, then it would be quite reasonable for citizens to make these connections also. Indeed, the connections made rhetorically by elites may be the major reason that citizens perceive some ideas as logically linked to others. These connections are those made in political discourse, and this, in turn, is often driven by social groups. The "social sources" of constraint are to be found in the major social divisions that generate political alignments – divisions based on social class, education, religion, and geography.

In the remainder of this chapter, we will empirically examine attitudinal constraint – with particular attention to logical connections at the psychological level. The role of major social divisions in structuring the debate will be illuminated in the next chapter.

The Core of the Belief System: Beliefs about Human Origins and Biblical Literalism

We begin our exploration of the structure of evolution beliefs by examining three core elements. First is the individual's belief about human origins. If one is skeptical of either the creation story in Genesis or scientific accounts of human origins, then we expect this skepticism to be reflected in policy preferences. Second, one's belief in creationism may be logically related to one's views about how to interpret the Bible. We explore these first.

Three polls contain questions asking about policy (what should be taught?), beliefs about human origins, and biblical literalism. These fit together logically and, if this logic governs the thinking of large numbers of people, we should see high correlations among these variables. With respect to human origins, most polls use a question offering respondents three choices.

☐ God created human beings pretty much in their present form at one time within the last 10,000 years or so.

☐ Human beings have developed over millions of years from less advanced forms of life, but God guided this process.

☐ Human beings have developed over millions of years from less advanced forms of life, but God had no part in this process.

We have scored those who give the first answer (young earth creationism) as 1, those who choose the middle option (commonly termed "theistic evolution") as 2, and those who select the materialistic or organic evolution option as 3. In polls since 1999, roughly 45% of the public has endorsed the young earth creationist position, 32% theistic evolution, and 13% materialistic evolution (Plutzer and Berkman 2008).[7]

Questions about the Bible typically offer three choices along the lines of:

☐ The Bible is the actual word of God and is to be taken literally, word for word.

☐ The Bible is the word of God, but not everything in it should be taken literally, word for word.

☐ The Bible is a book written by men and is not the word of God.

We also score these from 1 to 3. The *Newsweek* 2004 survey has a yes/no question in which respondents are asked, "*Do you believe that every word of the Bible is literally accurate – that the events it describes actually happened, or not?*" This is scored as a 1 for yes, and 2 for no.

Table 2.7 reports polychoric correlations among these three questions, calculated separately from three different data sources. Polychoric correlations are appropriate for estimating correlations from ordinal and dichotomous items, and they are interpreted in the usual way: correlations run from −1 to +1 with a value of 0 indicating statistical independence and scores of −1 and +1 indicating a perfect

---

[7] This poll question is far from ideal. The second option in particular might be selected by many who identify as creationists as well as those who accept evolution. For example, "old earth" creationists – those who believe in human's special creation but subscribe to different interpretations about the length of biblical "days," for example – might plausibly give either of the first two answers. Nevertheless, it provides a useful ordering of ordinary citizens and, as we will show in Chapter 7, public school science teachers as well.

Table 2.7. The structure of evolution–creationism belief systems: Polychoric correlations among idea elements

	Teach what?	Human origins	Is Bible true?
A. Newsweek 2004 poll			
What should be taught in public schools (1–5)	1.00		
Beliefs about human origins (1–3)	.49	1.00	
Is Bible literally true (1–2)	.52	.75	1.00
Mean polychoric correlation = .59			
B. VCU Life Sciences Survey 2005			
What should be taught in public schools (1–3)	1.00		
Beliefs about human origins (1–3)	.64	1.00	
Is Bible literally true (1–3)	.65	.74	1.00
Mean polychoric correlation = .68			
C. Pew Religion and Public Life Survey 2005			
What should be taught in public schools (1–5)	1.00		
Beliefs about human origins (1–3)	.50	1.00	
Is Bible literally true (1–3)	.46	.67	1.00
Mean polychoric correlation = .54			

Sources: See Appendix 2.

correlation. As a matter of convenience, all survey questions examined in this section are scored such that the low score represents the creationist or socially conservative response and high scores the pro-evolution or more liberal response. Scored this way, high *positive* correlations will indicate constraint consistent with historical linkages, elite discourse, or logical inference.

The results show that, in all three surveys, the attitudes are tightly structured. The average inter-item correlation ranges from 0.54 in the Pew Survey to 0.68 in the VCU Life Sciences Survey. Americans who are biblical literalists tend to reject evolution entirely in favor of a "young earth" creationist position, whereas those who see the Bible as a human achievement are most likely to adopt a materialistic view of evolution (average correlation among these two elements is 0.72). Not surprisingly, personal beliefs about human origins are strongly correlated with preferences for what should be taught (average correlation is 0.54). Thus, we see a logical basis for the policy preferences expressed by ordinary Americans.

Of course the correlations are far from perfect. We expect some departure due to random measurement error and because citizens undoubtedly bring other considerations into play when reporting their policy preferences. Thus, we need to ask why someone who is a biblical literalist and believes in a "young earth" might nevertheless endorse the teaching of evolution (perhaps in addition to creationism). And, conversely, why would those who believe in a materialist view of evolution agree that creationism should also be taught in public schools? One obvious answer concerns church–state relations and civil liberties. The ACLU and other civil libertarians have consistently argued that there is nothing wrong with *believing* in the teachings of the Bible, so long as those beliefs are not implicitly or explicitly endorsed by government institutions such as schools. Fundamentalist Christians who find this argument persuasive might logically believe that God created Adam and Eve roughly 6,000 years ago but not wish to have that story taught in high school science classes. On the other side of the spectrum, citizens who accept evolution but are not concerned about the introduction of religion in public schools might find proposals for "equal time" to be quite reasonable.

To see whether this is the case, we turn to the 2004 CBS–*New York Times* poll. This contains the two-question-format measure of teaching preferences, the standard question about belief in human origins, and four questions that address church–state relations. These ask respondents whether the federal government should fund "faith-based" organizations to carry out social programs, whether such programs should promote their religion if they accept such funds, whether they are worried about close relationships between religious leaders and politicians, and whether politicians should legislate religious-inspired policies. These questions are not perfect, but they do allow us to construct a scale running from 0 to 4 that distinguishes those who see a need for closer linkages between religion and government (scored 0) and those who are concerned about all four aspects of church–state relations (scored 4). The scale has only a modest degree of reliability (alpha = 0.58), which would have the effect of masking strong correlations.

To see how church–state attitudes influence policy preferences, we examined the association between church–state liberalism and

Table 2.8. The association between church–state liberalism and preferences for teaching evolution and creationism

	Number of liberal church–state answers					
	0 (%)	1 (%)	2 (%)	3 (%)	4 (%)	Total
A. Citizens with young earth creationist beliefs						
1. Teach creationism or ID only	64	63	61	49	26	54
2. Teach creationism for sure (DK instead)	11	10	6	6	7	7
3. Teach a combination	24	20	25	33	37	28
4. Teach evolution for sure (DK along with)	0	0	2	2	0	1
5. Teach evolution only	0	7	7	10	30	10
	100%	100%	100%	100%	100%	100%
(N)	(45)	(86)	(127)	(116)	(54)	(428)
Polychoric correlation = .19						
B. Citizens with theistic evolution beliefs						
1. Teach creationism or ID only	–	23	38	19	6	20
2. Teach creationism for sure (DK instead)	–	3	9	3	2	4
3. Teach a combination	–	52	29	56	44	47
4. Teach evolution for sure (DK along with)	–	6	2	4	2	3
5. Teach evolution only	–	16	22	17	47	27
	–	100%	100%	100%	100%	100%
(N)	(1)	(31)	(45)	(98)	(66)	(241)
Polychoric correlation = .17						
C. Citizens with materialistic evolution beliefs						
1. Teach creationism or ID only	–	–	8	7	6	6
2. Teach creationism for sure (DK instead)	–	–	0	0	0	0
3. Teach a combination	–	–	23	26	29	29
4. Teach evolution for sure (DK along with)	–	–	8	7	1	4
5. Teach evolution only	–	–	62	61	64	61
	–	–	100%	100%	100%	100%
(N)	(0)	(5)	(13)	(46)	(69)	(133)
Polychoric correlation = .01						

Source: CBS/*New York Times* Poll (2004); see Appendix 2 for details.

policy preferences separately for young earth creationists, theistic evolutionists, and materialistic evolutionists. The results appear below in Table 2.8. The first panel reports the results for the 428 respondents who said, "*God created human beings in their present form.*" This is a conservative group, generally, with 54% endorsing creationism only. But there is considerable diversity of views about the separation of church and state, and these views make a substantial difference. Support for creationism only is much lower, and support for evolution only is much higher, among those who take the liberal position in three or four of the church–state questions. Here, we see evidence that competing considerations are in play among those who do not accept evolution personally.

We see a similar pattern among those who believe that *"Human beings have evolved from less advanced life forms over millions of years, but God guided this process."* However, there is no impact of civil liberties attitudes among the small group of those endorsing evolution without God's guidance. This is due mostly to the lack of variance on the church–state questions – there are no church–state conservatives in this group.

WHAT, EXACTLY, DO CREATIONISTS WANT?

This chapter has focused on seven surveys and polls that each asked about teaching evolution and creationism in public schools. We have argued that the opinions expressed by ordinary Americans are stable, structured ideologically, and would not be altogether different if there were a major increase in general scientific literacy. For those who tell us that they want evolution eliminated from the curriculum – a minority of 25–30% – the policy implications are quite clear. But when citizens say that they want creationism taught in public schools, what precisely is the implication for public policy? Do they simply want a brief mention of creationism, to let students know that there is another explanation? Or do they want a detailed curriculum covering flood geology, evidence for irreducible complexity, and a detailed inventory of missing transitional forms in the fossil record? And do all of these citizens really want creationism taught *as science* in the required general biology class? Or would it be enough if students had an opportunity learn about creationist perspectives in a social studies or philosophy class?

Although none of the major university or media polls address these questions, we can get some sense by examining the results from the 2000 survey conducted by the Daniel Yankelovich Group for the liberal advocacy group PFAW (though see footnote 4). According to their published report (PFAW 2000), 29% of the public wants creationism taught in science classes as a "scientific theory." This includes those who would ban evolution and those who would teach the two perspectives side-by-side as scientific approaches.

This same poll estimates that only 20% of the public supports teaching only evolution, with 46% supporting the teaching of creationism as something other than science – as a "belief" or as a "religious explanation" for human origins. Such instruction could conceivably pass constitutional muster if presented in the context of comparative religion (e.g., a discussion of creation stories from many faiths), history, or history of science. But if offered as an endorsement as a valid alternative to evolution, such instruction would likely be ruled outside the bounds of the constitutionally permissible. It is unfortunate that we lack greater detail on the preferences of the public. However, this lone study suggests, again, that only about 20% of the public endorses current policies; a larger number, 30%, support teaching creationism *as science*. The remainder is divided among softer alternatives that accommodate creationism to some extent and straddle the boundary dividing constitutional from unconstitutional policies.

It is perhaps easier to get a handle on what creationists *do not* want: they do not want their children exposed to the idea that evolution and common ancestry are universally accepted facts. While recognizing that the many surveys we reviewed here show support for teaching both, or for teaching what is often misleadingly referred to as "the controversy" (even though there is no controversy among scientists), we suspect that much of this actually represents what is seen as the only way to get nonscientific alternatives into the classroom. But from its origins, the *anti-evolution movement*, as Lienesch (2007) terms it, was one founded on opposition more than the promotion of any particular alternative. And that opposition is very clearly based on religious concerns with what it means to expose schoolchildren to the secular and materialistic view that God was not involved in the origins of man. As Eugenie Scott of the National Center for Science Education puts it, animosity toward evolution is founded "on a strongly held religious conviction that acceptance of evolution (or 'belief' in evolution as it is commonly put) causes children to abandon their faith in God..." If a child loses faith, "that child is lost to salvation" (Scott 2009, 371).

Michael Ruse puts this view in perspective when he writes of Darwin's *Origin of Species* that, "The Origin was one of the most significant and controversial work of the age – of any age – most particularly because the book was seen to challenge long-held views about religion, specifically the Christian religion and its claims about creation and about the nature of God, of humans, and of our relationship to God" (2005, 1). Anti-evolutionism was important to early twentieth century fundamentalist Christianity and it remains so because an "important element of evangelicalism is tension with a secular society that evangelicals perceive as antithetical to their values" (Campbell 2006, 106). Schools, according to many religious conservatives, are a source of immense danger to them and their children (Apple and Oliver 1996). Instruction in evolution was and continues to be perceived as a particular peril that reinforces "tension with a secular society that evangelicals perceive as antithetical to their values" (Campbell 2006, 106, paraphrasing Smith 1998). Campbell contends that "this group might consider itself threatened" because of this tension (2006, 106).

A sense of persecution at the core of American fundamentalism (Binder 2007; Smith 1998) is critical to understanding its strong opposition to the imposition of such a clearly secular and threatening perspective as evolution. In the next chapter, we explore this more systematically by demonstrating how important religious identification is to anti-evolution attitudes.

SUMMARY

In this chapter, we have explored the policy preferences of American citizens. Because any particular survey may have important limitations, we conducted detailed analyses on data from seven different studies, and we employed seven other surveys and polls for supplemental analysis. With one exception, we were able to obtain the original respondent-level data files, and this permitted us to conduct our own analyses. But more important, it permitted us to compare surveys so that we could estimate potential bias stemming from question wording and format, question order, question preambles and introductory sentences, and the general theme of the poll or survey. We uncovered several possible sources of bias – in which question wording or the theme of the survey could change the level of support for creationism by five or even ten percentage points. However, we also saw substantial evidence of consistency and evidence that deliberate attempts to manipulate answers had meager effects.

We found no compelling evidence that opinion on this issue is "manufactured" by the pollsters themselves and therefore an "illusion." To the contrary, we found considerable evidence that respondents have logical reasons for the answers that they give. Respondents who believe in a fairly literal interpretation of the Bible tend to be skeptical of evolution and endorse the introduction of creationism into America's classrooms. But among this group, their policy preferences are tempered if they show support for the separation of church and state on other issues. Scientists might prefer that citizens use other criteria in reaching their policy preferences. But the fact remains that citizens have a reasonable basis for their preferences, given their more general beliefs about religion, the Bible's creation story, and civil liberties.

On the other hand, there is mixed evidence for whether scientific understanding plays a major role in forging individuals' policy attitudes. There is some evidence that citizens who are better informed about what "evolution" means – that humans and apes share a common ancestry and not that humans evolved from apes – are more supportive of evolution in the classroom. Yet, most creationists understand that there is a scientific consensus regarding evolution, and they *nevertheless* reject its inclusion in the curriculum.

Although any particular data set may have limitations, analyzing many different polls provides valuable insights into what Americans want and allows us to conclude that these desires merit respect and consideration in the democratic process. Even if the actual percentages might differ from poll to poll, there can be no doubt that the large majority of Americans want creationism taught in the public schools. A large plurality of this group wants creationism taught *as science and in science classes*, whereas others apparently would be satisfied to see some ideas of creationism validated by their discussion as a religious perspective or belief. But current legal decisions rule out *all* such possibilities. And as we will see in later chapters, their preferences are nowhere realized in official content standards of the U.S. states. Many citizens, therefore, perceived these standards as hostile toward their values. This keeps the issue alive and keeps evolution opponents mobilized and motivated to influence standards in more subtle or creative ways that do not raise constitutional issues.

On the other side, we find a small but growing number of citizens who support the teaching of evolution and only evolution; and we find a shrinking group occupying the middle position. This is evidence of a nation divided. This division is reflected in attitudes, beliefs, and policy preferences. But its roots lie in *social divisions* that derive from religious affiliation, education, and geography. Understanding these roots – the "social bases" of the evolution conflict – is essential to understand the resulting politics and to understand the challenges facing the nation's high school teachers. Thus, our next chapter includes an analysis and description of how the nation is socially divided about evolution and creationism.

3 A Nation Divided by Religion, Education, and Place

Question: Why do so many people believe in the theory of evolution?

Answer: Some people believe in evolution because that's all they know. In school, at home, on T.V. – everywhere they look – that is all they hear. They don't know there are problems with the theory, or that there are good reasons for believing that God created everything. Other people believe in evolution because they have studied science and believe the evidence supports the theory. Often, these people have not considered the wonderful evidence for creation. Sadly, some people believe in evolution because they think it supports their denial of God's existence.

Digger Doug, *Discovery Magazine (Scripture and Science for Kids)*[1]

Question: So many people resist believing in evolution. Where does the resistance come from?

Answer: It comes, I'm sorry to say, from religion. And from bad religion. You won't find any opposition to the idea of evolution among sophisticated, educated theologians. It comes from an exceedingly retarded, primitive version of religion, which unfortunately is at present undergoing an epidemic in the United States. Not in Europe, not in Britain, but in the United States.

Richard Dawkins (2005)

D ARWIN PUBLISHED *On the Origin of Species* (or simply, *The Origin*) in 1859 and *The Descent of Man* in 1871. By the late

[1] Digger Doug is quoted from the Web-based *Discovery Magazine* (http://www.discoverymagazine.com/digger/d95dd/d9508dd.html; accessed March 16, 2008). The Dawkins quote is from an interview by Gordy Slack for Salon.com, April 30, 2005 (http://www.salon.com/news/feature/2005/04/30/dawkins/index.html; accessed December 21, 2009).

1920s, anti-evolutionism in the United States was a complex and well-developed social movement (Lienesch 2007), and the controversy over teaching evolution was highly divisive (Ginger 1958; Larson 1989; Numbers 1992). The most important lines of division concerned religion, education, and geography. The popular view, reinforced by the images of the *Scopes* trial in the public imagination, is that opposition to evolution was a distinctive product of southern, poorly educated fundamentalists.

Of course, the social divisions underlying the evolution conflict were not so clear cut then. In the 1920s, there were differences within Protestantism (Marsden 1982); fundamentalism was not the only Christian tradition opposed to evolution (Ruse 2005); the leaders of the anti-evolution movement were themselves well educated and drawn from the middle class (Numbers 1992); and, although the movement only achieved legislative success in the South, it had considerable popular support throughout the nation (Larson 1989; Lienesch 2007). What we can say *as a generalization* is that anti-evolutionism was most prominent among those caught up in the nascent fundamentalist movement and in the non-metropolitan areas of the South and the Midwest (Larson 1989; see also Woodberry and Smith 1998 on the migration of southern conservative Protestants to other parts of the country).

It has now been 151 years since publication of *The Origin* and 85 years since the *Scopes* trial. Yet, the controversy over teaching evolution in public schools remains a feature of U.S. domestic politics. During the years 2006–2008 alone, legislation bearing on the question was introduced in nineteen state legislatures[2]; this is in addition to controversial decisions by state boards of education, textbook commissions, and many local skirmishes. In broad terms, religion, education, and geography remain central lines of cleavage, and we will examine these in this chapter. Yet, there is reason to believe that cleavages may be more blurred and more complex than they were in the 1920s. Fundamentalist ideas are now held by many individuals who attend mainline Protestant churches (Wilcox 1986). Education levels of evangelicals and fundamentalists have risen faster than

[2] National Center for Science Education, News Search (http://ncse.com/news; accessed November 6, 2009).

those of other faith traditions, and substantial residential mobility has complicated the geographic bases of cultural politics (Woodberry and Smith 1998).

Understanding how religion, education, and geography structure the conflict among members of the public will help us understand how the hostility of many toward evolution can be traced to specific lines in Christian theology. The social dimensions also illuminate the politics of both writing curricular policy at the state level and implementing those policies in the nation's classrooms.

DIVERSITY IN PROTESTANT AMERICA

How did the nation become so divided in just sixty years following the publication of *The Origin*? Part of the answer lies in rapid social change within Christianity in North America. Between the end of the Civil War in 1869 and the turn of the century, deep divisions formed within American Protestantism along four key dimensions: orientation toward modernity, biblical interpretation, ideologies of progress, and eschatology. Northern evangelicals and those associated with older Protestant denominations tended to have a more accommodating approach toward modernity, an interpretive approach to the Bible, and believed that good works to better society were an expression of faith and piety (Marsden 1982; Ruse 2005; Woodberry and Smith 1998). This wing of American Protestantism became active in the abolition and temperance movements, was instrumental in the emergence of social work as a profession, and actively participated in socially progressive efforts. Southern, white Protestants were more traditional and gradually became differentiated from their northern counterparts. At the same time, the nation saw the development of parallel Protestant church institutions for African Americans and the rapid immigration of Roman Catholics to America's cities.

The formation of the Fundamentalist movement contributed to institutionalizing the divisions among white Protestants. Expressed in a series of pamphlets, *The Fundamentals of Christian Religion* (or simply, *The Fundamentals*), this movement "argued for the authority of Scripture, the veracity of Biblical miracles, and salvation through Christ alone" (Woodberry and Smith 1998, 28). A major step in institutionalization can also be seen in the 1909 publication of the Scofield Reference Bible by Oxford University Press (Bray 1996, 453; Marsden 1982, 119). The Scofield Bible "was meant to explain the vagaries of dispensational premillennialism to the masses" and "was arguably the most important event in the development of fundamentalism in the twentieth century" (Balmer 2002, 511). Widely used throughout the twentieth century, the Scofield Bible contained notes throughout emphasizing the principals of biblical inerrancy and premillennial eschatology. Most relevant, it also included in its notes the calculation of Archbishop James Ussher that the earth was created in the year 4004 BC. At the same time, mainline Protestants gained control of major religious institutions in the North. As Bray describes it, those with the most orthodox interpretations of the Bible "lost control of the major denominations, and were driven from Princeton Theological Seminary, which had been their great stronghold" (Bray 1996, 376).

Within secular thought, an ideology of progress has always been present in American culture. In this view, industriousness and scientific progress are seen as the sources of steady improvement in the human condition. The ideology of progress fit well with northern evangelicals' emphasis on good works and societal improvement.

Reinforcing these divisions were differences in *eschatology* that emerged during the late nineteenth and early twentieth centuries as well. Two different interpretations of the Book of Revelation were widely held at the turn of the century. Postmillennialists believed they were living through a thousand-year period of heaven on earth and that biblical prophecies concerning the defeat of the anti-Christ (often seen to be the Pope) would soon be fulfilled. Christ would return at the end of this period of spiritual and cultural progress. Postmillennialists believed that humans could actively help to bring this about by their good works, and such a view was quite compatible with a secular ideology of progress. Promoted by preachers such as Jonathan Edwards during the Great Awakening, postmillennialism was "the most prevalent view among American evangelicals between the revolution and the Civil War" (Marsden 1982, 49).

Premillennialists, in contrast, believe that Jesus will return first, before his thousand-year reign, but only after a horrific battle of good versus evil on this earth – Armageddon. Traditionalism, fundamentalism, and premillennialism all flourished in the period during and immediately after the First World War. As Woodberry and Smith summarize, "many fundamentalists viewed the rise of Bolshevism as the natural outcome of modernism, and barbarity of 'civilized' Europe during World War I as a resounding disproof of modernist beliefs in the perfectibility of society and the goodness of human nature. Society was not becoming better, it was becoming worse; social reform and education could not overcome human sinfulness" (1998, 28; see also Ruse 2005).

The notion of organic evolution as it was conceived by many scientists and lay people had implications for each of these two dimensions. It was a modern, scientific perspective that was linked to historical advancement – with humans being seen by most early evolutionists as evidence that evolution brings biological "progress" (Ruse 2005). Thus, evolution was embraced by both theological postmillennialists and those who most fervently embraced an ideology of progress – whether secular or religious. Because Christians in these traditions typically took a more interpretive approach to Scripture, evolution did not pose a challenge to their faith.

In contrast, evolution came to be viewed as incompatible with Christianity by premillennialists, because they viewed the Bible as authoritative, inerrant, and literally true. Into this theological context, one additional element would be needed to turn a general hostility toward evolution into a full-blown political movement: the unprecedented expansion of public education. The teaching of evolution – or any doctrine hostile to fundamentalist adherents – would have generated little controversy in the years immediately following the Civil War because so few Americans attended more than a few years of school. The rapid expansion of education meant that the children of almost all conservative Protestants would potentially be exposed to Darwinian ideas that posed a challenge to their faith (Scott 2006). This was the perfect storm that provided the conditions for anti-evolutionism to grow into a vibrant social movement characterized by strong nationwide organizations, prominent leadership, impressive fundraising, massive rallies, and the widespread distribution of books, pamphlets, and reprints of sermons (Lienesch 2007).

Religion and Anti-Evolutionism Today

The denominational landscape in the United States is complex and not easily mapped – either theologically or geographically. Woodberry and Smith argue that the term *fundamentalism* "properly refers to a small subset" of conservative Protestants who "emphasize a strict literal interpretation of the Bible, dispensational theology, premillennial eschatology, and institutional separation from . . . liberal Protestants and Catholics" (1998, 28). However, doctrines associated with the early fundamentalist movement – biblical inerrancy in particular – are also widely embraced by individuals in other denominations (Wilcox 1986), a tribute to the effectiveness of fundamentalist clergy and laity in spreading their ideas to the wider community.

In this section, we will focus on the denominational bases of pro- and anti-evolutionism in the United States. Denominations serve as potential bases for political mobilization and can influence public opinion – not only among their own adherents but also among members of the broader community. Thus, understanding the denominational bases of the evolution conflict is critical.

Unfortunately, the fragmentation of American Christianity complicates our efforts. There are well over a thousand distinct Protestant denominations in the United States, and any analysis of denominational impact must reduce this to a manageable number of denominational families or "faith traditions." A valid taxonomy must meet two conditions – one conceptual and one empirical. Conceptually, a valid taxonomy must be based on criteria relevant to the topic being investigated. In the present case, we must distinguish among denominations based on their doctrinal positions with respect to modernity, the Bible, and eschatology. Empirically, we need to have sufficiently detailed information of individual survey respondents so that we can confidently place them in the proper faith tradition.

Most of the media polls we examined in the previous chapter do no more than ask respondents if they are "Protestant, Catholic, Jewish, or something else." Such polls will not allow us to investigate splits within Protestant America. Others allow more choices, but, as Woodberry and Smith note, even "generic categories of Baptist, Lutheran, Presbyterian, etc., mask [important] distinctions and muddy statistical results" (1998, 34). Thus, surveys must make fine distinctions, for example, between the mainline *Evangelical Lutheran Church of America* and the fundamentalist *Wisconsin Synod Lutheran Church*.

Social scientists have developed many different ways of classifying denominations. Smith's (1990) review of different approaches to classification identified twelve distinct taxonomies dating from the 1950s through the 1980s. Most of these divide Protestants into three categories – a conservative or fundamentalist group, along with either (1) liberal and moderate groups or (2) a liberal group and a group of black Protestant churches. We rely on the *Religious Traditions* coding scheme (RELTRAD) developed by Brian Steensland, Jerry Park, Mark Regnerus, Lynn Robinson, W. Bradford Wilcox, and Robert Woodberry (2000). We use the RELTRAD taxonomy because the criteria it uses to classify Protestant denominations are based primarily on doctrinal differences that others independently have identified as central to the origins of anti-evolutionism: stance toward modernity, authority of and strict adherence to the Bible, dispensationalism, and eschatology (see Steensland et al. 2000, especially pages 293–294). These criteria mirror the religious doctrines most closely associated with anti-evolutionism historically, giving this scheme greater face validity than any other alternative.

The RELTRAD scheme will allow us to divide survey respondents into seven categories based on their religious affiliation: (1) mainline Protestant churches, (2) doctrinally conservative Protestant churches, (3) traditionally black Protestant churches, (4) the Roman Catholic Church, (5) Jewish congregations, (6) congregations of other religious traditions, and (7) a category for individuals who are not affiliated with any religious tradition. Among the respondents classified as mainline, the largest denominations represented include Methodists, Lutheran (excluding Missouri and Wisconsin Synods), Presbyterian, and Episcopalian. Among the doctrinally conservative churches, the largest number of individuals come from Southern Baptist, Pentecostal, and independent churches not affiliated with national denominational organizations. Of course, not all respondents who we identify as attending a "doctrinally conservative" church will identify themselves as "fundamentalist," "evangelical," or a "conservative Protestant." But all predominantly white churches with linkages to the fundamentalist or traditional evangelical traditions are included in this category.[3]

Religious Tradition and Support for Teaching Evolution

To classify Protestants into traditions likely to be either hostile toward or accommodating to evolution, we need surveys that ask respondents a series of follow-up questions that distinguish among the many different denominations containing the words Baptist, Evangelical, Lutheran, and so on. To our knowledge, only one data set contains this level of denominational detail and also contains a question about *teaching* evolution – a 1998 survey conducted by the University of North Carolina (UNC). In addition, the General Social Survey contains an extremely detailed denominational coding scheme and also contains questions asking about respondents *beliefs* about human origins. We will use both of these studies to explore the religious, geographic, and educational sources of political conflict.

We applied the RELTRAD classification scheme to respondents in the 1998 UNC survey and then examined support for teaching creationism *along with* evolution (the only teaching question available). The results (shown in the left-hand columns of Table 3.1) show that, among adherents to doctrinally conservative churches and traditionally black denominations, roughly 90% endorse creationism in the classroom. Support is substantially lower (though still well over a majority) among both mainline Protestants and Roman Catholics. Only Jews and those with no religious affiliation are clearly opposed to the introduction of creationism.

The right-hand columns of Table 3.1 report support for creationism, but only for those who attend church regularly (operationalized as at least 2–3 times each month). This breakdown gives us a better sense of the mobilization potential of the various denominations as it is easier to mobilize regular participants. But more importantly, this shows that, within *every* faith tradition, there is not that much

---

[3] There is considerable controversy over the label given to these churches. Many typologies refer to these churches as "Fundamentalist" (e.g., Smith 1990), Steensland et al. (2000) use the term "Evangelical," whereas others use the term "Conservative." We will use the term "doctrinally conservative Protestants" as this seems closest to the actual criteria used to classify the denominations.

Table 3.1. Support for teaching creationism *along with* evolution, for all respondents and those attending religious services at least 2–3 times each month, 1998

	All respondents		Regular attendees	
	%	N	%	N
Doctrinally conservative Protestant	90	304	91	201
Black Protestant	88	53	91	40
Mainline Protestant	58	232	66	136
Roman Catholic	57	339	63	198
Atheist/Agnostic	38	107	–	11
Jewish	12	26	–	5
Other faiths	–	9	–	8
All respondents	65	1055	75	599

Source: Southern Focus Poll (UNC); see Appendix 3 for details.

of a difference between regular and occasional participants in church services. This suggests that doctrine is far more important than a general concept of religiosity in structuring policy preferences concerning evolution.

The breakdown suggests that, when Roman Catholics and members of mainline Protestant churches attend religious services or informal gatherings, they will be in environments characterized by substantial diversity in opinions regarding evolution in the classroom. The distribution of opinion in these churches is slightly more opposed to teaching creationism than the nation as a whole, and the diversity of views would suggest that few mainline or Catholic congregations would be fertile ground for anti-evolution activities. Such activities, even if supported by a slim majority, would potentially alienate more than 40% of the congregation. In contrast, there is near uniformity of opinion in the doctrinally conservative congregations, making these ideal locales for political mobilization.

The black Protestants are also characterized by a near uniformity of opinion on this issue. However, their churches have never played a major role in evolution politics. This is likely due to two factors: (1) the greater salience and priority of politics concerning racial and economic justice and (2) a long-standing separation from predominantly white Southern churches that share many doctrinal beliefs (Lincoln and Mamiya 1990).

Table 3.2. Belief that "Human beings developed from earlier species of animals," by religious tradition, 1993–2004

	Definitely false (%)	Probably false (%)	Probably true (%)	Definitely true (%)	Total	N
Doctrinally conservative Protestant	62	14	19	5	100%	1,348
Black Protestant	46	20	28	7	100%	378
Mainline Protestant	27	18	38	16	100%	879
Roman Catholic	24	18	39	19	100%	1,253
Other Faiths	38	12	30	20	100%	326
Atheist/Agnostic	15	14	41	30	100%	584
Jewish	9	7	41	43	100%	120
All respondents	36	16	32	16	100%	4,888

Source: GSS (National Opinion Research Center, University of Chicago); see Appendix 3 for details.

It is unfortunate that, of the many polls and surveys that asked *something* about evolution or creationism in the classroom, the UNC survey is the only one that permits a detailed and valid denominational breakdown. The UNC survey is limited because it is now more than a decade old, asked but a single question about teaching creationism, and has a sampling scheme that limits statistical power (an oversample of southern states that requires substantial weighting of the data). In contrast, the best data source for studying religious differences in the United States, the University of Chicago's General Social Survey (GSS) has never asked a question about evolution *in the classroom* in its distinguished history from 1972 to the present. The GSS has, however, periodically asked questions about *beliefs* about human origins. Because beliefs are so highly correlated with policy preferences – in the last chapter, we estimated the correlation to be between 0.49 and 0.64 – we can use the GSS to complement our analyses of the UNC data.

In Table 3.2, we use the GSS to show how belief in human evolution is strongly associated with religious tradition (using the same RELTRAD typology). The tabulation reinforces our conclusion that religious traditions form one important source of cleavage in the evolution conflict. As in the case of policy preferences, respondents who are affiliated with doctrinally conservative churches are both conservative and relatively homogeneous in their opinions. Only 5% of this group thinks it is definitely true that "human beings developed from earlier species of animals," whereas 62% believe this is definitely false. In contrast, a majority of mainline Protestants and Roman Catholics think that evolution is "probably" or "definitely true." We see considerable diversity of opinion among the mainline Protestants and Catholics, again suggesting that political activism – in support of either side – is unlikely to emerge in these congregations.

Table 3.2 also contains a sufficient number of Jews and those unaffiliated with organized religion to make strong generalizations. Both groups are strong believers in human evolution, and neither group has substantial diversity of opinion, again suggesting that pro-evolution political mobilization is likely to emerge from and target these groups. In most communities, however, the Jewish community will simply be too small to be either effective or attractive to political entrepreneurs. And the "community" of nonreligious individuals is not a community at all – there is no weekly meeting of agnostics. Thus, the mobilization of these individuals will necessarily be facilitated by other kinds of institutions.

Overall, these two descriptive analyses show us which religious traditions show the strongest support and strongest opposition to evolution. But they also show substantial diversity within each camp. For example, doctrinally conservative Protestants comprise only 47% of all those who believe evolution is "definitely false."[4] Thus, a majority of those with anti-evolution beliefs come from the other religious traditions. Similarly, Roman Catholics comprise 31% of those who believe evolution is "definitely true," making them numerically the largest block in the pro-evolution camp, ahead of unaffiliated (23%) and mainline Protestants (19%). Thus, both the anti-evolution and pro-evolution coalitions are religiously diverse. While there is some truth behind the fundamentalist stereotype, the actual political landscape is a bit more complex. Nevertheless, this analysis suggests that public opinion in areas with high concentrations of doctrinally conservative churches will tilt more heavily against evolution and toward teaching creationism either alone or in tandem with it. These areas will also have the highest potential levels of political mobilization against

---

[4] The percentages reported in this paragraph are based on the same tabulation shown in Table 3.2 but are based on column percentages (which we omit to save space but can be recalculated from the information in Table 3.2).

the teaching of evolution in public schools. Both have important implications for policy making at the state level and policy implementation in classrooms located in specific communities.

EDUCATION AND IGNORANCE

The second part of the anti-evolutionist stereotype suggests that those who do not accept the evidence for evolution are poorly educated, ignorant, and unintelligent. H. L. Mencken was the most widely read American journalist during the 1920s, and his daily dispatches from Dayton made him the most influential journalist reporting on the *Scopes* trial. As Ginger characterized his reporting, "Mencken daily referred to the people of Rhea County as 'morons' and 'hillbillies' and 'peasants.' He wrote about 'degraded nonsense which country preachers are ramming and hammering into yokel skulls'" (Ginger 1958, 129). With Mencken's character re-created by Gene Kelly in the Hollywood version of *Inherit the Wind* and the frequent revivals of the stage version (most recently in 2007 on Broadway), this view of anti-evolutionists remains a part of the popular culture. In contemporary debate, Richard Dawkins, quoted at the beginning of this chapter, has proven to be as colorful as Mencken. He writes, for example: "It is absolutely safe to say that if you meet somebody who claims not to believe in evolution, that person is ignorant, stupid or insane (or wicked, but I'd rather not consider that)" (Dawkins 1989). In this section, we will see whether there is some truth to this stereotype by examining three potential indicators of ignorance and knowledge: general cognitive ability, general scientific literacy, and formal educational attainment.

General Cognitive Ability

Is it possible, as Dawkins suggests, that those who doubt that humans evolved from earlier species of animals are simply unintelligent? In the previous chapter, we argued that Americans are sufficiently knowledgeable about evolution to have an opinion on the matter. But Dawkins raises a different point, and that is that scientific illiteracy and general intelligence distinguishes among those who are strong supporters of evolution and those who are anti-evolutionists. In other

Table 3.3. Belief that "Human beings developed from earlier species of animals," by score on the Thorndike Verbal Intelligence Test, 1993–2004

	Definitely false (%)	Probably false (%)	Probably true (%)	Definitely true (%)	Total	N
Low (0–5 correct)	41	20	30	10	100%	1,457
Medium (6–7 correct)	39	17	32	12	100%	1,622
High (8–10 correct)	26	12	34	28	100%	991
All respondents	36	17	32	15	100%	4,070

Source: GSS (National Opinion Research Center, University of Chicago); see Appendix 3 for details.

words, not only must people be intelligent to come to an informed opinion, but being intelligent also leads to *supporting* evolution. We cannot explore this thoroughly, but we can examine the association between one type of cognitive ability and acceptance of evolution. The GSS has always included a version of Thorndike's "test of verbal intelligence" – a multiple-choice vocabulary test adapted for use in a survey or poll (Thorndike 1942; Thorndike and Gallup 1944). Tests of this kind are highly correlated with tests of general intelligence (Kvaal et al. 2001; Miner 1957), but researchers who employ this measure more typically refer to it as a measure of cognitive ability or vocabulary knowledge (e.g., Alwin 1991; Alwin and McCammon 2001). Regardless of the precise interpretation, the popular stereotype would lead us to expect that individuals scoring low on this scale would be less likely to accept that humans evolved from other animals.

In Table 3.3, we put this expectation to the test. Using the GSS (again using data from 1993, 1994, 2003, and 2004), we examine the relationship between cognitive ability and belief in human evolution. For the purposes of presentation, we have divided individuals into low ability (zero to three questions correct), middle ability (four to six questions correct), and high ability (seven to ten correct answers). The results show an absence of a strong linear relationship (using the raw score of verbal ability, Pearson's r is 0.18). We can see that those with high scores are much more likely to say that humans "definitely" evolved from earlier species; although, even in this group, there is diversity and considerable skepticism about evolution. But the low-scoring individuals are virtually identical to those with medium scores.

Cognitive ability has a small association with beliefs about human origins, but skepticism about evolution is *not concentrated among the low scorers*. Rather, doubt is characteristic of the 76% of the population having low or average scores on this test.

Scientific Literacy

If disbelief in evolution cannot be attributed to low levels of cognitive ability, then perhaps it is due to a specific intellectual deficit related to science. Scientific illiteracy is widespread in the United States (Miller 1998, 2004; National Science Board 1982), and support for creationism may be a specific manifestation of this more general sense of scientific illiteracy. To determine whether this is so, we again use data from the GSS. In 1993 and 1994, respondents were given a five-item scientific literacy "quiz." First, respondents were told:

For each statement below, just check the box that comes closest to your opinion of how true it is. In your opinion, how true is this?
  a. All radioactivity is made by humans
  b. Antibiotics kill bacteria, but not viruses
  c. Astrology – the study of the star signs – has some scientific truth
  d. Human beings developed from earlier species of animals
  e. All man-made chemicals cause cancer if you eat enough of them.

Using only the four questions that do not address evolution, we can form a highly reliable scale (Cronbach's alpha = 0.93) of general scientific literacy. We gave each respondent four points for a perfectly correct answer (definitely false for items a, c, and e; definitely true for item b), three points for a nearly correct answer (probably false for items a, c, and e; probably true for item b), and so on. Averaging scores gives each respondent a score ranging from one (all items completely wrong) to a possible high of four points (all items correct). For purposes of presentation, we have grouped respondents into low, medium, and high scores on this quiz. Table 3.4 reports belief in human evolution by scores on the scientific literacy quiz and shows that the association is essentially zero (Pearson's r and the polychoric correlation are both under 0.02 and not statistically significant). The data show that belief in human evolution is highest among *both* the most scientifically literate and the least scientifically literate.

Table 3.4. Belief that "Human beings developed from earlier species of animals," by levels of general scientific literacy, 1993–1994

	Definitely false (%)	Probably false (%)	Probably true (%)	Definitely true (%)	Total	N
Low (scores 1.0–1.9)	30	18	33	18	100%	629
Medium (scores 2.0–2.9)	35	19	34	11	100%	1,237
High (scores 3.0–4.0)	38	10	31	21	100%	702
All respondents	35	16	33	16	100%	2,568

Source: GSS (National Opinion Research Center, University of Chicago); see Appendix 3 for details.

Research by Jon Miller – who used a much larger and more sophisticated battery of questions to measure scientific literacy – shows statistically significant but low correlations, also suggesting that general scientific literacy does not lead to an acceptance of the fact of human evolution (Miller 2004). What the foregoing analyses tell us is that the stereotypes of those who do not accept evolution are quite misleading. Those who say that humans "definitely" did not evolve from earlier species are not distinctively unintelligent, and they are similar to those who accept evolution with respect to knowledge about other scientific facts.

These analyses make clear that anti-evolutionists do not lack the opportunity or ability to learn the scientific facts concerning the origins of species; opposition to evolution is not simply a specific instance of scientific illiteracy. Rather, it appears that anti-evolutionists *choose* not to accept evolution, *choose* to ignore scientific arguments demonstrating evolution, or express skepticism ("probably true" or "probably false") as a hedge between what they have been taught in school and seen in museums on the one hand, and what they may have heard in church, on the other.

Formal Education

If evolution skeptics are not distinctively unintelligent or scientifically illiterate, then we might not expect to see dramatic differences when we compare individuals based on their formal education. But here we see a much stronger association. Table 3.5 analyzes the same GSS

Table 3.5. Belief that "Human beings developed from earlier species of animals," by formal educational attainment, 1993–2004

	Definitely false (%)	Probably false (%)	Probably true (%)	Definitely true (%)	Total	N
Less than high school	38	20	32	9	100%	747
High school diploma	42	17	31	10	100%	2,679
Associate degree	39	19	30	11	100%	337
College degree	27	11	36	26	100%	918
Graduate degree	18	10	33	38	100%	420
All respondents	36	16	32	15	100%	5,101

Source: GSS (National Opinion Research Center, University of Chicago); see Appendix 3 for details.

data that we have used in previous sections. It shows that those with a graduate degree (in any subject) are nearly four times as likely to believe that humans "definitely" evolved than are those whose highest credential is a high school diploma.

However, the relationship here is far from perfect (the polychoric correlation is 0.28). There is considerable diversity of opinion among those holding a college degree, with nearly equal numbers believing that human evolution is "definitely false" (27%) and "definitely true" (26%). This suggests that even communities with a high percentage of college graduates will have a degree of polarization. The data suggest that the ranks of pro-evolution activists are likely to be drawn from those with graduate degrees, the only group with substantial numbers who view human evolution as "definitely true." The highly educated have also been identified as the most fervently "anti-fundamentalist," whose politics is, at least according to some research, increasingly oriented toward opposing the very religious fundamentalists who we have shown most support evolution (Bolce and de Maio 1999a, 1999b).

GEOGRAPHY

As we noted previously, the early anti-evolution movement of the 1920s was prevalent throughout the nation but enjoyed legislative success only in the South. In the last three decades, legislative battles have been most frequent in the southern states, but controversies

Table 3.6. Belief that "Human beings developed from earlier species of animals," by Census region, 1993–2004

	Definitely false (%)	Probably false (%)	Probably true (%)	Definitely true (%)	Total	N
East South Central	51	20	20	9	100%	359
West South Central	47	14	26	13	100%	514
South Atlantic	43	17	28	12	100%	959
East North Central	39	16	33	11	100%	870
West North Central	36	15	35	14	100%	363
Mountain	34	17	30	18	100%	313
Pacific	29	17	34	20	100%	772
Middle Atlantic	24	16	40	20	100%	752
New England	20	13	42	25	100%	213
All respondents	36	16	32	15	100%	5,115

Source: GSS (National Opinion Research Center, University of Chicago); see Appendix 3 for details.

have also been common in the Midwest and in smaller communities throughout the nation. In this section, we describe the regional variation of anti-evolution sentiment to show that anti-evolutionism is not solely a southern phenomenon. Of course, geography does not *cause* people to have particular beliefs. And there will be regional variation that is "spurious" due to factors such as religion and education (e.g., doctrinally conservative Protestant churches are more prevalent in the South; educational attainment is highest in New England; Roman Catholics have high concentrations in large metropolitan areas, etc.). But we are not interested here in establishing cause and effect relationships. Instead, geography is indispensable to fully *describe* the attitudinal landscape.

Because of its large sample size, we again turn to the GSS, but we will then move to incorporate a wider array of polls. Table 3.6 shows how views about human evolution vary across the Census Bureau's nine major divisions, ordered from the most to least skeptical about human evolution. In the East South Central United States, a *majority* of citizens think human evolution is "definitely false," with nearly identical attitudes in the West South Central. These two regions include the states that passed most of the key anti-evolution legislation both in the 1920s and in the post-Sputnik era (Arkansas, Louisiana,

Table 3.7. Belief that "Human beings developed from earlier species of animals," by urban–rural classification, 1993–2004

	Definitely false (%)	Probably false (%)	Probably true (%)	Definitely true (%)	Total	N
Other rural	50	17	25	7	100%	566
Other urban	38	17	32	13	100%	2,043
Core of 13–100th largest metro areas	35	17	30	17	100%	726
Suburb of 13–100th largest metro areas	33	16	35	16	100%	720
Core of 12 largest metro areas	29	15	33	22	100%	359
Suburb of 12 largest metro areas	28	14	36	22	100%	700
Total	36	16	32	15	100%	5,115

Source: GSS (National Opinion Research Center, University of Chicago); see Appendix 3 for details.

Mississippi, and Tennessee) and includes Texas, whose statewide textbook selection commission has been influential in watering down treatments of evolution. These are followed by the South Atlantic states and the two regions of the Midwest. Only three regions show a majority believing that human evolution is either "definitely" or "probably" true: the Mid-Atlantic, Pacific, and New England states. Yet, even in New England, only a quarter of the general public believes that human evolution is "definitely true."

We can also examine the geographic distribution by considering the degree of urbanization. The GSS classifies respondents into four types of communities: central cities of metropolitan areas, the suburbs of those metropolitan areas, small cities that lie outside metropolitan systems, and non-metropolitan rural communities (rural areas that fall within metropolitan counties are grouped with the suburbs). The GSS further divides metropolitan areas by separating the twelve largest from the others. This classification (though arbitrary in some respects) provides a second window into the geographic bases of the evolution conflict. Table 3.7 shows that belief in human evolution is rare in rural America (only 7% say it is "definitely true") and increases steadily with metropolitanization. However, even the most metropolitan areas show substantial diversity.

Public Opinion in the Fifty States

Although certain regions and locales enjoy significantly higher concentrations of anti-evolutionists, overall this sentiment can be found throughout the country. This variation may be significant to policy outcomes because the curricular policies that guide textbook selection, student examinations, and teacher lesson plans are the responsibility of state governments. In order to understand if and how public opinion may play a role in the creation of these policies, we require state-level estimates of public support for teaching creationism and evolution (readers with less interest in the technical details of how we do this may want to skip ahead to Figure 3.1).

The science of estimating public opinion at the state level has advanced remarkably during the time that the two authors have worked as social scientists. The challenge of doing so is well known in political science and other fields, such as epidemiology, in which estimating opinions, attitudes, and behaviors for small areas is important. In the ideal situation, fifty identical surveys would be fielded (one for each state), and each would have a large enough sample size – say 600 or more per state – to permit fairly accurate estimates of the opinions in the state. Of course, such a survey, involving over 30,000 completed interviews, would be enormously expensive. Historically, surveys of such scope have only been possible as part of large government studies.

Political scientists rarely have the resources to conduct such studies or the media and public interest polling organizations that have generated the bulk of useful data concerning evolution in the classroom. Instead, political scientists have typically taken many different surveys – often covering many years – and combined them into a single data set. Then, individuals are classified by their state of residence – essentially creating the equivalent of fifty identical polls. Even so, the number of individuals in the smallest states might still be quite small, and the estimates of opinion in these states would have large margins of error. For example, a typical national media poll might include three to five interviews with residents of Delaware or North Dakota. So even when combining ten such surveys, we might have only forty respondents in each state, with a corresponding margin of error of roughly plus or minus 15%.

A second challenge occurs if the representativeness of the samples is different across states. For example, if highly educated people on the East and West Coasts are more likely to screen calls with an answering machine than similarly educated people in the South and Midwest, then low-education respondents will be over-represented in some states but not others. Because education is a strong predictor of attitudes toward teaching evolution, this could substantially confound our estimates.

Fortunately, the last decade has seen an explosion of new research to address these challenges. The newest techniques for small-area estimation of public opinion combine two well-established methods to dramatically improve our opinion estimates, particularly of small states. The first step is to estimate opinion not by taking the simple means – which can have very large margins of error in small samples – but to estimate "Empirical Bayes" opinion estimates with multilevel models. Empirical Bayes estimates are a blend of the observed data for a state and national opinion, and these estimates turn out to be both valid and much more reliable than traditional estimates. In this paper, we estimate the opinion of different types of individuals in each state – for example, young, highly educated, white women – and then recombine the estimates of each demographic group in proportion to their share of the actual population. This recombination, the second step in the process, is called "poststratification." Poststratification is an old technique that re-weights survey data to match the population and is used in virtually every major poll and survey. But in this case, we do not weight based on the national population (e.g., to ensure that our percentage of African Americans matches the national proportion) but instead match the proportions in each state.

This technique is known by the rather long name "Multilevel Modeling with Imputation and Poststratification" or the briefer "Multilevel Regression with Poststratification" (MRP). It was introduced by Gelman and Little (1997) and has been validated and used by many political scientists (Lax and Phillips 2009; Pacheco 2008; Park, Gelman, and Bafumi 2006). In an earlier book, we used a variation of this technique to validly measure public opinion for roughly 10,000 school districts (Berkman and Plutzer 2005). Others have shown that these techniques can reduce margins of error by 30–40% and reduce overall error (including bias) by as much as 50% (Pacheco 2008; Park et al. 2006) in comparison to the older aggregation method.

To estimate public opinion for each of the fifty states and the District of Columbia, we used data from every national poll or academic survey that met three conditions: (1) the survey contained a standard question asking specifically about *teaching* evolution, (2) the survey recorded the state of residence of each respondent, and (3) the original data records were available to us to analyze. In total, we were able to use nine different studies from 1998 through 2005 that included 9,533 respondents. The specific surveys and questions used in the estimation procedure are documented in Appendix section A3.8. For each survey, we recoded the question about evolution so that respondents who supported teaching only evolution (about 25%, depending on the question wording) could be compared with all others who expressed an opinion.

We then estimated a multilevel logistic regression model that allowed us to get a preliminary estimate of the average support in each state. This model also included four demographic variables – education, age, race, and sex – and the effects of these variables were modeled as well. This permitted us to estimate the support for teaching only evolution for 64 different types of citizens in each state. For example, within the state of California, we not only estimate the average opinion, but also the opinion of a Californian who is female, black, a college graduate, and under thirty years old. In fact, because the logistic regression slopes and state intercepts each are estimated with uncertainty (each has a margin of error), we did each estimate 1,000 times to simulate random draws from sampling distributions. Thus, for each of the 64 types of people in California, we have 1,000 different estimates. These estimates are then combined using poststratification weights derived from the U.S. Census, giving us 1,000 estimates of opinion in each state. We report the mean score from this simulation, a step typically called *imputation* – hence the moniker of Multilevel Models with Imputation and Poststratification (MLM-IPS).

This type of estimation procedure has two advantages over traditional methods of simply combining surveys and estimating support for each state (the classic example is Erikson, Wright, and McIver 1993; see also, Brace et al. 2002; Norrander 2001). First, Bayesian estimation substantially reduces the random error component for states with small numbers of respondents. For example, the confidence interval for Vermont, with only 24 respondents, would typically be plus or minus 15%. However, the confidence interval for our imputed estimate is half that size, plus or minus 7.5%. Second, the method of poststratification weighting adjusts results for nonresponse bias at the state level, rather than using a single poststratification weighting scheme for the entire country.

A modeling approach has yet a third advantage for our study. We can also introduce variables for the type of question used. We know that a single question asking whether respondents want to teach creationism "along with" evolution will produce a higher estimate of evolution supporters than questions that offer more choices. Our modeling allows us to take this into account, and we can report the results in terms of any particular question wording. For example, let us take the most liberal state, Massachusetts. Assuming that we use the single-question format used by the Harris poll (see Table 2.1), we estimate that 27.5% of Massachusetts citizens support evolution only, with a margin of error of plus or minus 5.4%. If we calculate our estimates using the single "along with" format (as in Table 3.1), we estimate support for teaching only evolution as 40.6%, with a margin of error of 7.1%.[5]

This approach is realistic and allows us to specify worst case or best case estimates for each state (what is worst and best may depend on your own perspective). In the case of Massachusetts, even if we take the question wording most favorable to evolution, and even if we take the maximum margin of error (plus 7.1%), we find that, at most, 47.7% support evolution only. Thus, even in the most liberal state in the nation, evolution supporters fail to reach a majority. We get very similar "best case" estimates for Connecticut (39% plus or minus 9%), New York (39% plus or minus 5%), and California (37% plus or minus 4%).

Perhaps the best way to get a sense of the geographic distribution of opinion is by mapping our estimates, as we have done in Figure 3.1. It

---

[5] In reporting these percentages based on the most liberal question wording, we are adjusting the data in a manner similar to the way economic reports adjust the final reports into "constant dollars." The rank ordering of the states is identical no matter how we scale the results, and on average our lower bound estimate is about 10% less than the high estimate in each state.

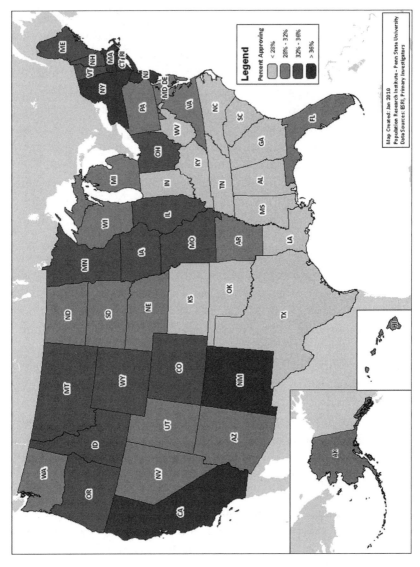

Figure 3.1. Level of support for teaching evolution only in public schools, by state, 1998–2005.

shows that pro-evolution sentiment is strongest in New England, the Mid-Atlantic states, and California. The lowest support for teaching only evolution is in the South and the Midwest. More specifically, we estimate that fewer than one in four citizens support teaching only evolution in West Virginia, Alabama, Indiana, Kansas, and Tennessee. This pattern reproduces the regional pattern of answers to the GSS for a question concerning *beliefs* about human origins. This reinforces the linkage between beliefs and also serves as an indicator of convergent validity. However, the results show diversity within regions. Citizens of Missouri, for example, are far more supportive of evolution (34%) than those in neighboring Kansas (24%); and Floridians are more supportive (32%) than Georgians (28%). Obviously, there is some validity to regional generalizations, but these estimates allow us to be more precise and will allow us to see if public opinion influences policy. Our estimates for all fifty states and the District of Columbia are reproduced in Appendix Table A3.1.

The Social Bases of State Differences

The distribution of public opinion across the states follows some general patterns, and of course there will be considerable heterogeneity within each state. But the pattern of public opinion is structured and anchored in the different social compositions of the various states. One way to see this is to examine how our estimates of state public opinion are associated with two key features of the states: (1) the percentage of the population holding masters or doctoral degrees and (2) the percentage of the population affiliated with doctrinally conservative Protestant churches.

The former is easily calculated from reports of the U.S. Census, but calculating the number of conservative Protestants is more difficult. For this we use the state-level data file from the Religious Congregations and Membership Study. The data were collected by the Association of Statisticians of American Religious Bodies and distributed by the Glenmary Institute (see Jones et al. 2002, for a complete report on the methodology). These data are based on a census of religious bodies and reported as a proportion of the adult population in the state. We again classify denominations based on the RELTRAD taxonomy. The proportions here do not reflect individuals' *self-identifications*

Table 3.8. What explains state-level public opinion concerning the teaching of evolution?

	B	SE	t	p
Intercept	27.44	3.15	8.71	.00
Conservative Protestant adherents (proportion of population)	−13.11	3.44	−3.82	.00
Proportion of adults holding advanced degrees	114.37	33.79	**3.38**	.00
Gross State Product/capita ($1000s)	−.06	.09	−.70	.49
Adjusted R^2	.47			

Dependent variable is public opinion concerning evolution ($N = 50$; DC is excluded). Bold entries are significant in expected direction at .05 level. Entries are slopes (B) and their corresponding standard errors, t ratios, and the probability of a null effect in the population.

but instead reflect reports of individual churches on the number of families who are affiliated with the church.

If the relationships we uncovered with survey data extend to the state level of analysis, our estimates of public support for teaching evolution should be well predicted by the relative concentrations of the highly educated and of doctrinally conservative Protestants. To see this, we estimated a simple regression model in which our estimate of public opinion is the dependent variable, and our two compositional variables are predictors. The results, reported in Table 3.8, indeed show that public opinion is driven both by the presence of the highly educated and the presence of conservative Protestants. Our measure of doctrinally conservative Protestants is roughly 2–3% in the New England states of Vermont, New Hampshire, Rhode Island, Maine, and Connecticut and is above 30% in virtually all of the southern states, excepting Virginia (25%) and Florida (20%). In Arkansas, Tennessee, Oklahoma, Mississippi, and Alabama, more than 45% of the population is affiliated with a doctrinally conservative church. The estimated regression slope suggests that, if the conservative Protestant population in state increases from 6% to 32% (approximately the difference between the tenth and fortieth ranked states on this measure), public support for evolution would drop by a little more than three and a third percentage points.

We get an equally strong effect of our measure of education. This measure is not as highly skewed with the twenty most agricultural states typically reporting that between 4.5% and 6% of their adult population holds a masters or doctoral degree. At the high

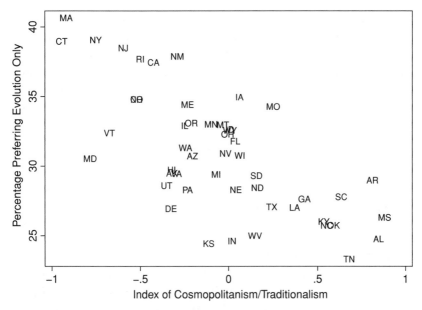

Figure 3.2. The relationship between public opinion and the degree to which conservative Protestants outnumber the highly educated.

end, Colorado, New York, Virginia, Massachusetts, Maryland, and Connecticut all register above 9%. Again, going from a value typical of the tenth state to the fortieth state would shift opinion by about 3%.

One way to illustrate the combined effect of these two variables is to construct a simple index that ranks states along a dimension running from highly traditional populations to highly cosmopolitan ones. To do so, we rescaled our measure of educational attainment so that the state with the most advanced degree holders was rated 1 and the state with the fewest was rated 0. Similarly we assigned a score of 0 to the state with the fewest doctrinally conservative Protestants and 1 to the state with the most. We then subtracted the index of highly educated from the index of doctrinally conservative Protestants to get a scale that can run, theoretically, from −1 to +1. In Figure 3.2, we plot each of the fifty states along the horizontal axis from most cosmopolitan to most traditional. The percentage supporting evolution is plotted on the vertical axis. We recognize that the labels of cosmopolitan and traditional are general terms that do not do justice to the subtleties involved in both education and the religious traditions prevalent in each state. Nevertheless, this simplifying device allows us to capture religion, education, and geography in one visual display. The graph clearly shows an unmistakable pattern characterized by a correlation of −0.72. In states with few conservative Protestants and many highly educated citizens, public support for evolution will be relatively high. Support falls as the relative balance of highly educated citizens declines. These three factors – religion, education, and public opinion – create a political context in each state within which curricular policies are established.

THE SOCIAL BASES OF THE EVOLUTION CONFLICT

Most major political conflicts have their basis in social groups. Groups can acquire different preferences that reflect their interests, their historical alliances with political movements, their values, and their culture. When groups line up on different sides of an issue, we have the makings of political cleavages, and these cleavages are transformed into political conflict by political parties, interest groups, social movements, and other organizations that represent the groups in political venues. In this chapter, we have shown that pro-evolution support is most prevalent among those who are not deeply involved in organized religion, among those with graduate degrees, and among those who live in urban and suburban communities. Highly urbanized states with many professionals and with few conservative Protestants – Massachusetts, for example – show the greatest support for teaching evolution, and only evolution, in the nation's classrooms. The less metropolitan states in which doctrinally conservative churches are prevalent tend also to have fewer highly educated citizens. Public opinion in these states, such as Alabama and Mississippi, generally supports the introduction of creationism into the public school curriculum.

The more cosmopolitan citizens are represented in politics by a number of different kinds of organizations. These include the major scientific and educational organizations, such as the National Science Teachers Association, the National Academy of Science, and countless other scientific societies across the United States. They are also represented by the American Civil Liberties Union, Americans United for

the Separation of Church and State, watchdog organizations such as
the National Center for Science Education, and a number of Catholic,
mainline Protestant, Jewish, and atheist activists – both clergy and
scientists.

In contrast, anti-evolution sentiment is most highly concentrated
in the smaller cities of the Midwest and South, particularly among
those who attend doctrinally conservative Protestant churches. These
groups are represented by organizations that stand as independent
anti-evolution organizations. Some, like the Discovery Institute, maintain few connections to organized religion. Most, however, have
histories closely connected to churches associated with the Fundamentalist movement of the 1920s or adhere to the premillennial doctrine that was central to the fundamentalist separation from northern
evangelicals. The Deluge Geological Society, for example, was originally founded by individuals with strong ties to the Seventh Adventist
Church (Numbers 2006, Chapter 7).

Like all other political battles, we expect that each side will enjoy
greater success in locales where their supporters are highly concentrated. Anti-evolution efforts are most likely to succeed in states with
large numbers of doctrinally conservative Protestants, whereas evolution supporters will have support in states with large numbers of
scientists and professionals. In each case, there are two possible means
for social groups to influence outcomes. One is through the exertion
of direct pressure on policy makers. In states with large numbers of
doctrinally conservative Protestants, their political organizations will
be able to mobilize individuals to protest, make campaign donations,
or directly lobby state lawmakers and bureaucrats. The other mechanism is public opinion. In states with large numbers of professionals,
public opinion will be relatively favorable toward evolution, and state
officials may heed the public's wishes when crafting state educational
policy.

However, there are strong anti-majoritarian forces operating. The
federal courts have considered many proposals advanced by opponents of evolution and have ruled them all to be unconstitutional.
Other, constitutionally permissible, proposals such as the watering
down of the evolution curriculum may be resisted by bureaucrats in
state departments of education. Still others will face intense lobbying

by national scientific organizations that insert themselves into local politics. Binder (2002) has argued that these forces may be too much for anti-evolutionists to overcome. In the next chapter, we will use our measure of state public opinion to see if, indeed, there is some degree of majoritarian democracy within the range of possibilities permitted by the courts.

4 Is Evolution Fit for Polite Company? Science Standards in the American States[1]

The recently proposed "Nature of Science" statement in the Science Curriculum Framework for California Public Schools represents an appalling imposition of the religion of evolutionary humanism upon our public school system and will be deeply resented and opposed by a very large number of concerned parents and other citizens if adopted.

> Henry Morris, and the faculty and staff of the Institute for Creation Research (1988)[2]

The proposed revisions to the commonly accepted definition of science are so far removed from the consensus views of scientists and science teachers that their inclusion in the state standards would seriously jeopardize the quality of science instruction in Kansas. Most troubling is the distinct probability that such changes would hamper students in their future quests for success in our increasingly technologically and scientifically advanced world.

> Robert Dennison, President, Texas Association of Biology Teachers (2003)

A S THE UNITED STATES entered the twenty-first century, more than forty years after Sputnik jump-started science education reform, the Ohio Department of Education did not think it necessary

---

[1] Parts of this chapter are adapted from Berkman and Plutzer (2009).
[2] Quotations from: Henry Morris and faculty and staff of the Institute for Creation Research. 1988. "Proposed California Science Framework: An Open Letter to Education Superintendent Bill Honig," Institute for Creation Research. http://www.icr.org/article/proposed-california-science-framework-open-letter (accessed March 6, 2009). Dennison, Robert. 2003. "Review of Proposed Revisions to Kansas Science Standards Draft 1." http://coalitionforscience.org/newsblog-archives/sciencereviewrobert dennison.pdf (accessed March 6, 2009).

that its public school students learn about biological evolution. Ohio's state curricular content standards, described on its Education Department's Web page as *"the what of what students should know,"* made no mention at all of the term "evolution." Under the auspices of the standards-supporting Fordham Foundation, a research team led by physicist Lawrence Lerner assessed the evolution content of states' science standards on an A to F grading scale and awarded Ohio one of twelve Fs reserved for states "who fail so thoroughly to teach evolution as to render their standards totally useless" (Lerner 2000b, 16). Ohio treats evolution, wrote Lerner, "as if it were not proper conversation in polite company" (2000b, 16).[3]

Public high school students in neighboring Indiana, on the other hand, were offered an "exemplary" treatment of evolution (Lerner 2000b). Science education scholars Gerald Skoog and Kimberly Bilica also reviewed state standards and found approvingly that Indiana required instruction in all eight concepts they identified as "central to understanding evolution" (Skoog and Bilica 2002, 448; see also Donnelly and Sadler 2009). When a new Fordham Foundation team led by biologist Paul R. Gross (2005) took a fresh look at slightly revised Indiana science standards – including not only biology but the entire science curriculum – Indiana again received a grade of A and was lauded relative to other states for its many "positive factors for which we looked in vain in many of the others" (38). But it was noteworthy that Gross, while acknowledging how Indiana "stands out" for its straightforward discussion of evolution generally and of human evolution specifically, gave voice to a warning: "Sad to say," he wrote, "we hear of political moves in this state to derogate or downgrade the teaching of evolution. Should this happen, Indiana will go the tragic way of Kansas" (Gross 2005, 38).

Kansas, of course, is the poster child for low-quality standards, earning from Lerner's team of experts their only F-minus for its "disgraceful paean to antiscience" (2000b, 16). *Scientific American*

---

[3] The Ohio standards in effect in 2000 were written in 1996 and are no longer available on the Ohio Department of Education Web page. The quote refers to Ohio's current standards. We have no reason to believe the purpose of the standards has changed, but they were revised in 2003. There are, however, now nearly 100 uses of the word "evolution." http://www.ode.state.oh.us/GD/Templates/Pages/ODE/ODEDetail.aspx?page=3&TopicRelationID=1696&ContentID=72&Content=56210 (accessed November 21, 2008).

editorialized that universities should be wary of accepting students from Kansas high schools because of the low quality of their state science standards (Rennie 1999). Gross's fears about Indiana were unrealized but not unfounded. Today, Indiana's content standards remain far superior to Kansas's. They retain much of the language that Skoog and Bilica (2002) highlight as strong examples for addressing the most critical and salient concepts for a thorough course in biological evolution; however, as we elaborate in Chapter 6, Indiana is no longer among the states to recommend the study of human evolution.

MAJORITARIANISM, GUARDIANSHIP, AND STATE STANDARDS

Standards do not *dictate* what is covered in a specific classroom, so many Indiana schoolchildren likely received significantly less instruction in evolution than this exemplary treatment might suggest. At the same time, in spite of its standard's silence concerning evolution, many Ohio students presumably heard their biology teacher at least mention evolution, and probably learned something about it as well. In Chapter 6, we use our National Survey of High School Biology Teachers to explore specifically the extent to which standards do or do not influence instruction in biology classrooms. But states certainly act as though standards are important, as do activists and organizations on both sides of the evolution debate. As a result, standards have become a critical battleground in the ongoing evolution–creation controversy.

Since the 1990s, state school boards and education departments have spent considerable time and effort on the writing and periodic revision of state standards. In many subject areas, these standards are "contested terrain" (Placier, Walker, and Foster 2002, 282), and their writing often makes news because the outcomes matter to teachers, parents, interest groups, and ordinary citizens.[4] The history curriculum, for example, might generate conflict on the proper balance between diversity and the perspectives of the nation's founders; indeed, it was controversy over President Clinton's *Goals 2000* history recommendations that catapulted standards into a central front in the

---

[4] Binder (2002) provides detailed case studies of standards revision in California and Kansas. For a more comprehensive set of examples of these political battles, see the Web site for the Center for Science Education (http://ncse.com), which keeps careful track of evolution issues throughout the American states.

culture wars. Similarly, a health class curriculum can teach comprehensive sex education or abstinence-only, also generating controversy. And, of course, the biology curriculum can place evolution squarely in the forefront or try to ignore it completely, with each option triggering praise from some and alarm and opposition from others.

By any measure, the process of drafting state content standards for high school biology is a *political* process that attracts the interest and input of ordinary citizens and a wide range of political actors. Interested parties range from local religious congregations, groups of concerned parents, teachers, teacher unions, and national scientific organizations. Given the many sources of input and political pressure, we ask: Are school board officials and other policy makers across the states guided by a desire to be responsive to public sentiment, as the majoritarian ideal would demand? Or are they largely guided by the scientific consensus and the advice of scientific and pedagogical experts, acting as guardians of the public good? We have already seen in Chapters 2 and 3 that public opinion toward evolution is structured and mapped along particular social and religious lines. The challenge for this chapter is to assess whether that opinion influences the writing of state standards, our first effort to identify the implications of "who decides."

Policy Responsiveness

Our approach in this chapter follows a long tradition of empirical research in American state politics that assesses *policy responsiveness*: the extent to which policy choices and state public opinion correspond (Brace et al. 2002; Erikson, Wright, and McIver 1993; Manza and Cook 2002; Mooney 2000; Mooney and Lee 2000). In this kind of research, scholars seek to determine whether measures of state public opinion are associated with state policies, after accounting for other plausible factors. Building on and extending some of our prior work (Berkman and Plutzer 2009), in this chapter, we will focus on state standards as they stood in the year 2000, after the first eight years of the standards and assessment movement stimulated by Presidents George H. W. Bush and Bill Clinton.

There are two reasons to expect that state science standards might be responsive to public opinion in this period. First, times of rapid policy change can create political opportunities for advocates of change; and, second, evolution is similar to other "morality policies" that have proven to be especially responsive to public opinion. But we know as well that the federal court decisions shown in Figure 1.1 limit the policy space for decision makers, making responsiveness more problematic.

Changing political opportunities

Whereas a few states, such as California, had detailed science standards in place for decades, many states in the 1990s were drafting them for the first time. Other states were substantially increasing the detail and sophistication of their standards or aligning them with newly introduced assessment tests. This flurry of activity, spurred by action in Washington and a keen interest in educational reform by the nation's governors, provided what social movement scholars call an opening in the political opportunity structure (Lienesch 2007). When either new policy-making institutions are created or existing policy-making institutions are given substantially new responsibilities, well organized groups of citizens can often overcome their outsider status and make inroads into public policy, sometimes taking establishment officials and bureaucrats by surprise. Their potential for succeeding is enhanced when outsiders enjoy considerable support from the general public. Thus, if we are to see evidence of policy responsiveness to public opinion at all, we are most likely to see it during this unsettled time. In Chapter 6, we will revisit these issues to see if responsiveness increased, declined, or stayed the same.

Evolution as morality policy

The second important reason why evolution standards in particular might reflect public opinion is that evolution is embedded within broader cultural conflicts in American politics that play out over issues like same-sex marriage and abortion. For these *morality* issues, public opinion tends to be especially critical and is often more important than factors such as state capacity, demographics, and economics. Morality issues are distinctive for their high salience to ordinary citizens and the strong opinions they elicit even in the absence of detailed policy knowledge. Like other morality issues, evolution is essentially a "debate over basic values" that "can grab citizen attention" (Mooney 1999, 676; see also Mooney 2000; Mooney and Lee, 2000; Smith 2002).[5]

Evolution's similarity to these other morality issues and the clear over-time stability in public opinion toward the place of evolution in public schools seen in Chapter 2 suggest that state governments should be responsive to public opinion in developing their standards, with much weaker or more cursory treatments of evolution apparent in the standards of states where public opinion is more strongly opposed. But a correlation between opinion and policy can occur only within the narrowed range of possibilities allowed by the courts. This, too, we have seen with other morality issues. For example, where different states would have settled on different approaches to abortion that would include outright bans, *Roe v. Wade* (1973) required all states to allow abortion until the third trimester; but within these parameters, abortion polices tend to align with state public opinion (Mooney 2000).

We expect a similar pattern with state evolution standards. Repeated losses in federal court have led creationism itself to evolve, or in Amy Binder's colorful analogy, every victory in the courts or elsewhere results in creationism "coming back, like a wounded soldier with even more fight in him" (2007, 555). Creation science and especially intelligent design are essentially modifications by opponents of evolution in response to changes in the legal environment (Scott 1994). As the courts have redefined what is allowed, evolution standards should align with public opinion within the parameters allowed by the courts, in the space defined by the upper panel of Figure 1.1; federal courts constrain state policy makers, but within the space

---

5 The testimony of Dover school board member Angie Yingling in *Kitzmiller v. Dover* offers a cogent example of how ignorance of both evolution and intelligent design need not stand in the way of strong opinions about the matter. Yingling admits in her deposition that she learned about intelligent design from publications like *People* magazine while "standing in checkout lanes at the grocery store and in Wal-Mart" (Humes 2007, 226). "Firm opinion in the absence of knowledge," writes Humes in his account of the Dover case, "were the rule, not the exception, among board members" (Humes 2007, 226). They voted in "favor of one scientific idea (intelligent design) and against another (evolution) that none of them really understood, denying publicly that religion had anything to do with their actions even as they privately admitted they were instituting this new policy as a service to God" (Humes 2007, 227).

available to them, they can adopt policies representing not necessarily what experts say is the best science, but rather their interpretation of public opinion.

Scientists and the Monopolization of Expertise

It is who these experts are, however, that makes the evolution issue different from many other morality issues. We can think of few highly salient issues where preferences of the public are so at odds with the preferences of established experts. And the experts – the scientific community – have clearly used this issue to assert their cultural and political authority (Binder 2007; Ruse 2005). Scientists insist that only they should be able to supply the "market" for specialized knowledge about the origins of life (Gieryn, Bevins, and Zehr 1985). In other words, scientists have fought hard to be the ones who determine what schools and students consume as knowledge about this and other scientific subjects. They seek to deny influence to their competitors, whether these be defined by public opinion generally or doctrinally conservative Christians in particular.

Scientists, of course, are not at all conflicted about the role and status of evolution. Few would disagree with the geneticist Theodosius Dobzhansky that, "Nothing in biology makes sense except in the light of evolution" (1973). Alternative approaches, whether intelligent design or variations of creationism, are labeled "hoaxes" or "faith" (Coyne 2006; Dennett 2006); in either case, the scientific establishment has argued that neither has any place in a science curriculum. Through their formal organizations, scientists have weighed in clearly on the side of rigorous public school instruction in evolutionary biology. The National Academy of Sciences calls evolution "the central concept of biology" (1999), and three national organizations have developed model curriculum standards and teaching resources. These include the National Science Teachers Association's report *Scope, Sequence, and Coordination* (1992), the American Association for the Advancement of Science's "Science for All Americans" (1989), and the National Research Council's *National Science Education Standards* (1996).

All three of these documents "provide evidence that evolution has attained its status as a unifying theme in science" (Skoog and Bilica

2002, 449), but among these, the National Research Council's *National Science Education Standards* (NSES) report has proven to be the most influential. As in the others, evolution is presented as a powerful scientific theory accepted by the scientific community, essential to understanding biology and other scientific fields, and an illustration of the role that theories play in the scientific enterprise (Lerner 2000a). The NSES presents evolution as one of five "unifying concepts and processes" that provide the "big picture of scientific ideas." The report further enumerates eleven benchmarks, such as natural selection and biological adaptation, for state policy makers and textbook publishers to use in determining the content for high school biology. The more closely a state adheres to the NSES benchmarks, the more evolution will be emphasized in its standards (Skoog and Bilica 2002). The prefaces to many state standard documents acknowledge the influence of the NSES.

Scientists go further than simply recommending curriculum for schools and states. They see the evolution debate more broadly in terms of its implications for the prestige, power, and autonomy of *science* as a social institution. Prominent scientists and their professional associations have therefore engaged in what is referred to by sociologists as "boundary work" to clearly demarcate what constitutes science and what lies outside of its domain, and thereby buffer policies at the state and local level from public opinion and organized groups (Gieryn et al. 1985). American courts have been a key venue for these efforts, where major legal battles over evolution have often centered on the very question of "what is science and what is outside of science?" Scientists use their support in these cases to establish, in effect, that those who practice creation science or advance the theory of intelligent design are not scientists at all (Binder 2007; Gieryn et al. 1985) and are therefore unqualified to determine what belongs in a science curriculum.[6]

For example, scientific testimony in *McLean v. Arkansas Board of Education* (1982) challenged an Arkansas statute requiring the

---

[6] Gieryn (1985) points to the 1925 *Tennessee v. Scopes* "monkey trial" as an example of this boundary work, although scientists' testimony was not actually allowed. Many scientific organizations contributed funding to Scopes' defense, and their prepared testimony – released by Scopes' attorney Clarence Darrow to the large media assembly in Dayton – detailed how science differed from religion (Gieryn et al. 1985; Ginger 1958).

side-by-side teaching of evolution and creation science. The ACLU-led case against the Arkansas law relied on two teams of experts: a religious team to establish the fundamentalist religious basis of anti-evolutionism and creation science, and a scientific team to testify that creation science was not science (Larson 2003, 161). Scientists effectively made the case that science is "a game that not just anyone can play. Only credentialed scientists can decide the validity of a scientific theory or method" (Gieryn et al. 1985, 402). The Court accepted their distinction between religion and the religious neutrality of science, dismissing arguments that evolution itself is a secular religion and therefore also subject to exclusion by the Establishment Clause (*McLean v. Arkansas* 1982).

This boundary work continues, as in the more recent case of *Kitzmiller v. Dover Area School District* (2005). This challenge to the school board's policy that biology teachers read a statement directing students to a text advocating intelligent design also featured scientific and academic testimony on the meaning of science and control over its practice.[7] Judge John E. Jones III's ruling found the board's policy in violation of the Establishment Clause because intelligent design "cannot uncouple itself from its creationist, and thus religious, antecedents" (*Kitzmiller v. Dover* 2005, 765) and "negative attacks on evolution have been refuted by the scientific community" (735). *Kitzmiller* followed the precedent of other cases where scientists win "boundary disputes that result in the loss of authority and resources by competing non-scientific intellectual activities" (Gieryn 1983, 754).

Policy Responsiveness and Professional Expertise

Cases like *McLean* and *Kitzmiller* are clearly important to the scientific community because they help to enhance support for science as an institution (Gieryn et al. 1985) and contribute to striking down anti-evolution laws and practices. But this does not mean that they are fully successful in the critical goal of "bounding" the science curriculum

---

[7] The witnesses for the plaintiffs in *Dover* were Brown University Biologist Kenneth R. Miller, Michigan State University Philosopher Robert T. Pennock, Georgetown University Professor of Theology John (Jack) F. Haught, Berkeley's Kevin Padian, McGill University's Brian Alters, and Southeastern Louisiana University Philosopher Barbara Carroll Forrest.

from public opinion or religious-based interests. *Scopes*, of course, led to much public ridicule of Bryan and the anti-evolution cause by secular elites. It was, however, followed by stepped up anti-evolution legislative activity and the virtual elimination of evolution from textbooks nationwide (Larson 2003; Skoog 1979). Despite the high financial cost and a severe scolding from Judge Jones, school board members in Dover only narrowly lost their re-election campaign.[8] And public opinion appears to still play a role in shaping evolutionary politics. "The controversy over evolutionary teaching," writes Larson in arguing for the continued importance of public opinion in driving the controversy, "is as lively today as ever" (2003, 210).

What would effective boundaries in the writing of state standards look like? We have plenty of examples of guardianship where policies are decided with little public awareness and little attention by policy makers to public opinion. The federal government, for example, sets standards for obtaining a pilot's license, and professional pilots and well-organized amateurs basically dominated the process since the origins of aviation (Budwig 1930, 242). Technical policies are developed throughout the federal and state bureaucracies through deference to expertise and without extensive involvement of ordinary citizens. State bureaucracies housing this expertise are most important to policy making when the issues are complex and technical (Barrilleaux 1999).

Were standards fully bounded, we would expect them to reflect the strong evolution consensus of the scientific community. But this is not to suggest that, even with impenetrable boundaries, all fifty states would make identical choices. We know our federal system better than that. States require infrastructure and capacity to turn recommendations from the NSES and other organizations into detailed curriculum standards, examinations, and teaching resources. Administration and public sector employment differ systematically across states, with wealthier and more urbanized states tending to support more professional bureaucracies (Barrilleaux 1999). States with this

---

[8] The *New York Times* referred to the loss by all 8 members of the school board as a "repudiation of the first school district in the nation to order the introduction of Intelligent Design in a science class" as the incumbents were "swept out" of office. In fact, the vote was actually quite close. Electoral systems scholar Burt Monroe argues that block voting overstates the size of their defeat: the election was roughly 51–49 against the incumbents (private correspondence, October 4, 2007).

greater bureaucratic capacity, usually measured in terms of financial resources and staff expertise, generally formulate different policies than states with less bureaucratic capacity (Barrilleaux and Brace 2007; Barrilleaux and Miller 1988; Leichter 1996). All states have departments of education that play central roles in writing their standards. Like all state agencies, these vary in terms of their capacity and design (Manna 2004; Manna and O'Hara 2005; Timar 1997).

With secure and impermeable boundaries, state science standards would follow an apolitical *technical policy-making model* in which interstate variation would result not from differences in how the public feels about evolution but rather from pedagogical philosophy and the overall capacity of the state to assemble the appropriate expertise to develop standards and revise them periodically. Boundaries would extend beyond the legally defined policy space to the actual policy-making process. The most rigorous and detailed standards and those that follow the most recent recommendations of experts would most likely be developed in states with highly professionalized and relatively large education departments, in those with significant financial resources, and in those that enjoy high public support for public education.

If scientists are not successful – that is, if the boundaries they fight for cannot overcome the intensity of anti-evolution forces – we would expect policy to be responsive to public opinion *within the policy space permitted by the courts*. Whereas previous studies on morality politics in the policy-making process have focused on the legislative arena (Mooney 2000; Mooney and Lee 2000; Sharp 2002), our argument extends to a largely administrative policy-making process, where decisions are typically made in the bureaucracy or board of education (with occasional involvement by state legislatures). But even so, standards are developed in sunlight, complete with citizen advisory groups, hearings, the formal and informal input of state legislators, and the participation of state education scholars and science educators.[9] Given such transparency, even a bureaucratic process can

[9] For example, the Ohio state standards discuss the process by which they were developed this way: "The people of Ohio played a key role in the development of the academic content standards. The Office of Curriculum and Instruction at the Ohio Department of Education facilitated the standards writing process and aggressively engaged the public in reviewing drafts of the standards throughout the development process. Thousands of

A. Technical Policy-Making Model

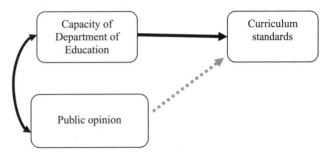

B. Court-constrained Responsiveness Model

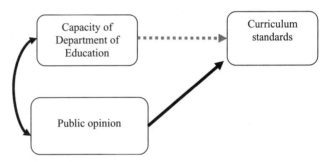

Figure 4.1. Technical Policy-Making Model and the Court-constrained Responsiveness Model (dashed lines indicate an expectation of no direct effect).

be influenced by the competition of groups that have strongly held values, reflected in state *public opinion*. Thus, state officials serving as bureaucrats in state departments of education, elected or appointed members on state boards of education, and members of various commissions and drafting committees may choose to work with an eye toward public preferences (policy responsiveness) or look to expert bodies of scientists and educators (technical policy making). Binder

Ohioans gave suggestions that were evaluated and incorporated, as appropriate, by the writing teams into the final adopted standards. We want to thank all of the people who took the time to comment on the standards and participate in the development process. The Science Advisory Committee and the Science Writing Team began work on the Ohio science academic standards by examining standards from other states. It became apparent that most states relied heavily on *Benchmarks for Science Literacy* and/or the *National Science Education Standards*. Ohio's science standards drew from national documents, state documents, the experience of Ohio teachers and other education professionals" (Ohio K-12 Academic Content Standards, Science, 2002, 1).

(2002) suggests that education policy makers have a strong standing commitment to the latter approach, making it difficult for anti-evolutionists to make substantial inroads in modifying the science curriculum.

These two models are illustrated in Figure 4.1. If scientists are successful in their boundary work, the standards directing teachers across the state would reflect the *technical policy-making model* in Figure 4.1A: Standards will not be influenced by public opinion. Variation among states will result from differences in the capacity of their state governments to closely align with the expectations of groups like the National Science Teachers Association, National Research Council, and the American Association for the Advancement of Science. In this model, the public does not have an opportunity to influence classroom instruction through curricular standards. If, however, scientists are less successful, standards should be responsive to public opinion, as illustrated in the court-constrained responsiveness model in Figure 4.1B. Here, boundaries are porous, allowing public opinion to influence policy makers.

TESTING THE RESPONSIVENESS AND TECHNICAL POLICY-MAKING MODELS

Are state evolution standards best described by the technical policy-making model or by court-constrained responsiveness? We can answer this question by estimating models of policy outcomes (the rigor of the standards) as a function of both public opinion and state capacity. However, we first fit the same models for standards in a *noncontroversial* area: the science curriculum for subjects *other than evolution*. Our expectation, of course, is that the content standards for science generally – for chemistry, physical science, earth science, and even biology *excluding* evolution – will be best explained by the technical policy-making model. These standards do not touch upon the fundamental values – such as biblical literacy or church–state relations – that underlie a person's attitude toward evolution. The three national science organizations that we mentioned earlier all make specific recommendations about how to teach all science, not just evolution.

According to our model, each state's general science standards should reflect the ability of state bureaucracies and governments to implement and integrate these recommendations. If scientists are also successful in bounding evolution, these standards will be treated just like these other science subjects. At first glance, however, the evidence suggests this will not be the case. Ohio's F in evolution standards stands in stark contrast to the grade of B that Lerner's expert panel awarded the state's science standards in all other subjects. Indeed, of the eleven other states that received Bs for their overall science curriculum three others also received Fs for their evolution standards, whereas two of the seven states that received As for their science standards received only Cs for their specific treatment of evolution.

Science and Evolution Standards

To test these two models, we need measures of the quality of general science standards – those for subjects other than evolution – as well as of the standards for evolution. For general science standards, we rely on the rankings reported by Gross (2005) under the auspices of the Fordham Foundation. In addition to letter grades, the report provides detailed information on seven criteria by which each state's overall science curriculum was evaluated.[10] Combined, each state could get a score ranging from 0 to 100, with an actual range of 13 to 67. One of the seven criteria was the treatment of evolution, and we subtract the evolution score to get an index reflecting standards in general. Because this is an arbitrary metric, we standardize this measure to have a mean of 0 and standard deviation of 1 (a z-score).

Gross's measure of *evolution* standards, excluded in the general standards measure, lacks detail and depth; therefore, for our measure of evolution standards, we rely on Lerner's published curriculum ratings (Lerner 2000b). These scores, which go well beyond the letter grades widely cited in the press and policy sectors, are based on

---

[10]   The seven criteria are (1) *expectations* that students will become scientifically literate, (2) the *organization* of standards by grade, (3) the *content* toward the interplay of data and theory, (4) the *seriousness* of the standards including whether or not pseudo-scientific or discredited proposals are included, (5) the *quality* of the standards in terms of their expectations, (6) the inclusion of material on *scientific inquiry* including the history or philosophy of science, and finally, (7) *evolution*, which we exclude. The rating team's combined expertise "covers elementary-secondary science, university science education through the postdoctoral level" and its "disciplinary coverage spans biology, chemistry, geology, and physics, as well as environmental science, epistemology, and logic" (Finn in Gross 2005, 9).

five evolution-specific content rankings and three semantic ones.[11] To assess the validity of these codes, we compared them to an independent set of ratings made by Skoog and Bilica (2002) and found them to be highly correlated.[12] The Lerner raw score has also been converted to a standardized measure with mean of 0 and standard deviation of 1.

Not surprisingly, from what we have already seen, the two dependent variables (general science standards and standards concerning evolution) are virtually independent, with a nonsignificant correlation of 0.21. This provides the first suggestion that the state-level determinants of the evolution curriculum and of the more general science standards are likely to be quite different.

State Education Agency Capacity

If the technical policy-making model holds, we expect states with greater administrative capacity to write science standards more in line with the model curricula and benchmarks developed by national organizations. To measure state administrative capacity, we combine two indicators about state education departments into a composite scale. The first reflects funding and is the 1998 administrative budget for education per student.[13] The second component is the ratio of students to full-time administrative education staff.[14] The two

---

[11] The content areas that states were expected to include in their standards include biological evolution, human evolution, geological evolution, cosmology, and connections among the historical sciences. Lerner (2000b) also noted the frequency and appropriate usage of the word "evolution," the presence and the extent of "creationist jargon" (e.g., use of "theory" in the colloquial, rather than scientific sense), and whether the state requires a disclaimer statement of some kind (only Alabama at the time of the data coding).

[12] Skoog and Bilica's goal was to evaluate each state's document for "the inclusion of salient concepts or topics deemed central to understanding evolution" (2002, 448). Their criteria were adapted from the National Research Council's *National Science Education Standards* (1996). Factor analysis suggested that individual ratings by Skoog and Bilica loaded on the same factor as the eight scores made by Lerner; however, when we created a scale combining ratings from the two different sources, it had slightly lower reliability so we use the simpler Lerner scale.

[13] Our indicator ranges from under $20 per student in Texas and Ohio to over $200 per student in Connecticut and Alaska (mean = $62 per student).

[14] The ratio of students to full-time administrative education staff ranges from over 3,000 in Indiana, Texas, Washington, and Ohio to under 600 in Alaska and Missouri (mean = 1,598).

Table 4.1. What explains the rigor and quality of state science standards?

	B	SE	t	p
Intercept	−.74	1.16	−.64	.52
State educational administrative capacity (Z)	.37	.15	**2.43**	.02
Gross State Product/capita ($1000s)	.02	.02	.76	.45
Public support for public education (Z)	.28	.15	**1.88**	.07
Public opinion concerning evolution	.01	.03	.19	.85
Adjusted R²	.14			

Dependent variable is rigor of state science standards, excluding evolution (N = 48; excluded are IA, HI, and DC). Bold entries are significant in the expected direction at the .05 level.

components are highly correlated, and the two-item scale has a reliability of 0.76 (calculated as Cronbach's alpha).

Our notion of state policy-making capacity extends beyond just the state bureaucracy, however. It includes state affluence as well, so we use a measure of per capita Gross State Product. We also include a measure of public support for public education spending. We expect that this, too, is a component of state capacity; where state administrators enjoy a general climate of support for public education, there should be greater support for their work. In an earlier work, we found that school districts spend more on public education when public opinion shows greater support for public education spending, and we use our measure of public support here (Berkman and Plutzer 2005). In effect, this particular component of opinion, totally distinct from the measure of public opinion toward evolution that we developed in Chapter 3, is a resource policy makers can draw upon in developing what they can argue are the best quality standards.

Regression Analysis

We estimate our models using multiple regression, which allows us to isolate the effects of several influences on state policy simultaneously. Table 4.1 shows the results for expert-rated rigor in state content standards for the sciences generally. Column "B" reports the estimated regression slopes – how much change in standards is associated with a one-unit change in each independent variable. We hypothesized that only measures of state capacity, and not public opinion, would have

Table 4.2. What explains the rigor and quality of state evolution standards?

	B	SE	t	p
Intercept	−3.86	1.13	−3.43	.00
State educational administrative capacity (Z)	−.02	.15	−.14	.89
Gross State Product/capita ($1000s)	.04	.02	**1.94**	.06
Public support for public education (Z)	.03	.14	.18	.86
Public opinion concerning evolution	.08	.03	**2.33**	.03
Adjusted R²	.19			

Dependent variable is rigor of state evolution standards (N = 48; excluded are IA, HI, and DC). Bold entries are significant in the expected direction at the .05 level.

significant effects on the rigor of general science standards. The model estimates, reported in Table 4.1, show that states with greater support for public education and greater capacity in the bureaucracies charged with developing standards tend to have the most rigorous general science curricula. As support for education and spending on bureaucracies increases, so too does the rigor of state science standards. But public opinion specifically concerning evolution does not have any influence on the standards.[15] These analyses show that the process of drafting these standards is insulated from cultural politics and consistent with deference to scientific expertise as anticipated by the technical policy-making model.

When we now turn to an analysis of state content standards concerning evolution in particular, we get dramatically different results. Table 4.2 again includes our three measures of state capacity, per capita Gross State Product, and public opinion specifically about evolution. The difference between Tables 4.1 and 4.2 is striking. The evolution opinion measure is a significant and positive predictor of state policy.[16] In contrast, the detail and rigor of the evolution sections of state science standards are not influenced by any of the more

[15] To see whether the general ideological tendency of the state might make a difference, we also examined the impact of Erikson, Wright, and McIver's measure of state ideology (1993). This measures the relative balance of self-identified liberals and conservatives in a state, and we found that when added to the model, it had no impact on general science standards (t = 0.67).

[16] To confirm that we were tapping into distinct, policy-specific public opinion – rather than general ideology – we again added Erikson, Wright, and McIver's (1993) measure of policy liberalism to the model. Ideology's impact was again zero (b = −0.001, t = 0.02), and the effect of our opinion measure was essentially unchanged.

general measures of administrative capacity. The zero-order correlation of evolution opinion and evolution content standards is a healthy 0.43, and the regression slopes suggest that a shift in opinion from that typical of the average state (31% support evolution only) to a level typical of California (the sixth most supportive state at 37%) would increase the rigor of the evolution curriculum by half a standard deviation. These two ways of looking at the effects both suggest modest responsiveness to public opinion and the inability of organized science to exclude politics from the process of defining what is appropriate material to include in biology and life science curricula. We know from the analysis in Chapter 3 that anti-evolution opinion is driven by values associated with doctrinally conservative Protestant denominations, precisely those competitors that scientists have targeted in their boundary work. Within the space provided by federal court decisions, public opinion does seem to play a substantial role in the curriculum development process. We can now conclude not only that public opinion toward evolution is real and structured, but that it has significant impact on the political process.

STANDARDS AS DEMOCRATIC CONTROLS

These differences in the sources of variation in states' overall science standards and those particular to evolutionary biology bring us back to the conflict in *Scopes* in the early twentieth century, *Kitzmiller* in the early twenty-first century, and the many judicial decisions in between. "Your honor," William Jennings Bryan pleaded to the court in his successful efforts to keep scientific testimony out of the *Scopes* trial, "it isn't proper to bring experts in here to try and defeat the purpose of the people of this state by trying to show that this theory that they denounce and outlaw is a beautiful thing that everybody ought to believe in" (in Larson 2003, 68). Although scientific expertise surely plays a role in shaping state evolution standards – many states acknowledge the scientists and science educators who assist them – it is also clear that public opinion can shape the choices states make about what should be taught in biology classrooms about evolution. Bryan would be pleased.

This belief that scientific expertise and teachers' professional discretion should be trumped by public preferences – by the majoritarian ideal – arose again when Susan Epperson, a young science teacher in Arkansas, challenged her state's law denying her the opportunity to teach human evolution. Speaking for the community, prosecutor Bruce Bennett defended the law as a simple and necessary "administrative control." Epperson, he argued, "wants to teach the Darwin Theory only when in fact there are dozens of other off-beat theories that other teachers might want to explain to their students. Someone has to administer the schools" (Larson 2003, 100–101). The state supreme court, acting, according to Larson, in response to public opinion, accepted this argument as a "valid exercise of the state's power to specify the curriculum in its public schools" (Larson 2003, 107). Eventually this Arkansas law, too, would be declared an unconstitutional establishment of religion when the case reached the Supreme Court as *Epperson v. Arkansas* (1968), significantly reducing the policy space for states to legislate. Thirty-seven years after that, when the popularly elected school board of Dover, Pennsylvania was eager to introduce intelligent design into its classrooms, it felt itself constrained by Pennsylvania's administrative controls. But, in this case, the controls ran the other way. The statement the school board expected teachers to read to their students spoke directly to the board's recognition that the Pennsylvania state government had chosen to promote a strong curriculum in evolutionary biology. Declaring in its opening line that Dover is a "standards driven district," the statement continued, "The Pennsylvania Academic Standards require students to learn about Darwin's theory of evolution and eventually to take a standardized test of which evolution is a part." These standards constrained the policy space even more than decisions by the federal courts, eliminating the local option of de-emphasizing evolution. And this may have led board members to endorse a policy that they really did not understand beyond the fact that it was an alternative to evolution and its teaching might undermine confidence that students might have in the findings of evolutionary biology.

Of course, the *Kitzmiller v. Dover* case would further restrict the policy space going forward; at least in the middle district of Pennsylvania, intelligent design cannot be introduced into the science classroom. And the board's efforts to de-emphasize evolution offer a particularly dramatic example of how standards can be important. But it does not really address standards' role in influencing classroom instruction.

Through their standards, states codify what students should learn. They promote and encourage curricular coherence across districts by directing local school boards, school administrators, and teachers in their choices of texts and lesson plans. Their influence over the organization and content of textbooks is especially significant in states like California, where textbook commissions select a small number of textbooks from which schools may choose (Bianchi and Kelly 2003). In many cases, standards are accompanied by state-wide exams that reinforce their ability to direct classroom behavior by imposing sanctions on schools that do not perform well. The importance of these exams was clearly stated by one Kansas science teacher in reference to his state's weak standards: "Many districts, not with any particular agenda, will leave out evolution because, obviously, it must not be important. Why spend our time teaching something that isn't going to be assessed?" (quoted in Lienesch 2007, 222). In all these ways, standards can be understood as democratic *controls* over schools and classroom instruction. They are a means through which the public, through its elected and appointed officials, tries to influence school instruction at the local level.

SUMMARY

In this chapter, we focused on the official curricular policies of the fifty states as they stood in 2000, after a flurry of curricular reform spurred by the national standards movement. Unlike earlier policies that were implemented through laws banning evolution or mandating equal time, these policies are expressed through official documents known as content standards. These are *political* documents in two important senses. First, they are the result of democratic political institutions and are subject to the influences of elected officials, their political appointees, and career bureaucrats entrusted to use their technical expertise to advance the values and priorities of the citizens. Second, they are political documents in the sense of having been politicized by highly motivated citizens, by organized interests, and by elected officials. Officials working in state departments of education can be fairly confident that the choices they make about the chemistry curriculum are unlikely to be controversial. But they can be equally confident that content standards concerning evolution will be scrutinized closely by anti-evolution activists, national scientific organizations, professional organizations representing teachers, and elected officials concerned with representing their constituents and concerned about their next election. The political mix in every state is different, and it is not surprising that the content standards for evolution vary substantially from state to state. In this chapter, we showed that some of that variation is explained by public opinion. In states where a majority of the public are hostile toward evolution, the standards tend to be cursory and vague; they invite teachers to spend only a minimum amount of time on evolution, and they provide no guidance to teachers who may wish to teach in ways that align with the recommendations of the National Academy of Sciences. In states where more people endorse its teaching in schools, we find the most rigorous evolution standards.

The responsiveness to public opinion suggests that scientists and their major national organizations have failed in keeping this portion of the science curriculum buffered from politics and popular control. Unlike the broader science curriculum, whose creation is well described by the apolitical technical policy-making model, content standards pertaining to evolution are influenced by the preferences of ordinary citizens within the policy space permitted by federal courts, a process well captured by our court-constrained responsiveness model.

But what is at stake in these debates? Certainly, citizens who become engaged by these debates take them very seriously. They are exhilarated if their side wins a victory at the state school board, at a textbook selection committee, or in a court case. And they feel the sting of defeat when these decisions are decided in favor of their opponents. Joseph Gusfield (1963) observed that, when legislatures or the courts rule on issues of moral concern, they bestow a kind of prestige on one group. And we have seen in many different policy domains that the vindication of a group's deeply held values by such institutions alone can motivate the highly charged politics of the culture wars.

But we want to pursue a more specific question: Do these standards actually influence the choices made by individual classroom teachers and the instruction received by children? If they do, and if teachers faithfully implement the policies set by government bodies, then our story of responsiveness and popular sovereignty consists of the courts on the one hand and the standards-making process on the other. But the public servants who implement public policies are a critical link in the democratic process (Mosher 1982). If a substantial number of teachers deviate from their prescribed lesson plans, then the story is more complex and, we think, far more interesting. Indeed, we will show that most teachers do not seem to adhere to the standards of their states, although there are important groups of teachers that do take the standards to heart. And if teachers do deviate from the standards, can we explain how and why? And what does this say about the ability of the public to control what goes on in the classroom? Does it stop at state standards, or can policy be responsive to them through the teacher as well?

To answer these questions, we surveyed 926 teachers from across the United States. These teachers took the time to provide detailed reports on what they teach, how much they teach it, what they emphasize, and what they personally believe about human origins. The next four chapters focus on what these teachers told us, and we use their reports and their extensive answers to open-ended questions to build a more complete understanding of democratic responsiveness, guardianship, and the culture war concerning evolution. In Chapter 6, we will see how standards influence the emphasis that teachers place on evolution in their classrooms. But first, we need to understand *how* they teach, how much attention teachers devote to evolution, whether they embrace the priorities of major scientific organizations, and the extent to which they introduce students to criticisms of evolutionary theory and potential alternative perspectives.

5 Teachers and What They Teach

One Hundred Years without Darwin Are Enough: When we say a thing is a fact, then, we only mean that its probability is an extremely high one: so high that we are not bothered by doubt about it and are ready to act accordingly. Now in this use of the term fact, the only proper one, evolution is a fact. For the evidence in favor of it is as voluminous, diverse, and convincing as in the case of any other well established fact of science concerning the existence of things that cannot be directly seen, such as atoms, neutrons, or solar gravitation ...

    Hermann J. Muller (1959)[1]

The scientific case against evolution: The fact that macroevolution (as distinct from microevolution) has never been observed would seem to exclude it from the domain of true science.

    Henry M. Morris (2000)

OUR INVESTIGATION INTO THE POLITICS of evolution and creationism has shown that, beginning with *Epperson v. Arkansas* (1968), U.S. federal courts have increasingly narrowed the range of acceptable public policies that state governments may enact concerning evolution. Today, states may choose to de-emphasize evolution in their curricula and select textbooks based on how extensively evolution is covered, so long as they do not also promote explicitly biblical creationism or "creation science." In addition, although the district court decision in *Kitzmiller v. Dover* only serves as a legally

---

[1] Quotations are from: Hermann J. Muller. 1959. "One Hundred Years Without Darwin Are Enough," *School Science and Mathematics* 59: 304–305. Henry M. Morris. 2000. "The Scientific Case Against Evolution–Part I," *Impact* #330: i–iv.

binding precedent within the Middle District of Pennsylvania, it is likely to discourage efforts to introduce intelligent design into public school curricula elsewhere.

Nevertheless, we showed in the previous chapter that this narrowed range still allows for enormous diversity in state curricular standards, with some of this diversity being a reflection of public opinion (less rigorous standards where opinion is most opposed to teaching evolution). Where standards are more rigorous than public opinion might suggest (e.g., Indiana and North Carolina), we see evidence of the success of scientific organizations to get state educational bureaucracies to enact model curricula. In states whose curricula are not as sophisticated as the public might demand (e.g., Maine), the explanation may be due to state bureaucratic capacity and limited resources.

The result is that standards create different teaching environments for teachers, depending on their state of employment. Biology teachers working in Maryland have quite different official mandates from those working in neighboring Virginia. But the fact that these standards reflect democratic processes or expert recommendations cannot be celebrated (or lamented, depending on one's point of view) if they are not implemented as intended. The same can be said for the decisions of the Supreme Court and other federal courts: although judicial opinions have a clear impact on state governments, do they similarly constrain classroom teachers? Thus, we ask, do these mandates make a difference in how these educators go about doing their jobs? We will seek to answer this question in this and the following chapter.

In trying to understand the role of teachers as the final stage in the policy-making and policy-implementation process, we read many previous studies of teachers. We examined twenty-five studies in all, including sample surveys of teachers in fifteen states. And yet these studies were not adequate for our task. Most of the previous studies are now dated, and the more recent ones each examine but a single state. Even collectively, their geographic coverage is limited because many states (most notably California, New York, and all of New England) have never been studied at all (see Donnelly and Boone 2007; Moore 2002b; Rutledge and Mitchell 2002 for comprehensive reviews of these single-state studies). In addition, the studies employed incomparable measures, and some of them sacrificed scientific sample survey methods in favor of higher cooperation rates (such as surveys of teachers attending conventions and professional meetings; e.g., Moore and Kraemer 2005). As a result, we lacked a systematic and coherent account of how instruction varies from teacher to teacher across the nation as a whole. And without comparable surveys in many states, it is impossible to see if the characteristics of states and communities make a difference in how evolution is taught, because any observed differences could be due to differences in questionnaire, sampling, or the time that the study was conducted.

THE NATIONAL SURVEY OF HIGH SCHOOL BIOLOGY TEACHERS

To supplement the many individual state surveys and to bring teacher reports up to date, we designed and fielded the National Survey of High School Biology Teachers in the spring of 2007. To do so, we acquired the names and addresses of a randomly selected group of 2,000 teachers of biology in U.S. public schools. Following the *Tailored Design Method* for mail surveys (Dillman 2000), we first sent all 2,000 teachers a prenotification letter explaining that they would be receiving a survey in 7–10 days. This letter explained the purpose of the survey and encouraged them to look for our mailing and complete the questionnaire. They were then sent a survey packet containing a questionnaire booklet, along with a cover letter, a postage-paid return envelope, and a two-dollar bill to get their attention and to express our thanks for completing the survey. Two weeks later, they received a reminder postcard, and (if they had not yet responded) we next sent a replacement packet with a second questionnaire and another postage-paid envelope. All respondents were also given a Web address that would allow them to complete the survey online. We had valid e-mail addresses for 1,500 teachers, and these teachers received two e-mail reminders as well; the e-mails included links to the online version of the survey. Additional technical descriptions of the sampling design, how we acquired the names and addresses of teachers, and detailed analyses showing that the survey is broadly representative of all public school teachers are reported in the Appendix to this chapter and in an earlier scientific paper we published in the journal *PLoS Biology* (Berkman, Plutzer, and Pacheco 2008, supplementary text S1).

Responses were received between March 5 and May 1, 2007. In some cases, we received blank questionnaires (or even partially completed ones) from teachers who told us that they were currently retired, no longer teaching biology, or otherwise ineligible. After excluding 58 such "out-of-scope" respondents, we calculated the response rate as 50% (see Appendix Section A5.1 for details).

The Questionnaire

Teachers completed a six-page survey containing questions about the content of their most recently taught biology courses, more specific questions about the teaching of evolution in particular, and a variety of background questions. The questionnaire was designed in the context of previous studies, and we adapted question wording from other studies whenever possible and appropriate. We then asked six high school biology teachers from our own community to look at the initial draft of the questionnaire and provide us with suggestions for improvement. The final questionnaire reflected the feedback we received and was six pages long, taking a teacher about 15 minutes to complete.

Representativeness of the Sample

The data set contains teachers from the District of Columbia and forty-nine states (no teachers from Wyoming), and we examined the sample to determine whether it was representative of the larger population of public school biology teachers. A sense of the geographic spread can be seen in Figure 5.2, which maps the school locations of all teachers completing the survey (some dots represent multiple teachers in the same city).

Although there is no census of teachers, the Common Core of Data (CCD) compiled by the National Center for Educational Statistics is a census of schools; we used this to see if our sample members' schools were representative of high schools nationally. Our teachers taught at schools with an average enrollment of 1,311 students, compared with the national average of 1,332. Similarly, our sample's schools had an average of 26% of their students qualifying for free lunch compared with 28% nationally. On the other hand, only 27% of our teachers taught at schools having more than 10% black students, and only 22% taught at schools with at least 10% Hispanic students.

PENNSTATE
1855

The National Survey of High School Biology Teachers

Tell us about your experiences. Share your opinions.

We are inviting you to participate in a study of high school science teachers. Your name was selected from a database of science teachers from all fifty states and the District of Columbia. Your participation in this study is very important to the success of this project and without your participation we will not be able to accurately describe the opinions and experiences of teachers in schools and communities such as yours.

Please use a blue or black ink pen to answer the questions and mail your completed questionnaire back to us in the postage-paid envelope.

A Confidential Survey of High School Science Teachers
conducted by the Survey Research Center at Penn State
and supported by a grant from the National Science Foundation

Figure 5.1. National Survey of High School Biology Teachers questionnaire.

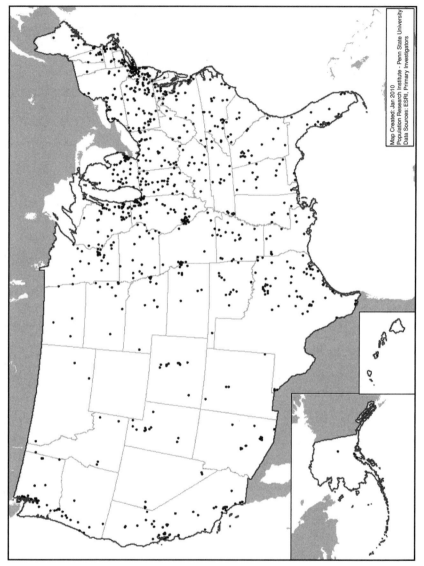

Figure 5.2. Geographic distribution of teachers completing the survey.

The corresponding national figures are 42% and 39%, respectively. In addition, we slightly over-represent midwestern and small-town schools, at the expense of slightly under-representing central city schools. Such departures from national characteristics could bias some of our inferences if, for example, teachers at all-white high schools teach differently from their counterparts at schools with more diverse student bodies.[2]

Quantitative and Qualitative Data

These data can be used to create a statistical portrait – a snapshot – of public high school biology teachers during the spring of 2007. But we are well aware that numbers can tell only part of the story. As a result, we invited teachers to add comments, suggestions, anecdotes, or anything else they wished to tell us in addition to their answers to the forced-choice survey questions. A total of 325 teachers took advantage of this, typically writing a short paragraph (the average comment was 68 words long). We will draw on these additional comments to help flesh out the statistical analyses based on the forced-choice section of the survey.

Evolution in Public School Classrooms

How much time should be spent on evolution in the typical high school biology class? There is no clear answer to this question. There are, for example, no national standards for high school biology, and neither the strongest nor the weakest state standards specify a precise amount of time that should be spent on any particular topic. As we noted above, there are three widely circulated documents that seek to fill the standards void at the national level (National Academy of Sciences

---

[2] The standard practice for adjusting surveys for differential nonresponse across groups is to calculate poststratification weights (Groves et al. 2004; Kish 1965; Lohr 1999). Nearly all media polls and scientific surveys use weights to ensure that the data are nearly identical to the larger population on key regional and demographic characteristics. We calculated poststratification weights to adjust the survey for regional and racial under-representation. However, the weighted and unweighted results never differ by more than 2.5%, and the same substantive conclusions emerged from both weighted and unweighted analyses. We have reported weighted analyses elsewhere (Berkman et al. 2008), but because the results are essentially the same, we will report only the unweighted data in this book.

1999; National Research Council 1996; National Science Teachers Association 1992). But these, too, refrain from offering directions on the amount of time that should be spent on evolution relative to other topics. In general, these national reports and state standards offer ideas for the *content* of high school science, biology, and life science classes, but not the *curriculum*; in other words, they enumerate and elaborate on outcomes – what students should learn – but not on any particular ordering or allocation of time for each subject.

It is clear, however, that all three of these reports expect a substantial investment in evolution and evolution-related topics. All expect science teachers to "provide evidence that evolution has attained its status as a unifying theme in science" (Skoog and Bilica 2002, 449). The National Research Council's 1996 *National Science Education Standards* (NSES), often used as a benchmark to evaluate the content of state science standards and textbooks, identifies evolution as one of the five "unifying concepts and processes" that provide the "big picture of scientific ideas." The NSES further identifies eleven benchmarks, such as natural selection and biological adaptation, for states and textbook editors to use in determining the content for high school biology.

We asked teachers to indicate the number of hours they devoted to human evolution, to general evolutionary processes, and to creationism or intelligent design (ID). The reports of instructional time for evolution are displayed in Table 5.1. The answers concerning human and general evolution were combined to get a summary measure of the number of hours devoted to evolution overall, which is reported in the third column. In addition, we used the answers to our forced-choice questions to generate a numeric variable; from this, we calculated the mean number of hours.[3] The data show that, on average, teachers devoted about 14 class hours specifically to evolution, and only one percent excluded evolution entirely. But significantly fewer teachers teach about human evolution, which is not included as an NSES benchmark and, as we explain in the next chapter, has disappeared as a benchmark in most state standards. Seventeen percent of teachers

---

[3] Teachers selected categories in order to indicate the number of hours devoted to evolution and creationism (see Table 5.1). Using category midpoints and assuming a mean of 25 hours for the last category (22 hours and more), we calculated the mean number of hours devoted to each of these three topics.

Table 5.1. Hours devoted to human evolution and general evolution in high school biology classes ($N = 926$), 2007

	Human evolution (%)	General evolutionary processes (%)	Human plus general evolution (%)
Not covered	17	1	1
1–2 hours	35	9	2
3–5 hours	25	23	8
6–10 hours	12	27	33
11–15 hours	4	17	19
16–20 hours	2	11	13
20 hours or more	2	10	22
No answer provided	2	2	2
Total	100%	100%	100%
Mean number of hours	4.1	9.8	13.8
Standard deviation	4.8	6.3	8.8

Source: National Survey of High School Biology Teachers.

surveyed did not cover human evolution at all in their biology class, whereas a majority of teachers (60%) spent between 1 and 5 hours of class time on it.

The Content of Evolution Instruction

However, the amount of time does not tell the entire story, or even the most important part. In order to understand how teachers navigated the cultural politics of evolution, we asked a series of questions about *how* they taught the class. In particular, we wanted to know how many teachers embraced an approach that would be consistent with three positions taken by the National Academy of Sciences (NAS) and other major scientific organizations: (1) that there is no dispute that evolution has occurred, (2) that one cannot properly understand other topics in biology without understanding evolution, and (3) that evolution should be the unifying theme of any class in general biology.

First, we wanted to address the distinction between evolution as something that has occurred – *a fact* – in contrast to theories accounting for how it did so. The NAS has made the point that, although *findings* are always tentative, there are some observations that have been verified hundreds or even thousands of times and that these are considered *facts*. The position was stated most forcefully by the eminent geneticist Richard Lewontin:

> It is time for students of the evolutionary process, especially those who have been misquoted and used by the creationists, to state clearly that evolution is a FACT, not theory, and that what is at issue within biology are questions of details of the process and the relative importance of different mechanisms of evolution. It is a FACT that the earth with liquid water, is more than 3.6 billion years old. It is a FACT that cellular life has been around for at least half of that period and that organized multicellular life is at least 800 million years old. It is a FACT that major life forms now on earth were not at all represented in the past. There were no birds or mammals 250 million years ago. It is a FACT that major life forms of the past are no longer living. There used to be dinosaurs and Pithecanthropus, and there are none now. It is a FACT that all living forms come from previous living forms. Therefore, all present forms of life arose from ancestral forms that were different. Birds arose from nonbirds and humans from nonhumans. No person who pretends to any understanding of the natural world can deny these facts any more than she or he can deny that the earth is round, rotates on its axis, and revolves around the sun. (Lewontin 1981, 559)

Lewontin, however, is hardly alone in this position, as the most eminent biologists of many generations have made similar points, including Theodosius Dobzhansky (1973), Stephen Jay Gould (1981), and others.

Although there is no scientific controversy over whether evolution has occurred, there is disagreement among scientists on the relative importance of several mechanisms that might account for it and the current diversity of species. For example, advocates of the "genetic drift" explanation place greater weight on how geographic isolation – rather than natural selection – combines with random mutations to produce new species. And horizontal gene transfer suggests yet another potential mechanism. Indeed, scientists are highly critical of those who use legitimate scientific debates about mechanisms to undermine the evidence that evolution has occurred. The

Table 5.2. Teacher support of key positions advanced by the National Academy of Sciences and other organizations (*N* = 926)

A. When I teach evolution (including answering student questions) I emphasize the broad consensus that evolution is a fact, even as scientists disagree about the specific mechanisms through which evolution occurred:

Strongly agree	30
Agree	44
Disagree	16
Strongly disagree	6
Not applicable/No answer	5
	100%

B. It is possible to offer an excellent general biology course for high school students that includes no mention of Darwin or evolutionary theory.

Strongly agree	5
Agree	7
Disagree	25
Strongly disagree	58
Not applicable/No answer	5
	100%

C. Evolution serves as the unifying theme for the content of the course.

Strongly agree	26
Agree	36
Disagree	25
Strongly disagree	9
Not applicable/No answer	6
	100%

Source: National Survey of High School Biology Teachers.

NAS addressed this in a recent publication, stating, "Because the evidence supporting it is so strong, scientists no longer question whether biological evolution has occurred and is continuing to occur. Instead, they investigate the mechanisms of evolution, how rapidly evolution can take place, and related questions" (2008a,18). It was this notion that we tried to tap into when we asked teachers, "*when I teach evolution (including answering student questions) I emphasize the broad consensus that evolution is a fact, even as scientists disagree about the specific mechanisms through which evolution occurred.*"

Table 5.2, panel A, reports that 74% of teachers emphasize the fact that evolution occurred, but only 30% agree strongly with this statement. Surely, the major proponents of this view would be disappointed to see that fewer than one in three teachers strongly agree that this characterizes their teaching. Moreover, more than one-fifth of teachers do not emphasize this point at all. As we will illustrate later in the chapter, some teachers explicitly reject the fact of evolution and share their skepticism with their students.

Asserting that evolution has occurred is central to the public science activities of major scientific organizations and is clearly intended to undercut a significant portion of debate about evolution by arguing that this aspect of the "debate" is not debated at all by scientists. A teacher from Illinois agreed, telling us that "Evolution is a fact and needs to be presented as such with supporting evidence." Or, as one of our teachers from Oregon put it, "I tell students that evolution will occur with or without their agreement." But, apparently, few teachers are this direct.

The NAS and other leading scientific organizations also call for the absolute necessity of including evolution in the biology curriculum. The oft-quoted line of geneticist Theodosius Dobzhansky, that "nothing in biology makes sense except in the light of evolution," (1973) is a widely accepted idea. As a result, the NAS and leading organizations not only advocate for the inclusion of evolution but its integration into the many different aspects of a typical course in general biology. In this view, evolution unifies disparate facts in subfields such as genetics, anatomy, ecology, and the study of health and disease.

Two questionnaire items on our survey get at this notion. One is "*I believe it is possible to offer an excellent general biology course for high school students that includes no mention of Darwin or evolutionary theory.*" This addresses the desire to remove evolution entirely from high school biology – often urged as appropriate in order to avoid offending or infringing on the rights of some Christians. But it also measures the extent to which practicing high school biology teachers embrace or reject a key goal of the NAS and virtually all other scientific organizations. The responses of our sampled teachers appear in panel B of Table 5.2 and show that only 12% believe an excellent class can exclude evolution entirely.

But the minimal inclusion of evolution is not really what establishment science recommends. They argue that a student's understanding of biology is enhanced when evolution is not just a short topic but a unifying theme that is woven throughout the biology curriculum. Our last question addressing scientific priorities asks teachers whether

Table 5.3. Support for core NAS positions and the number of hours devoted to evolution ($N = 903$)

	Distribution of teachers (%)	Mean number of hours devoted to evolution
"Strongly" endorses all three positions	12	19.7
Endorses all three positions, but not necessarily "strongly"	35	15.4
Does not endorse all three positions	53	11.4
	100%	13.8

Source: National Survey of High School Biology Teachers.

"Evolution serves as the unifying theme for my course." Panel C of Table 5.2 shows that 62% of our teachers report that evolution is the unifying theme for their course (26% strongly agreeing).

All told, we see substantial variation on each of the questions. Moreover, when taken together, we see important differences within the teaching profession. Just under half (46%) of the teachers in our survey agreed or strongly agreed with the first and third questions and disagreed (or strongly disagreed) with the second. That is, the profession seems to be divided roughly 50–50 between those who embrace national organizations' recommended pedagogical approach and those who do not. If we look only at teachers who *strongly* endorsed these positions, they comprise only 12% of the sample (112 of 926 teachers).

Not surprisingly, there is a strong linkage between the adoption of the NAS positions and the amount of time devoted to evolution. As Table 5.3 shows, those who do not consistently embrace these positions spend an average of 11 hours on evolution, whereas those who strongly endorse all three positions devote 20 hours a year to evolution. This table also tells us that only 12% – roughly one in eight – public high school teachers are teaching evolution in a manner totally consistent with the recommendations of the most prominent national scientific organizations.

Among the core group of NAS supporters, many elaborated on their teaching. One teacher from Indiana who reports devoting about 20 hours to evolution noted, "I tell students that I teach evolution as a topic in biology because all other biological functions are based in evolution." A teacher from Oklahoma wrote, "I feel that evolution is a key concept and theme in biology and that the course cannot be adequately taught without teaching evolution." She continued by saying, "I would not be willing to teach the course if I were unable to present evolution as a key concept." A teacher from Montana emphasized the pedagogical benefits, explaining, "When working with a textbook such as ours that uses it as a continuing theme I feel that students benefit more than if it is covered as a separate unit." And a teacher in Maine who devotes about 21 hours to evolution summed up this position well: "I pretty much discuss Evolution all year – it's the unifying theme of Biology."

Although some teachers credited their textbook for integrating evolution, others pointed specifically to their own discretion in integrating evolution throughout the class even beyond the presentation provided in their assigned textbook and assigned curriculum. A Pennsylvania teacher, for example, reported, "The natural selection process is interjected into almost every topic I cover. The actual chapters on evolution are reserved for the end of the year, if time remains."

But more than half the teachers rejected one or more of these three positions. What does it mean to cover evolution without embracing the positions of the nation's most prestigious scientific organization? We have already seen that it means spending considerably less time on evolution. Based on our open-ended questions, it appears that, for many teachers, this entails confining instruction to *within-species* change – what is often called *microevolution*. Microevolution is a major focus of evolutionary biology, and the NAS devotes considerable attention to it in its public science communications (e.g., NAS 2008a). More important to the *politics* of evolution, microevolution is accepted by many in the creationist and ID camps. For example, chemist Jonathan Sarfati addresses the claim made in NAS's *Science, Evolution and Creationism* that an understanding of evolution was essential to quickly identifying solutions to the spread of severe acute respiratory syndrome (SARS). Writing on the Web site of Creation Ministries International, Sarfati notes, "Certainly combating the SARS virus was great medical science, but was evolution really necessary? Even if they were right, all they found was a virus changing into a virus, which says nothing about how viruses might have evolved into virologists" (Sarfati 2009; see also Sarfati 2008).

Several of our teachers likewise echo this theme. A Nebraska high school science teacher who devotes just 3–5 hours to evolution took the time to explain to us that, "In my classroom I distinguish 'micro' evolution from 'macro' evolution." A teacher from Indiana explains how his teaching directly contradicts the position elaborated by Lewontin. He explains that, "I distinguish microevolution as fact, macroevolution as theory." A Maryland science teacher elaborated on her minimal conception of evolution, "I do teach that animals can adapt behaviorally, but not necessarily physically (i.e., giraffes migrating to find food vs. growing long necks)." And a Tennessee teacher who devotes less than 4 hours to evolution over the course of the year told us, "I teach to the standard. I don't believe the standard. Huge difference in macroevolution and microevolution."

It is useful to point out, however, that some teachers appear to use the micro–macro distinction in order to make the material less controversial to students, rather than as a method of narrowing the scope of instruction. For example, a Wisconsin teacher who devotes about 15 hours a year to evolution explained, "I divide evolution into two units: microevolution (change to populations) and macroevolution (change between species). My biggest reason for this is because it is easier for students to learn the material if it is divided into two smaller units, rather than one large unit. However, I also point out to students that there is no reason for a person to feel that microevolution would offend their beliefs. When we get to macroevolution, there are some students who do not accept the premises, even though I teach both macro and micro as established ideas with solid evidence. At the very least, I feel my method gets students to accept at least half of evolution (micro), rather than no acceptance at all." A teacher in California has also given this considerable thought, telling us:

> I teach evolution through a cellular and molecular approach. I find students are less offended by it. The minute you start off with evolution showing primates or fossil evidence, students immediately shut down. On the other hand, when I teach students the mechanisms of cells and that all cells basically are similar, then I can suggest evolution without so much opposition. When covering DNA and Protein Synthesis in particular, it is easy to get students to consider evolution. It leads naturally into genetics, which then naturally leads into

Evolution using the fossil evidence. To start with fossil evidence is not very effective with a majority of the students. I don't even mention the word 'Evolution' in the beginning of the term.

But more generally, it appears that teachers use the micro–macro distinction as a specific way to narrow the scope of instruction. Reflecting the more general position, a Texas teacher who devotes only 3 class hours to evolution summed it up, "We teach evolution mostly as a series of changes thru time and do not dwell upon more controversial issues." In this way, teachers can cover at least some textbook material and several of the NSES benchmarks, including concepts like species change over time, random mutation, adaptation to the environments, and extinction. They can discuss the impact of geographic isolation and the concept of genetic drift, using breeds of domesticated animals, antibiotic-resistant viruses, and the origin of new *varieties* as examples of "change over time." As a result, teachers who confine discussion to the less controversial examples of microevolution will necessarily omit discussions of dramatic changes in body structure and function.

Pacing

A second method of avoiding controversy is to schedule the topic of evolution as the last major unit of the academic year. In doing so, delays of various kinds would have the effect of pushing evolution off the schedule. Before designing our study, we had heard anecdotal evidence that some teachers deliberately did this, and we therefore asked all teachers to react to the following statement: "*I have paced my class so that the evolution chapters in my textbook would be covered only minimally at the end of the academic term.*" Indeed, one of our respondents was advised to take this approach when she was a student teacher: "My advisor suggested I cover evolution quickly." As Table 5.4 shows, 12% of teachers report having done so at least once, although only 3% of our sample reports having done so "frequently." This small group of frequent deliberate avoiders spends, on average, only 7 hours a year on evolution-related instruction. But all those who report having done this teach somewhat less than the national average.

Table 5.4. Teacher reports of deliberately avoiding evolution by pacing and the impact on the number of hours devoted to evolution ($N = 903$)

I have paced my class so that the evolution chapters in my textbook would be covered only minimally at the end of the academic term	Distribution of teachers (%)	Mean number of hours devoted to evolution
Never	86	14.4
Once or twice	6	11.9
A few times	4	11.6
Frequently	3	6.8
No answer provided	2	9.8
Total	100%	13.8

Source: National Survey of High School Biology Teachers.

Others have little control over the sequencing of topics, which may be directed from higher administrators. A Michigan teacher reported, "I would agree that the teaching of evolution often occurs at the end of the year and therefore is slighted in our curriculum." But whether from outside forces, the chapter sequence of the textbook, or their own discretion, leaving the topic of evolution to the end of the course appears to be a tactic of avoidance and may well be a good indicator that a school district, science department, or individual teacher is hoping to either avoid controversy or deliberately give only minimal coverage to evolution.

Confronting Student Sensitivities

Almost all teachers recognize that evolution can be a sensitive and controversial topic for at least some of their students. And almost all teachers seem to have ways of proactively addressing these concerns and responding to students. Among the NAS endorsers who took the time to add comments to the survey, the most common approach is to discuss in detail the nature of scientific inquiry, emphasize its difference from religion, and argue that science and religion are not necessarily in conflict, a position taken by biologist Kenneth Miller (2000, 2008), author of one of the most widely used high school textbooks (see also Ayala 2007). An Ohio teacher who reports devoting over 30 hours to evolution told us, "Covering the nature of sciences the first couple weeks of school helps to avoid conflict with religion a great deal." And another teacher from Ohio, which has had its share of evolution controversy, explained, "I preface Evolution while we look at the Nature of Science. We compare the process, knowledge, societal value and types of questions that are answered by both organized religion and science. We recognize each serves a different purpose and they do not conflict. I have always had good results using this approach early in the school year."

Others more explicitly demarcate the domains of science and religion – what Stephen Jay Gould referred to as two *nonoverlapping magisteria* (1997). A Massachusetts teacher told us, "Entertaining the notions behind creationism is fine in so far as the students are made to understand why a (creator) God must remain outside of scientific inquiry. My objective, thus, is to make clear that science is NOT anti-God." A California teacher elaborated on this same theme: "I emphasize that science is one way of 'knowing.' It deals only with the physical world and can only answer specific kinds of questions." And a teacher in Arkansas explained, "I try to introduce evolution from a 'ways of knowing' perspective which emphasizes that religion is based on faith and non-measureable observations while science is based on measureable observations."

In fact, quite a few teachers also used the open-ended question in our survey to explain their personal comfort with their own faith and their understanding of science, but also with their firm belief in demarcating these two domains. One Michigan teacher told us this story: "The other day a student saw me wearing a bracelet with the Christian fish symbol. The student was amazed. She asked 'How can you teach biology, believe in evolution, and still be a Christian?' My response was 'The teaching of science neither proves nor disproves the existence of God. Why does … your religion attempt to disprove the existence of science?'" And a New Jersey teacher tells his students, "that all of science is based on careful observation and testable experimentation – i.e.: scientific evidence. There is no scientific evidence for creationism or intelligent design – yet as a scientist I still believe in God."

Still other teachers emphasize the different domains, but without using this as an opportunity to provide a detailed discussion of the nature of scientific inquiry. A Pennsylvania teacher told us, "But I am a fundamental Christian so I believe in creation. I never impose my personal beliefs on my students, but in certain situations, I do let the students research and debate the issue in class. I do not think that teaching creation or 'intelligent design' is appropriate in the public school. It would be as foolish as having my pastor explaining evolution to his Sunday school class." One teacher from Texas was even more emphatic. She wrote, "I teach BIOLOGY not Sunday school! I start by explaining that my job is to teach SCIENCE and if my students want to argue their views they can do so outside of my classroom."

Downplaying the Importance

Among the larger group of teachers that do not embrace the NAS goals, the most common type of conflict avoidance we came across was the minimization of the importance of the topic by telling students that it is okay to "not believe in" evolution while, at the same time, encouraging them to *understand it* sufficiently well to pass examinations.

Some emphasized the need to understand evolution to be considered educated, but more emphasized that students needed to study evolution to pass the class. For example, an Illinois teacher made this point: "I emphasize to my students (who are mainly Catholic) that they do not need to agree with evolution, but they should be able to have an intelligent conversation with someone who does agree. Basically, they should hear all perspectives to be a better, well-rounded individual & of course, for the state tests." A teacher from Connecticut was more narrow in her focus: "I tell my students that they are not required to BELIEVE the theory, just to study it," as was this teacher from New York: "I have always started the evolution unit by telling the kids that I don't care if they believe in evolution or not. I tell them that I'm not trying to change their beliefs. If they don't want to accept any of the topics we discuss, that's all right; just understand it enough to answer the Regents test questions."

This type of approach to students varies substantially from teacher to teacher. Some continue to assert the essential validity of evolutionary biology. Many others, however, appear to subtly, or not so subtly, undermine it in the students' minds. After all, a teacher would never tell students they did not care if they actually believed that light simultaneously has the properties of waves and of discrete particles, or that the movement of massive plates is the cause of earthquakes. A Texas teacher notes that the evolution benchmarks in the Texas state standards "are taught only as a theory and I tell my students to learn the information for purposes of only passing the state test to graduate." A Michigan teacher candidly reports this approach to teaching, explaining, "I do tell kids I can't force them to believe evolution, and all the details, but they need to understand it... [because] Biology is organized *as if* evolution is true" (emphasis added). And one Pennsylvania teacher even equated evolution with the philosophy of Hitler's Third Reich: "Students are always told that they do not have to believe in evolution, just learn it. They don't have to believe in Nazism but they do learn it."

Still other teachers encouraged their students to learn enough about evolution so that they could use the knowledge to more effectively defend their previously formed beliefs about creation. A Minnesota teacher explains how he asks students "to listen to the concepts and learn them well. I do not tell them that they have to change their beliefs but I do tell them they are accountable for the information. I tell them a benefit of learning this material is that they will be better equipped to discuss creationist concepts with others if they understand evolutionary perspectives. To debate effectively you must know the 'other side'."

What these approaches all have in common, however, is the abdication of science as a superior form of reason about the natural world and a rejection of the idea that science and faith speak to distinct and nonoverlapping domains. Unlike teachers who believe that their faith in God is consistent with the methods, findings, and conclusions of evolutionary biology, these other teachers are telling students that they may ignore scientific evidence and conclusions without sacrificing an accurate view of nature and natural history. Indeed, the equation of evolution with a political philosophy – something that can be debated in terms of personally held values, like situational ethics – seriously undermines the legitimacy of science. Students are no doubt smart enough to pick up the message that underlies "just learn it for the test." We have no way of quantifying the precise proportion of high school teachers who take this tack, as we did not include a specific question about this on our survey. But the frequency with which it comes up in the open-ended comments suggests that this is a fairly common approach among teachers who do not embrace the NAS's goals.

Teaching Evolution – Diversity Within the Constitutionally Permissible

The reports of individual teachers describe a wide range of behaviors – wider than is reflected in the official policies of the states. Some teach rigorous classes that reflect the NAS priorities, devoting 20 or more hours per year to evolution, while weaving evolutionary biology into the discussions of the cell, genetics, morphology, ecology, and other topics. Others teach only some aspects of evolution – apparently the least controversial aspects. This can be the result of narrowing the scope of evolution to within-species change or simply due to the fact that teachers find that they have only a few class hours for evolution as the academic term ends. These reports, then, span the entire range of constitutionally permissible choices and confirm earlier observations that the teaching of evolution is frequently cursory (Rutledge and Mitchell 2002). For example, the Tennessee teacher who told us, "I teach to the standard. I don't believe the standard. Huge difference in macroevolution and microevolution," also told us that she spends no time on creationism in her formal instruction – 0 hours. She only devotes 4 hours to evolution, and she rejects all three NAS positions. But her teaching is not unconstitutional, and she does not cross the bright line demarking constitutional from unconstitutional practices. Yet if this teacher, obviously hostile to macroevolution, does not teach creationism or ID, it raises the questions of how many teachers actually teach creationism and how they do so. We turn to that next.

CREATIONISM IN THE CLASSROOM

We asked teachers how much time they spend on creationism or ID, and the results, reported in Table 5.5, show that 75% report 0 hours and 22% report various amounts. This latter number will strike many as quite high; however, it can be misleading because some teachers may cover creationism to expose students to an alternative to evolutionary theory, whereas others may bring up creationism in

Table 5.5. Hours devoted to creationism or intelligent design in high school biology classes (*N* = 926)

	Number	Percent
Not covered–0 hours	691	74.6
1–2 hours	159	17.2
3–5 hours	36	3.9
6–10 hours	6	.7
11–15 hours	3	.3
16–20 hours	3	.3
No answer provided	28	3.0
Total	926	100.0%

Source: National Survey of High School Biology Teachers.

order to criticize it or in response to student inquiries. Just as the hours devoted to evolution can mislead about the quality of the instruction, questions that simply ask about time devoted to creationism in the formal lesson plans may therefore overstate support for creationism or ID by counting both those holding it up for ridicule along with creationism supporters.

On the other hand, creationism or ID may occupy class discussion as a result of student questions even if not part of the formal curriculum. So, just as we wanted to understand the emphases of teachers when they discuss evolution, so we must again dig beneath the reports of time devoted to creationism. To do so, we first want to see how many teachers who discuss creationism, even if just in response to student questions, also endorse positions taken by the major advocates for creation science and ID. Two of our survey questions get at this. First, teachers were asked to agree or disagree with the following statement, "*When I do teach about creationism or intelligent design (including answering student questions) I emphasize that this is a valid, scientific alternative to Darwinian explanations for the origin of species.*" The second statement was similar and contained the same introductory phrase, but focused on the opinions of scientists, "*... I emphasize that many reputable scientists view these as valid alternatives to Darwinian theory.*" These two statements directly get at claims that these approaches merit inclusion in the *science* curriculum; our results are reported in Table 5.6.

Table 5.6. Teacher orientations to discussing creationism or intelligent design in high school biology classes (*N* = 926)

A. *When I do teach about creationism or intelligent design (including answering student questions), I emphasize that this is a valid, scientific alternative to Darwinian explanations for the origin of species.*

Strongly agree	3
Agree	11
Disagree	12
Strongly disagree	20
Not applicable/No answer	53
	100%

B. *When I do teach about creationism or intelligent design (including answering student questions), I emphasize that many reputable scientists view these as valid alternatives to Darwinian theory.*

Strongly agree	3
Agree	15
Disagree	17
Strongly disagree	13
Not applicable/No answer	52
	100%

C. Summary of responses to both questions

Agrees with both questions	11
Agrees with one question	10
Agrees with neither question (includes those responding "not applicable")	79
	100%

Source: National Survey of High School Biology Teachers.

Nearly half of the teachers (47%) declined to answer both questions, indicating that they do not teach creationism in their lesson plans or more informally through student questions. Fourteen percent of all teachers agreed (or agreed strongly) with the first statement, which indicates their *personal endorsement* of creationism or intelligent design, and 18% agreed with the second, which emphasizes the endorsement of "many reputable scientists." These proportions are somewhat less than the percentage of teachers who report devoting one or more hours to creationism or ID, suggesting that a portion of the initial report represents class time devoted to criticizing these approaches.

The relationship between formal class time and endorsement of creation science is elaborated in Table 5.7. Of the teachers who do not endorse creationism *as science* (those in the left column), 80 – or 11% – devote some time to creationism or ID. On the other hand, we

Table 5.7. Hours devoted to creationism or intelligent design in high school biology classes, by endorsement of these as valid scientific approaches ($N = 926$)

	Does not endorse creationism or ID in the classroom	Agrees with at least one statement concerning creationism or ID as a valid scientific approach
Not covered–0 hours	627	64
1–2 hours	*71*	**88**
3–5 hours	*8*	**28**
6–10 hours	*0*	**6**
11–15 hours	*1*	**2**
16–20 hours	*0*	**3**
No answer provided	25	3
Total	732	194

Source: National Survey of High School Biology Teachers.
Note: Italics represent teachers who do not endorse creationism but report spending class time on the topic (9% of the total). Bold entries refer to teachers who endorse creationism and report at least one class hour devoted to creationism or intelligent design (14%).

see that, of the 194 teachers who agreed with at least one statement (those in the right column, comprising 21% of the total), 64 teachers did not report instructional time for creationism but clearly spend some time on it as an addition to their formal lesson plans. One teacher from Louisiana, referring to restrictions on discussing creationism noted, "I believe we should be able to discuss creationism in classes along with evolution. The students bring it up anyway." Thus, if we count those who report 0 hours, but also report, *"When I do teach about creationism or intelligent design (including answering student questions)"* that they endorse these as *"valid scientific alternatives,"* we estimate that 21% of all science teachers endorse creationism or ID in their classrooms (that is, all teachers in the right column of Table 5.7). If we restrict ourselves only to those teachers who both support one or the other statements and report spending at least an hour on these topics, our lower bound estimate is 14% (both estimates have a confidence interval of plus or minus 3%). In either case, this is a substantial proportion of all public high school biology teachers.

Based on the reaction to a preliminary report of these data (Berkman et al. 2008), we know that many readers will focus on these particular estimates as being especially important and revealing. That original paper reported our lower-bound estimate only, and this drew considerable attention. From members of the establishment scientific community, there was considerable shock and anger. On the other hand, a brief report on the Christian Broadcasting Network regarded the estimate of roughly one in eight teachers endorsing creation in the classroom as positive news and a sign of progress in their efforts to change science instruction. Still others, such as the scholar Randy Moore, felt that our estimate might even be too low, and our higher estimate suggests that he may have been correct (Monastersky 2008).

In light of this, it is important to explore what these numbers mean and do not mean – first by providing a fuller treatment of their quantitative meaning, and then by getting under the surface with qualitative accounts from the teachers themselves. Additional context will be provided in the following chapters as well, as we illuminate the factors that lead to different approaches to teaching the topic.

First, we want to emphasize that these are estimates, based on a scientific sample survey of 926 teachers. As such, there are several potential sources of error. The first is random sampling error, and these estimates – 14% for the lower bound and 21% as an upper bound – each have an associated degree of uncertainty, a confidence interval, of plus or minus 3%. Whatever the true value is, this means that there is a 95% probability that each estimate is within 3% of that true value. Second, we discussed earlier the possibility of sampling bias due to the under-representation of schools with substantial minority populations and the slight over-representation of Midwest and smaller communities. When we weight the data to account for these, our corresponding estimates are essentially the same: 14% and 22% (also with confidence intervals of plus or minus 3%). Third, there is the possibility of measurement bias, of systematic over- or under-reporting by the teachers. This we can never know, but we find considerable evidence in the open-ended questions that teachers were candid and felt they could trust our promise that their answers would remain confidential. Most published case studies also estimate the prevalence of creationist instruction in the range of 15–20%, and this also gives us confidence in these estimates.

Ultimately, there is the question of exactly what these numbers connote. They do not mean that 14% or 21% of public high school science educators are teaching a creationism-rich curriculum – as one might find in private schools associated with doctrinally conservative Protestant faiths. Rather, we find that 14–21% of teachers are *endorsing* the validity of creation science or ID. The higher estimate includes teachers whose total formal instruction on ID is less than an hour. Of those who do report an hour or more of formal class time, the majority report 1–2 hours. These relatively brief endorsements do not constitute "equal time" but do confer legitimacy on these alternatives. Because legitimacy and prestige cannot be granted equally to competing approaches, those who teach creationism *as science* necessarily undermine the legitimacy of science. And this is what inflames this as a *political* controversy.

Balancing Creationism and Evolution in the Classroom

For the 14–21% of teachers who endorse creationism or ID, how does this endorsement fit into their broader approach to teaching general biology? Unfortunately, very few of the teachers who endorsed creationism in their classes provided significant detail on their pedagogy. What they did tell us is that they typically take a "teach the controversy" approach. An Indiana teacher who reports spending 30 hours on evolution and 4 hours on creationism or intelligent design told us, "In teaching biology, I do not impart my belief on this subject to my students, I present *each idea* as a theory and let the students decide which one they want to believe in" (emphasis added). And a teacher from South Dakota who devotes 8 hours to creationism and 10 hours to evolution explained, "I teach evolution/creation as an inquiry process. I use classroom text as well as other sources backing evolution/creation. I have several useful videos backing both areas. My goal is to make students analyze and think to arrive at their own educated decisions."

Although these teachers report providing students with some kind of balance, they actually devote far more time to evolution (11.9 hours) than to creationism or ID (an average of 2.0 hours). Nevertheless, they seem to think this is adequate so that the students have at least some basis for making their own choices (and "balance" can also be achieved by covering evolution topics in a way that suggests gaps or weaknesses in evolutionary biology).

Teaching Creationism as Good Science and Evolution as Bad Science

Interestingly, those who endorse creationism in their classrooms almost always defend their decisions as consistent with good science.

In particular, they take issue with Lewontin, Gould, and the National Academy of Sciences for their misuse of the term "fact" in describing the evolution of modern species. An Oklahoma teacher was emphatic about this: "To be a true scien[tist], you have to present both evolution and creationism!" A teacher from California explained his goals this way: "I feel much of the scientific community is afraid to allow the debate to happen. Good science looks at all possible explanations of the facts and evaluates each on its merits and picks the one that best explains the facts. High school students understand this and should be exposed to alternative explanation[s] of the facts and given the tools to evaluate and make up their own minds." Another teacher, from Iowa, described her approach: "I let the students know up front that I have a creationist view point of how life was created. I use the word 'model' to explain evolution ('evolution model'). I bring in the 'intelligent design model' to question the 'evolution model.'" A teacher from Nebraska makes a similar point, though he seems to adopt a lay definition of theory: "It surprises me that many science educators do not understand the difference between scientific theory and scientific law. Scientific theory should be taught as such. However you will have those that teach theory as if it is the absolute answer. Until scientists change the definition of scientific theory then Evolution must always be taught as a theory."

Evolution is further denigrated as a sound scientific theory by teachers accepting the scientific validity of creationism or ID through their emphasis on evolution's *supposed* inability to explain the development of complex organs and biological systems. We see this in their response to a question we asked about *irreducible complexity*, an idea central to intelligent design which essentially argues that incremental evolution of complex biological organs and systems is not plausible because it is not possible for natural selection to produce a series of partial mutations that are not themselves beneficial without subsequent mutations. Our question – *"Please tell us if you have ever done the following: I have encouraged students to consider how unlikely it is that complex organs (e.g., the eye) or biological processes (blood clotting) could have occurred simply by random mutation and natural selection"* – focuses on the conclusions of the irreducible complexity argument rather than the reason (that intermediate forms of organs that lack a crucial, not-yet-evolved element, will not be functional and not aid adaptation). It does, however, provide a sense of the

Table 5.8. Teacher reports of raising the possibility of irreducible complexity (N = 926)

I have encouraged students to consider how unlikely it is that complex organs (e.g., the eye) or biological processes (blood clotting) could have occurred simply by random mutation and natural selection.	Does not endorse creationism or ID in the classroom (N = 732) (%)	Agrees with at least one statement concerning creationism or ID as a valid scientific approach (N = 194) (%)
Never	79	48
Once or twice	5	11
A few times	6	22
Frequently	6	16
No answer provided	3	3
Total	100%	100%

Source: National Survey of High School Biology Teachers.

prevalence of this idea among both those who accept ID arguments and those who do not.

Roughly one-fifth of teachers who *reject* ID raise this question, suggesting that some teachers may use them as a devil's advocate or to be provocative without endorsing any particular position. But a significantly larger percentage – over half – of those who do endorse at least one statement concerning creationism or ID also raise the unlikelihood of complex organs evolving naturally, with one-third of these teachers doing so frequently. One explicit ID supporter from Florida shared his personal view: "I believe that science will never be able to answer everything, simply because the 'Intelligent Designer' will not allow it; how ironic?" Scientists, of course, vehemently reject the irreducible complexity argument as a valid critique of evolution (Dorit 2007; Miller 2008; Travis and Reznik 2009). Yet, raising this – along with other issues intended to throw doubt on evolution – allows many teachers who accept creationism or ID as an alternative to argue that they, rather than evolutionists, are arguing from a sound scientific basis. Rather than simply argue that creationism or ID is good science meriting equal treatment, they emphasize arguments that they believe devalue mainstream evolutionary biology. One Minnesota teacher explained it this way: "I don't teach theory of evolution in my life science classes, nor do I teach the Big Bang Theory in my earth science classes. There is just too much science and inquiry that we do not have time to do something that is at best poor science."

Evolution and Creationism as Belief Systems

Although most creationism or ID endorsers defended these alternatives as good science, others take the opposite tack: rather than treating evolution and creationism as both instances of science, they regard both as faith-based belief systems, with the validity of evolution as ultimately a question of faith and values and not of evidence. This position was explicitly stated by a Virginia teacher who argued, "I do not think [the] scientific viewpoint of Human Evolution is accurate or ethical. I do not teach Human Evolution nor do I impose my religious beliefs on the educational setting. Humans will never solve the knowledge God possesses." Likewise, an Illinois teacher told us, "I am always amazed at how evolution and creationism are treated as if they are right or wrong. They are both belief systems that can never be truly or fully proved or discredited as man was not present at the beginning to satisfy his or her curiosity as to the nature of the situation."

The notion that science is simply a belief system finds its way into many classrooms. As one teacher from Arkansas explained, "I try to emphasize to my students that their personal beliefs have value and that it is their personal responsibility to make up their minds about evolution and intelligent design." And another from Iowa recounted, "Even with a strong faith in God, I feel the evolution model requires a stronger faith. But, with the national benchmark and standard we teach the evolution model and try to point out many of the flaws."

MONKEY BUSINESS

Up until now, we have not distinguished between teaching the overall evolution curriculum and the particular topic of human evolution. As we elaborate in the next chapter, human evolution does not appear in the NSES benchmarks and is largely absent from the curricular standards of almost all states as they apply to general biology taught to ninth or tenth graders. We have also seen earlier in this chapter that teachers regard macroevolution especially as inherently more controversial than microevolution. And as we explained in the first chapter, the earliest anti-evolution laws in the United States applied only to the teaching of human evolution. For all these reasons, it may be the trickiest aspect of evolution for teachers to navigate in the classroom.

Yet Table 5.1 showed that 83% of teachers do cover the topic, typically for an average of 4 classroom hours. Human evolution is covered in most high school biology textbooks, and this creates a framework for its inclusion, but clearly teachers exercise discretion and there is considerable variation. Much of this variation stems from the different ways that teachers deal with the misconceptions that students bring to the classrooms. One Indiana teacher spoke directly to this, saying that the "number one biggest misconception students can't get out of their head is evolution means man came from a monkey." Indeed, several teachers told us that they deliberately "don't get into the 'man-from-monkey' issues, etc," as a teacher from New York phrased it. Or as a Wisconsin teacher explained, "We do not cover Neanderthal and . . . human ancestors due to the conservative nature of our town."

Yet others feel that these misconceptions are precisely why they must devote time to the human evolution. As a Texas teacher explains, "Most of my students are hung up on 'Darwin equals we come from monkeys.' I spend time discussing this and using other evolution-ary patterns to show how such a similarity occurs." As a California teacher told us, when her students "say, 'I don't think we came from monkey' . . . I constantly correct them, 'me neither' I come from a common ape-like ancestor."

One of the most interesting patterns in the data is that the overall emphasis that a teacher brings to the class is not related to the amount of time devoted to human evolution in the way that we expected. Table 5.9 divides our teachers into three groups: the 21% who endorse creationism or ID, the 12% who strongly embrace all three NAS posi-tions on evolution, and everyone else. This is a rather crude method of classification, and we will introduce more sophisticated numeric scores in the next chapter. But for now, this provides a useful classification. The table shows that endorsers of creationism or ID spend nearly as much time on human evolution as do the strongest supporters of the NAS program. Indeed, as a proportion of all time devoted to evolu-tion, the creationist endorsers devote a third of their classroom discus-sion to human evolution, whereas other teachers devote only about a quarter of the evolution discussions to humans and human ancestors.

Table 5.9. Coverage of human evolution by general teaching orientation (N = 903)

	Percentage of all teachers (%)	Mean number of hours devoted to human evolution	Human evolution as a percentage of all class time devoted to evolution (%)
Endorses creationism or ID in class	21	4.2	34
All other teachers	67	3.8	27
"Strongly" endorse all three NAS positions	12	5.3	24
	100%	4.1	28

Source: National Survey of High School Biology Teachers.

This may seem to be a contradiction, but it is fully consistent with what we have seen throughout this chapter. Recall that many creationism endorsers cover evolution in ways that may serve to undermine the confidence that children have in evolutionary biology as science, including emphasizing the "problem" of irreducible complexity or denigrating evolution as bad science. For those who intend to undermine students' confidence in establishment science, why not dwell on the most controversial part, the part most likely to lead students to *reject evolution*? In other words, when creationists teach evolution, they devote a disproportionate share of time to the topics that are most controversial in the public mind and which they know their students are least likely to accept. None of our teachers volunteered this as an explanation for their unusual attention to human evolution in class, but it is broadly consistent with our data.

SUMMARY AND DISCUSSION

General biology is generally taught in the ninth or tenth grade and is offered at nearly every high school in the United States. The NAS and other organizations have called for evolution to be a unifying theme of these classes and have called for curricula that emphasize the scientific method and the roles of theory, evidence, and inference. Central to this approach is the distinction between evolution as a fact – tens of thousands of individual findings all point to the fact that the diversity of species we see today are all descendents of earlier species of animals – and evolutionary theory, which is steadily revised in light of new evidence. Yet not all teachers emphasize these points to the same extent, and many express disagreement with these national organizations' assertions that an understanding of evolution is essential to understand biology more generally.

The result is an extraordinary range of actual classroom behaviors. By our estimation, 14–21% of teachers cross the line into unconstitutional instruction by explicitly endorsing creationism. Many others who remain within constitutional bounds nevertheless teach in ways that serve to undermine modern evolutionary biology. Others practice avoidance and provide students with only minimal exposure to the key ideas in modern biology or cover the basics in the least controversial manner. And we find that only a small portion of the science teaching profession fulfills the expectations of the scientific establishment.

To what can we attribute this enormous range in classroom behaviors? To answer this we must return to the question we raised in Chapter 1: Who Decides? In the remainder of this book, we empirically explore several kinds of proposed answers to this question. In the next chapter, we return to state content standards – perhaps the classroom practices of teachers vary because teachers teach to the standards in their state. These standards, we saw in Chapter 4, are strongly related to the preferences of each state's taxpayers. If teachers teach what the taxpayers want, as Bryan urged, then the rigor in state standards ought to account for much of the difference in rigor displayed in America's classrooms. But perhaps it is unreasonable for us to expect every teacher in a state to teach the same way; perhaps the teachers decide, so the individual characteristics of the teachers – their educational background, science training, and their personal beliefs – account for some of the variation in teaching practices. And perhaps there are environmental pressures based on the prevailing culture of a school district. We take up these alternative explanations in Chapters 7 and 8. But first, we examine the impact of the standards that attract so much interest from advocacy groups on both sides of the conflict.

6 State Standards Meet Street-Level Bureaucracy

In the state of Virginia, we have the state SOL's (standards of learning) that students must pass to earn their diploma. We do not have any choices on what we want to or should teach, it is already outlined for us.

Virginia Teacher (2007)[1]

Although standards for teaching science have been touted as important for the reform of science education, they often mean little in biology classrooms.

Randy Moore (2002)

FROM BIOLOGY CLASSROOM to biology classroom, American students in the same grade receive very different instruction in evolutionary biology. For some, evolution will be the central organizing concept of the entire biology class, consuming considerable classroom time throughout the academic year, taught by teachers who endeavor to communicate the scientific consensus. Other students will have teachers who address it only briefly, or with characterizations of scientific discovery that bear little resemblance to what practicing biologists believe is most important; evolution in these classrooms may be presented skeptically if not fundamentally undermined. Some even teach nonscientific alternatives.

Our National Survey of High School Biology Teachers does not distinguish among the many pedagogical techniques and tools for

---

[1] The teacher provided this quotation as part of completing the National Survey of High School Biology Teachers. The second is from Moore (2002b, 380).

teaching evolution and biology (Alters and Nelson 2002; Ingram and Nelson 2006; Wilson 2005), but our first look in Chapter 5 does show significant variation on the attention given to it, in terms of time, and whether teachers emphasized perspectives that bear on its overall legitimacy. This variation in teaching practices does not come from the scientific community, where no controversy exists except over the details of how evolution works. So what does explain it? We begin our exploration of that question in this chapter by examining whether the differences in state content standards that we identified in Chapter 4 can account for some of the variance among teachers.

Certainly state policy makers adopt academic standards because they believe they will matter, that school districts will respond to them, and that teachers will implement them. When standards were first introduced in the 1980s, they "represented an unprecedented assertion of state control over school and classroom curriculum decision-making" (Archbald and Porter 1994, 21), and the purpose of this centralized control was to encourage more challenging and more coherent academic content (Spillane 1998). The standards of some states adhere closely to the recommendations of professional organizations affiliated with scientists and science educators. But we saw as well in Chapter 4 that state policy makers respond to prevailing public opinion, which in most cases runs counter to these recommendations. Expectations of what students should learn – and therefore what teachers should teach – differ substantially across the states.

Do teachers follow the standards? Is the question of "who decides what students should learn" answered at the state level, where standards are written and developed, as the advocates of standards-based education implicitly argue it should? To answer this question we need an updated version of the coding of state standards that we used in Chapter 4 – one that assesses the rigor and detail of standards that were in effect in 2007, when we interviewed our sample of teachers. Our updated coding also needs to be more specific, focusing only on the portions of standards that pertain to the general biology class typically taught in the ninth or tenth grade. Combining a more contemporary ranking of state standards with our survey of 926 teachers allows us to see how standards influence teaching.

TEACHERS AS STREET-LEVEL BUREAUCRATS

Teachers "ultimately decide the fate of national and state science standards" (Spillane and Callahan 2000, 401–402). In this way, they are really no different from other unelected public servants who are responsible for implementing policies and programs developed in rule-making or law-making bodies. And what nearly every elected official has discovered is that public servants do not always implement policies exactly as they are written and were intended. Teacher implementation of standards therefore presents what is commonly referred to as a *principal–agent* problem (Brehm and Gates 1997; McCubbins, Noll, and Weingast 1987): Principals are those who write laws and rules subject to electoral constraints – for example, the state policy makers and their appointees who develop standards – whereas agents are those who are relied on to carry them out.

Under this "top-down" model of democratic control, bureaucrats are expected to be responsive to those who make laws and set policy (Meier and O'Toole 2006). The relationship is problematic because agents (teachers) may not act as their principals (state policy makers) intended or would have intended had they foreseen the circumstances. When the agents have particularly wide latitude in implementing policy through their daily interactions with the public, they are often referred to as *street-level bureaucrats,* a term that has been applied to various social service employees, police, corrections workers, mental health counselors, and teachers (Keiser 1999, 2010; Lipsky 1980; Maynard-Moody and Musheno 2003; Meier and Bohte 2001; Meier and O'Toole 2006; Smith 2003). These street-level bureaucrats all make decisions that "matter in profound ways to the everyday lives of American citizens" (Brehm and Gates 1997, 1).

In this and subsequent chapters, we treat teachers as the *agents* of state-level policy makers (the principals). After all, it is the teachers who are most directly responsible for policy implementation, through "the curricular and instructional decisions they enact within the specific, particular contexts of their own classrooms" (Goldstein 2008, 449).[2] Standards in many states leave a great deal of room for

---

[2] Of course, teachers are not the only ones responsible for implementing state curricular policy. State school boards, the schools, and academic departments are also important and have received considerable scholarly attention, especially in terms of implementing

interpretation, and they contain no direct coercive power over teachers, although we will show that some have more bite than others. In a comparison of teacher autonomy across several disciplines, Stodolsky and Grossman (1995) find that science teachers retain more control over curriculum content than teachers of other subjects. The curricular decisions of science teachers, therefore, are of greater importance in understanding how it is taught than some other subjects.

As teachers interpret the range of "state-, district-, and school-led policies" affecting their work, they, in effect, *make* education policy (Goldstein 2008, 449). To the extent that standards influence teacher choices, even at the margins, then we can say that teachers are *implementing* policy. The limited extant research on evolution standards in particular, however, suggests that teachers are doing what they want *irrespective* of their state's standards. Randy Moore (2002b) reviewed twenty-one studies of how teachers in fifteen states taught evolution between 1983 and 2002. He compared the results of these studies with the "grades" the states received from Lerner's 2000 assessment and concluded that, "although standards for teaching science have been touted as important for the reform of science education, they often mean little in biology classrooms" (Moore 2002b, 380). More recently, Bandoli (2008) surveyed college students about their high school biology classes in Indiana and Ohio. He concluded that, despite the higher quality of the Indiana standards, "the coverage of evolution in public high schools in Indiana and Ohio is not influenced by state standards" (2008, 214).

One of the advantages of our National Survey of High School Biology Teachers is that we have a standard set of questions about evolution instruction across teachers in nearly all fifty states. By matching each teacher's 2007 interview with their state's standards, we can explore how standards may influence teacher choices in the classroom. But measuring these state standards, as they stood in 2007, requires some attention, and we turn to that first.

HIGH SCHOOL EVOLUTION STANDARDS IN 2007

To assess whether the quality of standards makes a difference in teachers' behavior, we need detailed knowledge of the standards in each

education reforms more generally (Spillane 1998; Spillane and Callahan 2000; Stodolsky and Grossman 1995).

state. In Chapter 4, we used the expert coding done by Lerner and his Fordham Foundation team (2000a, 2000b). The Lerner scores proved useful in understanding the political sources of standards, but they are not adequate for our analysis of teachers' behavior. Most states require that standards be revised regularly, on schedules ranging from every five to ten years. Between Lerner's 2000 study and the 2007 distribution of our survey, half of the states significantly revised their standards.[3] To assess the role of standards operating on teachers in 2007, we need measures of these revised standards.

In developing our own rankings, we made a conscious decision to restrict our attention only to standards that applied to ninth and tenth grade biology. These are the standards that the ninth and tenth grade teachers who we surveyed would consult. In contrast, Lerner (2000b), Skoog and Bilica (2002), Gross et al. (2005), and Swanson (2005), all of whom produced quantitative rankings of state evolution standards, all looked at either the entire K–12 or 9–12 science or biology curriculum. One example highlights the importance of using standards specifically written for grades 9–10 rather than those for all grades. Lerner (2000b) and Skoog and Bilica (2002) both made careful note that Pennsylvania is one of the few states that expects instruction in human evolution. Indeed, the instructions in the standards are quite clear: teachers should "examine human history by describing the progression from early hominids to modern humans" (Pennsylvania Code § 4.83. 3.3.12). But this does not mean that the teachers surveyed in *our* study will find this in the standards directing their classroom instruction. Rather, a close reading of Pennsylvania's standards reveals that this guideline is not expected until the students enter twelfth grade biology – in effect, this expectation only applies to the small number of students enrolled in advanced placement biology courses. Pennsylvania's curriculum standards for ninth or tenth

---

[3] We estimate that twenty-five states changed their standards between Lerner's study (2000b) and 2007 (including Iowa, which first adopted standards after 2000). To determine the standards in effect for the teachers at the time of the distribution of our survey, we checked each state's Department of Education Web site. None of the standards we found were dated later than 2007, although the exact dates at which standards were adopted is not always a straightforward matter. To determine whether the standards we found were the same as those used by Lerner, we contacted the state Department of Education if it was not clear on the Web site. In most cases, Lerner lists the date of the standards that he used; in those few cases where he does not, we assume they were adopted no later than 2000. We then compared the dates of the standards with the dates of Lerner's.

grade, those that apply to the basic biology course taken by the vast majority of students, make no mention of human evolution at all. Had Lerner and Skoog and Bilica also restricted their attention to ninth and tenth grades, Pennsylvania would have had slightly lower ratings.

Coding State Science Standards

To operationalize the guidelines and controls operating on the teachers in our survey, we undertook our own content analysis. The differences among standards are often stark but just as often subtle. Iowa's standards are just a few pages long and contain no explicit mention of evolution; rather, under the bullet point reading "Students can understand concepts and relationships in biological science" (Iowa Department of Education 2009, 6), there are three references to the scientific process (e.g., "making inferences and predictions from data") but no content-based recommendations. Neighboring Illinois's standards also fail to mention evolution; Illinois teachers are encouraged instead to discuss some aspects of the unnamed theory in a subsection of concepts that "explain how living things function, adapt and change" (Illinois State Board of Education, 1). Without mentioning the phrase "natural selection," the Illinois standards call for instruction in describing "the processes by which organisms change over time using evidence from comparative anatomy and physiology, embryology, the fossil record, genetics and biochemistry" (1).

The challenge in scoring standards is to distinguish between the absence of attention to evolution in Iowa, the marginal and coded attention it receives in Illinois, and its prominence in New York and Utah's standards. In New York, for example, one of the "Key Ideas" in science includes the simple statement that "Individual organisms and species change over time." Within this section, we see mention of evolution in the first sentence; indeed, in the first word: "Evolution is the change of species over time." The standards then go on to list, virtually word for word, the benchmarks from the *National Science Education Standards* (NSES) under the general heading "explain the mechanisms and patterns of evolution" (New York State Education Department, 16). Utah, not among the states receiving the highest grades for earlier versions of its standards, now is comparably straightforward in its presentation of evolution.[4] One of the main science benchmarks is the statement, "Evolution is central to modern science's understanding of the living world" (Utah State Office of Education, 10). The standard goes on to list multiple objectives that forthrightly introduce the elements of evolutionary biology.

We rated the content standards of each state on three criteria, generating numerical scales for (1) the *prominence* of evolution in the curriculum, (2) the extent to which evolution served as the or one of several *guiding themes*, and (3) the degree to which standards were sufficiently *specific* to guide teacher behavior (see Appendix section A6.1 for details on our coding procedures). These three numeric ratings were then combined into a standardized scale (having a mean of 0 and a standard deviation equal to 1) that measures the rigor with which evolution is addressed in each state's standards. High scores indicate states whose content standards give significant attention to evolution, identify evolution as a major theme, and provide very specific guidance to teachers on the specific evolution topics that students are expected to learn. The scale has an estimated reliability of 0.88 (Cronbach's alpha).

We assessed the validity of the scale in two ways. First, we calculated the correlation between our measure and the scores generated by Lerner's team of expert raters for the twenty-five states *that did not revise their standards in the intervening seven years*. The correlation of 0.65 suggests that, even though our content domains and grade spans were different, both scales are measuring the same general construct. Second, we compared our scale with three independent assessments of content benchmarks and showed a positive correlation in each instance. The details of how we conducted our content analysis, assigned numeric values to our observations, and assessed validity are detailed in Appendix section A6.1.

---

[4] Lerner awarded Utah a "B" for its evolution standards in 2000 and said "Satisfactory coverage of biological evolution, but only in Grades 9–12. The implications for the life sciences are not made clear" (2000b, 15). We are using standards adopted in 2003, which appear to offer a richer treatment. This is not simply the view of our coders. The Fordham Foundation's "State of State Standards 2006" does not offer a detailed review of the state's evolution standards but does say that, although many of Utah's standards in other science topics earn only a "C," "biology gets the best treatment, and evolution is presented forthrightly" (http://www.edexcellence.net/detail/news.cfm?news_id=358&pubsubid=1323; accessed December 21, 2008).

Changes in the Quality of Standards, 2000–2007

With confidence that our coding of recent state standards measures the same general construct as those of the fuller K–12 science curriculum by Lerner in 2000, we can look at whether state content standards concerning evolution have become more rigorous, less rigorous, or remained essentially the same. To date, the limited evidence bearing on this question is mixed. Gross concluded that "the teaching of evolution hasn't changed much" from 2000 to 2005 (Gross 2005, 7). However, Gross's study did not investigate evolution in great detail. In addition, Gross's assessment, though only a few years older than our own, is now dated because fifteen states have changed their standards since 2005 alone (see footnote 3). In contrast, a recent *New York Times* article reported that "over a dozen states have ... given more emphasis in recent years to what has long been the scientific consensus: that all of the diverse life forms on Earth descended from a common ancestor, through a process of mutation and natural selection, over billions of years" (Harmon 2008).

Certainly, the times have been ripe for reform in the direction of increased rigor. The passage of No Child Left Behind (NCLB) in 2001 further elevated the importance of state standards as student performance became tied to federal funding. NCLB therefore put new pressure on states to revise their academic standards (Spillane, Reiser, and Reimer 2002), and provisions within the act calling for state assessments in science by 2007–2008 led to a renewed focus on science standards in particular (Labov 2006). (As of 2010, NCLB has yet to be reauthorized, so this testing is not currently federally mandated, but the process of pushing states to take a hard look at their standards was nonetheless in full swing in 2007.) In addition, curricular assessments, such as Lerner's widely publicized report, have themselves had an impact on states that undertake regularly scheduled revisions of their standards. *Education Week* reported that, "in the absence of a national body that could evaluate standards," different groups, with different conceptions of what makes good standards, "stepped into the fray" (Olson 1998). State education leaders from states that received low grades from Lerner found themselves in the position of either defending their state's standards or pledging to improve them. Lerner himself has been active and prominent in the revision process.

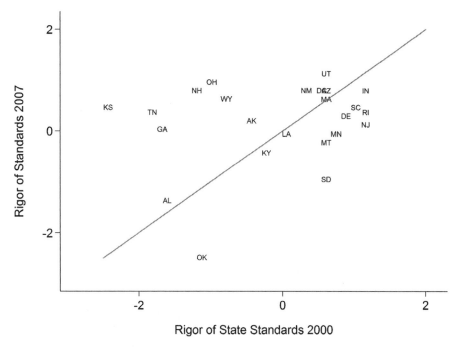

Figure 6.1. The rigor of state evolution standards in 2000 and 2007, for states that revised their standards.

For example, when Ohio produced an initial draft of revised standards, Lerner approvingly noted, in a report for the National Center for Science Education, "The new draft treats evolution in exemplary fashion" (National Center for Science Education 2002). And in the recent debate in Florida over standards revision, Lerner read and commented on a draft and awarded it a "B," writing that, "With a little bit of extra effort, Florida could bring that up to an A" (National Center for Science Education 2008). In short, policy makers in some of the states receiving poor marks in the 2000 report apparently viewed these as an embarrassment and were motivated to get better marks the next time around.

Because our 2007 and Lerner's 2000 scores use different scoring schemes, we cannot quantify absolute changes. But we can standardize each measure, and this will allow us to show how much states that revised their standards changed *relative to those that did not*. Consider Figure 6.1, which plots Lerner's 2000 rankings (standardized with a mean of 0 and standard deviation of 1) on the east–west axis and our 2007 rankings on the north–south dimension. This graph examines only states that revised their standards. If states had maintained their relative position, they would lie roughly on a 45-degree line drawn through the origin of the graph and extending upwards and to the right. Indeed, several states around the line retain their relative position; Arizona, Indiana, and Alabama have the same quality standards relative to other states in 2007 as they did in 2000. However, we also see a block of states that have improved quite significantly; many states with notoriously bad standards, including Ohio, Kansas, and Tennessee, moved from having scores in the lower quartile (all below −1) to scores that are above average (that is, greater than 0). Of the states that revised standards, only a few dropped at all and only Oklahoma dropped substantially relative to other states. This is borne out by comparing the difference in standardized scores from 2000 to 2007; the twenty-five states that did not change their standards dropped in their relative position by an average of 0.14 points, whereas the twenty-five states that did change their standards gained an average of 0.24 points. This relative improvement of a net shift of 0.38 points (analogous to a net shift of 38 points on the SAT), does not represent a sea change in content standards. But it is nevertheless reflective of a changed policy and political environment.

We have shown elsewhere (Plutzer and Berkman 2008) that public opinion concerning evolution has been remarkably stable for the last quarter century. Thus, public preferences cannot account for the increased rigor in the standards of states like Kansas, Tennessee, Georgia, Ohio, New Hampshire, and Wyoming. The changes must therefore lie in the increased effectiveness of scientific interest groups along with the motivation of state educational bureaucracies and legislators to conform to the goals of the scientific community. This would suggest less of a role for public opinion, and, indeed, the observed correlation between opinion and state standards has declined from 0.43 in 2000 to a marginally significant 0.26 in 2007.

We should reiterate that the two rankings of states are not strictly comparable, so our conclusions about change should be viewed as tentative. Yet, if we are correct, it would suggest that the influence of public opinion on the substance of policy is historically contingent (Jacobs and Shapiro 2000), with scientists and the public alternating in cycles of influence. Scientists continuously seek to play the decisive role in formulating science policy, and their efforts to establish firm boundaries are more successful in some periods than in others. This does not mean that state policy makers are free to ignore public opinion entirely but may respond in various ways. As Jacobs and Shapiro argue, politicians who are committed to a particular public policy may rely on the results of public opinion polls to package their policies in a way that resonates with the public and avoids inflaming strong opposition (2000).

Indeed, we see some evidence that the general improvement of standards (going against public opinion in most cases) was accompanied by strategic consideration of public opinion in the development of what Jacobs and Shapiro call "crafted talk" (2000). For example, a careful reading of the standards current in 2007 shows that at least six states eliminated all mentions of *human evolution* after 2000.[5] One of these states, Indiana, had long been recognized as a leader in writing high-quality standards generally (Jacobs 2006) and high-quality evolution standards more specifically. Human evolution was prominent and explicit in the Indiana standards coded by Lerner in 2000, and others, prior to revision in 2006. But Indiana's standards today no longer call for such instruction; rather, the standards now contain only more general language that easily allows its science teachers to avoid teaching anything about the relationship between humans and earlier hominids.[6] Of all the inferences and conclusions of evolutionary biology, the idea that humans and apes have common ancestors is the one that triggers the most visceral reaction. Eager to avoid "red flag" terms that might incite conservatives (Placier, Walker, and Foster 2002), human evolution is eliminated even as the standards

---

[5] We searched in the standards current in 2007 for the language that Lerner (2000b) identifies in earlier studies as making "explicit" mention of human evolution. We could find such language only in Michigan, Rhode Island, and Pennsylvania.

[6] This specific language is no longer included in the Indiana standards: "Fossil evidence is consistent with the idea that human beings evolved from earlier species and that the similarity of human DNA sequences and the resulting similarity in cell chemistry and anatomy identifies human beings as a single system" (Skoog and Bilica 2002, 10). The current Indiana standards instead read: "Describe how life on Earth is thought to have begun as simple, one-celled organisms about 4 billion years ago. Note that during the first 2 billion years, only single-cell microorganisms existed, but once cells with nuclei developed about a billion years ago, increasingly complex multicellular organisms evolved" (http://dc.doe.in.gov/Standards/AcademicStandards/PrintLibrary/docs-science/2006-science-biologyi.pdf; accessed December 9, 2008).

become relatively stronger in most other respects. Indeed, there is even a reluctance to use the word "evolution." And, as noted above, Illinois replaced the word "evolution" with the phrase "change over time" to maintain, according to the then Superintendent of Public Instruction Joseph Spagnolo, "broad public support" (Larson 2003, 201).

STANDARDS AND THE TEACHING OF EVOLUTION

In Chapter 5, we explored the teaching practices of teachers in substantial detail and revealed a great variety of approaches to teaching evolution. In order to test standards' impact in the classroom, we will focus on two summary measures that broadly distinguish among teachers in how they instruct their students in evolution. As an indicator of the *quantity* of attention to evolution, we look at the number of hours that teachers devoted to evolution, including human evolution, calculated as class hours per year and treated as a numeric variable (we examined this variable in Chapter 5). Our second variable is a composite of three questions that reflected on the *quality or the emphases* of teaching, measuring the extent to which teachers embrace three key goals of the National Academy of Sciences (NAS) and other scientific organizations.[7] This variable ranges from 0 (does not endorse any NAS positions) to 100 (strongly endorses all three NAS positions), with a mean score of 55. Teachers vary considerably on this scale, with 17% scoring under 20 points and 28% earning a score of 80 or higher. Because no state uses its standards to authorize or direct instruction in creationism, creation science, or intelligent design, we do not expect any effects from standards on teacher's instruction in these areas, although we do return to their place in classroom instruction in the next chapter.

Our key independent variable throughout this chapter is the rigor of ninth/tenth grade evolution standards measured in 2007 and scaled as a standardized variable (as in the vertical axis of Figure 6.1). Linear regression models can estimate how a given difference in standards (for example, comparing a state with a score of 0 and a state with

---

[7] The three emphases are: (1) The necessity of teaching evolution, (2) its role as a unifying theme of the year-long general biology class, and (3) the emphasis that evolution is a fact, even as there is legitimate disagreement about specific mechanisms.

a score of 1) is associated with an increase or decrease in quantity or quality of evolution instruction. Multivariate models also allow us to account for other potential influences of teacher behavior and to examine how the effect of standards may depend on certain conditions. Because we expect some similarity of teachers within each state (they share the same certification process, may have attended the same colleges, and use the same textbooks), we generally employ random intercept multilevel regressions, estimated by maximum likelihood.[8] Appendix section A6.3 explains why multilevel models are appropriate, reports diagnostic "null models," and provides some explanation to help readers navigate a table reporting multilevel regressions. The tables reporting slope estimates, slope standard errors, and variance components are also reported in section A6.3. Although we will refer to these models, we will summarize the key results from these models by graphs or tables that highlight the key substantive findings.

Our first look at the impact of standards is based on simple models that assess the linear increase in time devoted to evolution and to teacher emphasis that correspond to increasingly rigorous standards. In these bivariate models, we find that state content standards have almost no impact at all. The regression slope for the effect of standards on hours devoted to evolution is very small in magnitude. The estimated slope of 0.89 ($t = 2.17$) tells us that, if states improve their evolution standards enough to go from being the mean state to a state a full standard deviation above average, teachers in that state would be predicted to devote almost 1 additional hour to evolution (see Appendix Table A6.1, panel B). Likewise, the effect of a standard deviation increase in the rigor of standards results in a significant increase of 2.4 points on the 0–100 NAS emphasis scale ($t = 2.18$). To illustrate the impact of standards in this chapter, we will sometimes report the estimated scores of teachers in the state with the tenth *least* rigorous standards (Texas, with a standards score of −0.60) and teachers in a state with the tenth *most* rigorous evolution standards (a score of 0.80, typical of several states essentially tied for tenth place such as Indiana, North Carolina, Connecticut, and New Hampshire). Table 6.1 illustrates our approach, which shows that teachers in states

---

[8] These were estimated using the xtreg procedure in Stata. We note, however, that virtually identical results are obtained by the use of OLS with robust standard errors.

Table 6.1. Predicted teaching outcomes in states with less and more rigorous standards

	Dependent Variable	
	Hours devoted to evolution	NAS Emphasis scale
Regression slope for effect of standards	.9	2.4
Standard error of the slope	.4	1.1
Predicted outcome for teachers in state with the 10th least rigorous standards	13.5	53.6
Predicted outcome for teachers in state with the 10th most rigorous standards	14.7	57.0
Effect of moving from the 10th worst to 10th best state	1.2	3.4

Sources: Based on estimates reported in Appendix Table A6.1, panel B.

with rigorous standards devote about an hour more to evolution and score about three points higher on the NAS emphasis scale.

These models suggests that state standards have only minimal impact in spite of all the efforts that groups put into molding them. It is true that an additional hour of instruction in every classroom in a state might have a small cumulative impact. But relative to the enormous variation among teachers (within-state standard deviations of 8.6 hours and 29 NAS points, respectively), such an impact is small in magnitude.

WHY DO STANDARDS HAVE SO LITTLE INFLUENCE?

Why do we not see a stronger effect of state content standards? Prior research suggests three broad types of answers. The first points to public employees' knowledge of and attitudes toward public policy. The second focuses on whether the policy contains mechanisms to monitor and sanction civil servants. The third directs our attention to the characteristics of individual teachers that may make them more or less likely to be influenced by state standards.

Attitudes and Knowledge

Like any other kind of street-level bureaucrat, each teacher may respond "differently to the same information when making decisions"

(Keiser 2010, 7). Differences may be rooted in how well they understand the policy directives they are asked to follow and partly on how they filter information through their own experiences and backgrounds. Among teachers and administrators in all academic subjects, there is evidence of confusion concerning the content of the standards, therefore leaving them discretion to do as they wish. As one teacher interviewed by Barksdale-Ladd and Thomas put it, "You know, we get dozens of printed flyers about various topics every day from all over, from the principal, from committees, from the district, from the state, from the supervisors, and I just can't remember when any one of those showed up" (2000, 388).

Thus, it may be that few teachers know their standards well. Unfortunately, we must confess that, when we began our study, we assumed that classroom teachers would be familiar with the content standards for the subjects that they teach. As a result, our teacher questionnaire did not include an extensive battery of questions focusing on each teacher's knowledge of their own state's standards; we did, however, include one question that allows us to investigate this possibility indirectly. We asked teachers,

So far as you know, do your state's science standards include evolution?
☐ Yes, but not human evolution (30%)
☐ Yes, including human evolution (62%)
☐ No (1%)
☐ I am not sure [and no answer] (7%)

The results here are quite revealing given that only three states included any mention of humans, hominids, or common ancestors of humans and apes (see footnote 5). We considered the possibility that teachers might have been thinking of older standards and therefore went back to Lerner's evaluation of standards that were in effect in the 1999–2000 academic year. Lerner classified states in three categories: no mention of human evolution, explicit discussion of evolution, and an intermediate category in which human evolution was strongly implied. Table 6.2 shows that the misperception of standards is not related to confusion with previous standards. Even in states that do not mention human evolution in either time period, 59% of

Table 6.2. Relationship between evolution standards in the 2000 content standards and teachers' perception of human evolution in current standards

Do your state's science standards include evolution?	Lerner Standards Classification		
	No human evolution (%)	Implied human evolution (%)	Explicit mention of human evolution (%)
Yes, but not human evolution	32	30	25
Yes, including human evolution	59	61	67
No	2	1	2
Not sure	7	8	6
	100%	100%	100%
N	480	179	250

teachers believe that human origins are indeed part of the recommended course of study.

In short, there is little relationship between the actual content of the standards and whether teachers believe that they include human evolution. Of course, we simply do not know if this misperception is unique to the question of human ancestry or whether it is typical of misperceptions of other portions of the content standards. But it does strongly suggest that teacher familiarity with the standards is quite limited. If teachers do not know what is included in the content standards, how can these policies guide their behavior? In this light, the irrelevance of standards makes sense.

BACKING STANDARDS WITH SANCTIONS AND MONITORING

It is, however, premature to conclude that standards do not matter. Teachers report otherwise, often stressing how standards *discourage* evolution instruction. "In the state of Virginia," reports one teacher who spends about 4 hours a year on evolution but would like to do more, "we have the state SOL's (standards of learning) that students must pass to earn their diploma. We do not have any choices on what we want to or should teach, it is already outlined for us. Our biology curriculum is so extensive, that we barely have time to finish it. So... evolution is taught at bare minimum per state standards." But this teacher is saying something more than that standards are important to her classroom choices; she is saying as well that the standards are linked to a test that students "must pass."

The small impact of state content standards confirms that the implementation of state curricular goals is a kind of principal–agent problem. In the comfort of their own classrooms, teachers are only indirectly monitored by their school principals and far more removed from the states' appointed and elected officials who wrote the standards in the first place. Teachers, in this respect, are similar to case workers who are expected to implement state laws concerning eligibility for welfare, or police officers who are expected to consistently enforce highway speed limits. Policy makers and executive branch officials inevitably experience the frustration with the uneven implementation of the state laws they helped to craft and for which they are responsible to administer. As a result, they typically seek to reform the "architecture of public policy" to better insure that agents implement policies as the principals intend (McCubbins, Noll, and Weingast 1987; Reenock and Gerber 2008). In the realm of curricular reform in the last decade, this means the introduction of student testing.

Testing, especially the kind of high-stakes examinations mandated by NCLB for mathematics and reading, should enhance the impact of standards on classroom instruction. A test is high stakes if a student's graduation or progression to the next grade is dependent on their test performance or if schools face sanctions if a certain number of students fall below a particular threshold. State policy makers may use testing as a way of monitoring the implementation of standards, sanctioning teachers and school districts who fail to adhere to them, or signaling the importance of different components of a state's standards. The specific choice of test questions adds "authority to selected goals and topics" (Archbald and Porter 1994, 22). In these ways, aligned examinations will "drive instruction" in the direction intended by policy makers (Airasian 1988, 305).

High-stakes testing in science was not a mandate of NCLB in the spring of 2007, but it was expected to become one in the following academic year. This expectation motivated many states to create new science tests, and a careful analysis by Editorial Projects in Education (2007) indicates that thirty-one states had science examinations aligned with their state standards at the high school level during

Table 6.3. Relationship between the existence of aligned assessment and teachers' characterization of state testing policy

Does your state currently have an assessment test covering high school biology?	Editorial Projects in Education Designation	
	No test (%)	Test (%)
No	44	14
Yes, limited reporting	7	2
Yes, school-level reporting	35	40
Yes, high stakes for students	10	40
No answer or Don't know	4	3
	100%	100%
N	270	656

Sources: Test designation from Editorial Projects in Education (2007).

the 2006–2007 school year. Although this list serves as an objective measure of testing, we also asked teachers if their state had an assessment test that covered high school biology. Interestingly, we again see here a certain amount of disagreement among teachers, as indicated in Table 6.3. In states with such a test, 14% of teachers told us that they did not. In some states, such as New York and Michigan, 100% of the teachers correctly told us that there was such a test. But in Illinois and Wisconsin, more than one-third incorrectly reported that there was no such test. Among teachers in states without an aligned assessment test, more than half told us that they did, in fact, have one.

We recognize that part of the disagreement could be a matter of legitimate interpretation. Consider a comprehensive science test in which biology is a small component. Some teachers may have answered "no" because they interpreted the question as meaning a test only on biology. Others may have characterized testing initiated at the local level in states without assessments. Still others may have been legitimately confused about new testing that had been announced amidst the flurry of activity spurred by NCLB but not yet implemented.

To help us understand why teachers in the same state gave us different reports about the existence of state tests, we contacted officials in those states in which we saw the least consensus. In nearly every case, the testing regime was in flux.[9] In Arizona, the state had approved its new "Science AIMS" test in 2007, but it would not go into effect until the following year. Because it is an "end of course" examination, students taught in spring 2007 would not be affected. In New Jersey, students were being tested for the first time in 2007, but these would be seniors and not ninth or tenth graders. By 2007, New Hampshire had approved participation in the New England Common Assessment Program (NECAP) Science Assessment. This comprehensive science test was approved and being piloted in 2007, and current ninth graders could expect to be tested as seniors. However, it did not go "on line" until a year after our survey, and teachers might have focused on this when answering our questions. In light of situations similar to these throughout the nation, it is perhaps understandable that teachers in the same state gave different accounts of whether their students or their schools would be held accountable for learning the state-recommended content. As a result, we will examine both the actual existence of tests and teacher perceptions about the tests.

We first examined the regressions of time devoted to evolution and NAS Emphasis separately for teachers in testing states and nontesting states. The model results, reported in Appendix Table A6.2, show that the mere presence of aligned examinations makes no difference at all for either dependent variable.[10]

We then repeated this analysis using teacher *reports* of whether there was a test that covered general biology, again splitting the sample based on whether teachers believed there was such a test (Appendix Table A6.3). Here, we again find no additional effect of standards on the *amount of time* devoted to evolution. However, for content

---

[9] Donnelly and Sadler encountered a similar problem conducting their study of teachers' use of standards in Indiana. They argued that, at the time of their study, "some uncertainty existed in terms of how these examinations would ultimately be used . . . the state had not adopted official policy regarding the use of the examinations or student or school-level data resulting from the examinations. When data were collected for the current study, the end-of-course assessments were not mandatory, but several schools had participated in pilot testing of such tests" (2009, 1053).

[10] The t-ratios for all four variables are below 1.00. As a specification check, these models were re-estimated without interactions and without other independent variables. No matter the specification, testing made no difference in the impact of standards or in the levels of the dependent variables.

Table 6.4. Effect of standards on NAS scales, depending on whether teachers believe there is a test

	Score on NAS Emphasis Scale	
	Teacher does not report a test	Teacher reports a test
Predicted outcome for teachers in state with the 10th least rigorous standards	54.2	50.3
Predicted outcome for teachers in state with the 10th most rigorous standards	53.8	56.5
Effect of moving from the 10th worst to 10th best state	−.3	6.2

Sources: Based on estimates reported in Appendix Table A6.3 (effects are calculated for teachers with mean level of seniority who do not rate themselves as exceptionally well qualified).

emphasis, we find a small but statistically significant enhancement of standards' effects for those teachers who believe there is an examination. Even so, we should emphasize that the effects are small, as illustrated in Table 6.4. The effect of going from the tenth worst to tenth best state is 0 for teachers who do not believe there is an assessment test, and is now 6 points on the NAS scale (up from 3.4 points for the entire sample, as we showed in the bottom row of Table 6.1).

TEACHERS' CHARACTERISTICS AND ADHERENCE TO STATE STANDARDS

These results on teacher *perceptions* about testing show that standards are more important for some teachers than for others. Indeed, prior scholarship on both street-level bureaucrats and curricular reform point not only to the institutional environment, but also to the individual characteristics of teachers. Certain professional background characteristics may either enhance or diminish the likelihood that state policy will be implemented as intended. As Cohen and Ball (1990, 335) conclude, "Any teacher, in any system of schooling, interprets and enacts new instructional policies in light of his or her own experience, beliefs, and knowledge."

One of the most frequently mentioned factors in both the curricular reform and street-level bureaucracy literatures is *experience*. Teachers with substantial seniority have the least incentive to embrace new reforms (Berends 2000) and are more likely to implement only those standards and programs that fit their current agenda (Spillane et al. 2002). There are many reasons to expect that high seniority teachers will be the least likely to embrace standards, especially new ones. For one, they have time and effort invested in their lesson plans and teaching approach. They therefore incur the highest costs, both in terms of these investments and the time needed to come in line with standards if they contradict the way they have been teaching for decades. Second, teachers with high seniority were professionally socialized in a different era than those with less, and developed their teaching approach when other standards were in place (or, in many states, before formal standards even existed). In contrast, new teachers are likely to reflect not only the latest trends in pedagogy but contemporary content expectations, which only younger teachers would have been exposed to in college. As a result, younger teachers are more likely to accept the legitimacy of standards-based education because they are a normal part of their understanding of the profession, as opposed to a "reform" that required adaptation (see Donnelly and Sadler 2009). And, of course, with experience often comes tenure, providing a buffer from principals or others who would seek to promote the state's curricula.

Further, a sense of professional identity entices those administering policy to substitute their own judgment for that of the elected officials who passed the policy in the first place. This is especially likely to happen with standards, which can be quite vague, leaving teachers a great deal of discretion. In addition, personal attitudes and experiences may lead teachers to, consciously or unconsciously, ignore information – leading to different decisions (Cohen and Ball 1990; Jones 2001). One of the most critical factors is a teacher's own sense of competence in evolutionary biology. We expect that teachers who lack self confidence in their understanding of evolution will teach it less and have greater motivation to avoid controversy (Griffith and Brem 2004; Rutledge and Mitchell 2002). We look at this in detail in Chapter 7, but this personal sense of competence should also affect how teachers process standards. In particular, we expect that teachers who view themselves as especially competent may be *less* likely to let state standards guide their classroom instruction, instead substituting their own judgments about content and emphasis.

Table 6.5. Effect of standards on time devoted to evolution, by levels of seniority

	Hours devoted to evolution, by seniority				
	1–2 years (1.5 %)	3–5 years (7%)	6–10 years (20%)	11–20 years (36%)	21+ years (36%)
Predicted outcome for teachers in state with the 10th least rigorous standards	13.9	13.5	13.2	12.8	12.5
Predicted outcome for teachers in state with the 10th most rigorous standards	17.8	16.7	15.4	14.2	12.6
Effect of moving from the 10th worst to 10th best state	3.9	3.2	2.3	1.4	.2

Sources: Based on estimates reported in Appendix Table A6.3 (effects are calculated for teachers who perceive a test and do not rate themselves as exceptionally well qualified).

To examine the impact of experience and self-rated competence, we again rely on multilevel regression models predicting time devoted to evolution and emphasis, which include measures of seniority and self-rated expertise along with perceptions about testing, and the interactions of these variables with the rigor of state content standards. The detailed results of our regression models are reported in Appendix Table A6.3. These models yield a number of substantive conclusions.

First, we find that seniority is unrelated to the arguments and themes emphasized by teachers. Seniority has no main effect on the NAS score, nor does it interact with how standards impact teachers' emphases when teaching evolution. In contrast, seniority has a very substantial impact on the amount of time devoted to evolution as the model estimates tell us that high-seniority teachers not only devote fewer hours to evolution but are less influenced by standards. These effects are illustrated in Table 6.5.

As we read across the first row of Table 6.5, we can see that, in states with weak standards, there is a very small decline in the time devoted to evolution as seniority increases. However, in states with very good standards, the impact of seniority is dramatic. The teachers who are newest to the profession will devote nearly 18 hours of class

time to evolution if they teach in states with rigorous standards –
a "tenth worst to tenth best" effect of nearly 4 hours. Yet, as one
examines the third row, which summarizes the effects of standards
on class hours devoted to evolution, we can see that this drops off
steadily. By the time teachers have been in the profession for more
than a decade, the influence of standards is very small, and the 36%
of teachers with more than 20 years of seniority appear to become
immune to standards altogether.

As we noted earlier, previous research also suggests that teachers'
self confidence is an important contributor to how they approach
their classes (Griffith and Brem 2004; Rutledge and Mitchell 2002).
To assess whether this self confidence also effects their adherence to
state standards, we asked teachers the following self-rating question:

I would rate my knowledge of the scientific evidence bearing on the
validity of evolutionary theory as:

☐ Exceptional, on par with many college-level instructors (13%)
☐ Very good compared to most high school biology teachers (48%)
☐ Typical of most high school biology teachers (37%)
☐ I know less about this topic than many other high school biology
teachers (2%)

As can be seen, the question produces a "Lake Wobegon" effect, as
61% rated their knowledge as "above average" or "exceptional" and
only 2% rated themselves below average. For the purpose of illustration in this chapter, we will simply dichotomize this as exceptional
versus all other teachers.

The multivariate models reported in Appendix Table A6.3 also
yield very dramatic results for the impact of self-rated expertise. These
effects are summarized in Table 6.6. Among those who rate themselves
as exceptional, the effect of standards is negative (but not significantly
different from 0 for either dependent variable). It appears that those
who are less confident in their knowledge of evolution rely on their
states' standards to guide their lesson plans, whereas those extremely
confident in their expertise substitute their own judgment for that of
their states' policy makers. By comparing across the rows, we can
also see that teachers who rate their qualifications as "exceptional"
devote many more hours to evolution and score much higher on the
NAS scale. We will explore this in greater depth in the next chapter,

Table 6.6. The effect of standards on teaching evolution, by teachers' self-rated expertise

	A. Hours devoted to evolution, by self-rated expertise	
	Teacher's self rating is "exceptional" (13%)	All other teachers (87%)
Predicted outcome for teachers in state with the 10th least rigorous standards	19.4	12.8
Predicted outcome for teachers in state with the 10th most rigorous standards	18.3	14.2
Effect of moving from the 10th worst to 10th best state	−1.1	1.4
	B. NAS Emphasis scale score, by self-rated expertise	
	Teacher's self rating is "exceptional" (13%)	All other teachers (87%)
Predicted outcome for teachers in state with the 10th least rigorous standards	70.8	50.3
Predicted outcome for teachers in state with the 10th most rigorous standards	71.4	56.5
Effect of moving from the 10th worst to 10th best state	.6	6.2

Sources: Based on estimates reported in Appendix Table A6.3 (effects are calculated for teachers who perceive a test and with a mean level of seniority).

examining how formal training in science is connected to both self confidence and teaching behavior.

Taken together, the cumulative impact of these findings suggests that state content standards influence the teaching practices of a small subset of teachers. Teachers with less than ten years of seniority, who believe their state has an assessment test, and who do not rate themselves as exceptional comprise only 20% of our sample. Thus, we estimate that four out of every five biology teachers nationwide are essentially immune from influence by state content standards. Put another way, standards appear to have their greatest impact on younger teachers who lack self-confidence in their understanding of evolution.

SUMMARY AND DISCUSSION

The history of conflict concerning the teaching of evolution is a dramatic one and has lent itself to insightful scholarly accounts, numerous documentaries, and entertaining dramatizations, such as *Inherit the Wind*. With few exceptions, however, narrative accounts of the evolution and creation conflict have focused on legislation, state educational policies, decisions of textbook commissions, school boards, and the often dramatic courtroom battles that result when these policies are challenged. Opponents of evolution as well as evolution's defenders have looked to these policy-making bodies to advance their agendas concerning instruction in biology. They have sought to influence policy by electing supporters to local school boards and state boards of education; they have drawn thousands of supporters to their rallies and museums in order to move public opinion and place pressure on state policy makers.

And yet, we have seen that these state-level policies seem to have only limited impact. This is because it is teachers who play the crucial role of policy implementation. Individual teachers have the autonomy to, in effect, rewrite state curricular policies in accord with their own interpretations of standards, their own beliefs about what constitutes effective teaching, and to advance their own opinions about what should and should not be taught in the general biology class. Standards, even in the presence of high-stakes examinations that are aligned with the curricular content, influence only a small portion of teachers – primarily those early in their careers. And even then, the impact of standards is hardly dramatic – once teachers have more than five years of seniority, a large improvement in standards (improving from tenth worst to tenth best) leads to an additional hour or two of instruction in evolution and changing the emphasis on teaching by a few percentage points.

Our data point to several reasons why the reach of standards is limited, and the more general literature on curricular reform suggests some additional reasons. We saw that there is little consensus among teachers in the same state about exactly what is included in the standards and about whether students will be held accountable for achieving the learning objectives established by the state. We have also seen that only the group of teachers with limited seniority are responsive to the mandates in state standards. And further, we have shown that teachers who are extremely confident in their own expertise are especially unlikely to adhere to the goals established by state policy makers. All three findings are consistent with what we might expect from street-level bureaucrats who work in a highly decentralized system.

In addition, we suspect that the efficacy of standards is also undermined by the constant flux in standards and examinations. Evolution instruction is in some ways a "political football," shifting from one orientation to another as different factions gain political control of the policy-making apparatus. We see this most clearly in Kansas, where very close elections to the state board of education have resulted in nearly regular changes in the state standards. Further, the routine revision of state standards sometimes leads to substantial changes in a handful of states. Finally, a majority of states have recently introduced new assessment tests, creating additional turbulence in the curricular environment. Front-line public servants, such as teachers, are especially likely to behave like street-level bureaucrats precisely when they perceive conflicting cues and expectations.

From this, we conclude that we may have well analyzed the implementation of state teaching goals at a time when the barriers to straightforward implementation were greatest. We can speculate that, if a state were to maintain fairly consistent standards and testing policies over a period of a decade or more, we would see a greater impact. We might expect to see fewer generational differences among teachers, and the stable environment would not create the pressures for teachers to improvise in their classrooms. Indeed, our findings that younger teachers are most likely to adhere to standards could indicate an important generational shift that indicates standards will be more important over time. When Donnelly and Sadler (2009) asked their small number of young teachers, "How would your instruction differ if standards were not in place?" the teachers "seemed genuinely surprised as if they had never considered the possibility of running a classroom without standards" (1067).

On the other hand, American educators have been inventing and re-inventing curricular content and pedagogy for decades – in all subjects and in all grades. Evolution is perhaps the most volatile subject because it is in the public eye and frequently subject to political pressures. These features of the U.S. system suggest that expectations about what students should learn about evolution are likely to be in flux in many states for years to come. This means that, even if standards become more important as more and more teachers socialized to them take their place in the classrooms, the specific expectations of teachers may change often enough to create substantial costs for teachers to regularly update their lesson plans.

In either case, the evidence suggests that teachers will always have significant discretion. And thus far, we know little about the factors that lead them to teach evolution one way or another. One possibility is that teachers are essentially free agents, guided by their individual characteristics, values, and judgments. A second possibility is that teachers are influenced by their social environments. This could be due to pressures emerging from their communities or because teachers come to function as *representatives* of the citizens comprising their school districts. We investigate these possibilities in the next two chapters.

7 When the Personal Becomes Pedagogical

It is the teacher's business to decide what to teach. It is not the business of the federal courts nor the state.

John Thomas Scopes (1970)[1]

Once you get into the classroom . . . the teacher is going to teach whatever she or he really thinks.

Supreme Court Justice Lewis Powell (1987)

DESPITE THE INTENSITY that often accompanies the formulation of state standards, Chapter 6 offers strong evidence that standards exert only limited control over what high school biology teachers actually do in the classroom. Yet, if standards do not explain the substantial differences among teachers both in the time they devote to evolutionary biology and their emphases while teaching it, what does? Two factors we examined in the previous chapter – teachers' seniority and their self-rated expertise in the subject matter – suggest that it is their personal and professional characteristics that may provide much of the answer.

In this chapter, we will explore two facets of teachers' personal characteristics. First, we will examine their formal teaching credentials: Do their college majors, their formal coursework in biology, or their type of teaching certification help explain their classroom approach to evolution and creationism? Second, we will see whether Justice Powell was correct in suggesting that "the teacher is going to

---

[1] Scopes, in his last public appearance, quoted in Moore 2002a, 223; Powell's comment is from the oral arguments in *Edwards v. Aguillard*, 482 U.S. 578 (1987); http://www.oyez. org/cases/1980–1989/1986/1986_85_1513/argument/; accessed December 21, 2009.

teach whatever she or he really thinks." Do teachers' personal beliefs about human origins play a major role in determining teacher choices in the classroom? Our survey of high school biology teachers allows us to answer both questions about what students learn when teachers decide.

EDUCATIONAL BACKGROUND AND CERTIFICATION

Teachers in all states are expected to meet certain minimum requirements for certification. But this does not mean that all science teachers are equally knowledgeable about evolutionary biology or science generally. Indeed, Rutledge and Warden find among a sample of Indiana biology teachers a rather low level of understanding of evolutionary theory, well below what would "have been expected" among science teachers and more "in league with what is reported among the general public" (2000, 2). They attribute this, at least to some degree, to the teachers' college education, arguing that many teachers are not sufficiently trained to "possess a thorough knowledge of evolutionary theory and its place in the discipline of biology" (2000, 29). Randy Moore, who has studied biology teachers in a variety of states, concurs. Moore argues that evolution-related courses would "improve the status of evolution-related education" and make a difference in how well teachers understand evolution (2002b, 380).

In general, teachers who understand a subject well will teach it differently than a subject they know less well. William Carlsen, for example, conducted a detailed study of the practices of four new high school biology teachers, all of whom had majored in biology. The teachers observed closely in this study used different pedagogical techniques and interacted differently with students when the lesson plan called for subjects they knew less well. They also devoted fewer lessons to topics with which they were less comfortable (Carlsen 1991). Indeed, teacher knowledge and understanding may be especially germane to classroom instruction when the topic is evolution. Evolution can be a highly stressful topic for many teachers, but less stressful for those teachers who are more confident and comfortable with the material (Griffith and Brem 2004). We can reasonably expect that these will be the teachers who are better trained in the subject.

Our survey allows us to look in some detail at our teachers' educational attainment so we should be able to determine the extent to which their understanding of evolution affects their instructional decisions. We know, for example, that 51% of the teachers in our sample earned a bachelor's degree in biology or another scientific field; of those, about one-third also received a graduate degree in a scientific field. That means that half of our teachers were not science majors at all, although most had a minor concentration in biology or another scientific discipline, and some later earned a master's degree in biology or a related field. Therefore, the sample can be divided into three groups: those who do not hold any degree in science (38%), those who hold a bachelor's degree in science (37%), and those who hold a master's or doctoral degree in science (25%). Along the same lines, we classified teachers by the number of college-level credit hours they completed in biology and classify teachers as having a low number (under 24 credits, about 6% of our sample), a medium number (25–40 credits, about 30%), or a high number (over 40 credits). We also asked about each teacher's certification status. Eighty percent of teachers (80%) held the normal teaching certification for their state, whereas the remainder had temporary, provisional, or nontraditional certification.

One aspect of teachers' college-level training that would likely make them more informed about evolution and more comfortable teaching it is whether or not they took a college course specifically in evolutionary biology. This is because, even though most college-level biology courses are likely to include discussion of evolution, a focused semester-long class may have a greater impact on how students think about evolution. Ingram and Nelson, for example, find that a stand-alone course in evolution leads to greater "acceptance" and "understanding" of evolution generally, and of human evolution in particular (2005; see also Bishop and Anderson 1990). Indeed, based on their study of Indiana teachers, Rutledge and Mitchell found that teachers who took a course in evolution had greater acceptance of evolution, taught more hours of it, and were able to demonstrate a more sophisticated grasp of the material through concept maps (2002). Among our teachers, 43% took a course in evolutionary biology; not surprisingly, most of these teachers either majored in a science or took an advanced degree in one.

Table 7.1. Random intercept, multilevel regression models assessing the impacts of teacher educational credentials

	Predicting Hours of Evolution (*N* = 869)			Predicting NAS Endorsement (*N* = 887)		
	B	SE	t	B	SE	t
Standards Index 2007	**.81**	.42	1.92	**3.85**	1.11	3.48
Seniority (centered)	−.59	.31	−1.91	−1.27	1.01	−1.26
Standards × Seniority	**−.64**	.27	−2.33	−.23	.88	−.26
Believes there is no test	−.08	.75	−.11	1.81	2.31	.78
Standards × Believes no test	−.60	.66	−.91	**−4.38**	2.03	−2.16
Teacher is female	−.48	.26	−1.87	**−1.77**	.83	−2.14
Credits earned in biology (0–2)	**1.08**	.50	2.15	2.19	1.62	1.35
Science degrees (0–2)	−.21	.39	−.54	**2.57**	1.25	2.06
Completed evolution class	**3.37**	.62	5.46	**10.23**	1.99	5.15
Has normal certification	−.40	.73	−.55	−.83	2.36	−.35
Intercept	11.68	1.11	10.53	46.98	3.49	13.47
Sigma (between states)	**1.54**	.48		1.49	2.62	
Sigma (within states)	8.44	.21		27.75	.67	
Rho (ICC)	.03	.02		.00	.01	

Bold entries are significant in expected direction at .05 level.

We can build on our models of classroom instruction from Chapter 6 to assess the impact of this evolution course and other aspects of teachers' college-level education. Our first models predicting both hours devoted to evolution and teacher emphasis are reported in Table 7.1. Unlike the previous chapter, we report the full table of model estimates. Each entry in the "B" column is an estimated regression slope, telling us how much the dependent variable changes when the independent variable increases by one. For example, the variable *credits earned in biology* is scored 0–1–2 (for low, medium, and high numbers of credits). The slope in the first column (1.08) tells us that, as teachers increase their score by 1 – for example, by moving from the lowest level to the middle level – we expect them to teach a little more than 1 additional hour of evolution. Slopes that are significantly different from 0 are printed in a bold typeface.

We start with models that include all variables examined in the previous chapter, except for self-rated expertise, which we will look at shortly. The results reported in Table 7.1 confirm that standards influence the time devoted to evolution for teachers with low seniority and show that female teachers spend slightly less time on evolution and rate about 2 points lower on the NAS-endorsement scale. Our main interest, however, concerns teachers' educational credentials, and here we see additional interesting effects.

Looking first at the time devoted to evolution, we see that teachers who earned more than 40 credit hours in biology tend to teach 2 additional hours of evolution compared with teachers in the lowest category (two times the slope of 1.08). Earned degrees in science seem not to matter, but we see a very large impact of having completed a course in evolution, with those who completed such a specialized course teaching an additional 3.4 hours of evolutionary biology – an increase of 25% compared with the average teacher in the nation.

When we look at the scale tapping teachers' emphases (on the right side of Table 7.1), we see that the number of credits alone does not achieve statistical significance but that holding a degree in a scientific field increases the likelihood that teachers will endorse NAS priorities in their teaching. Yet here, too, the strongest effect by far is having completed a college level course that focused on evolution.

As a generalization, we can say that the more immersed education students are in science – by majoring in biology or another science and by taking many classes – the more likely they are to both teach more evolution and teach it in a way that comports with the norms and priorities of the scientific establishment. These effects are small, however, in comparison to the very large effect of having completed a semester-length class on evolution.

Exactly how might an education student's coursework influence their classroom teaching many years later? We suggest that formal training can operate in two different ways. One way is to simply give teachers more confidence, thereby reducing their anticipation of stress that might result from teaching evolution. In many districts, teachers understand that each additional class period devoted to evolution increases the likelihood of offending a student or getting an angry visit from a parent. Teachers with limited scientific training may be less confident that they will emerge unscathed in any such episode. Consider a Pennsylvania teacher who majored in biology, but with only an average number of biology credits and no specific course in evolution. Elsewhere in the survey he reports being pressured by parents and local religious leaders to teach creationism or intelligent design, and by a school administrator to teach evolution. He teaches somewhat fewer hours of evolution than most (about 9.5 hours) and told us, pleaded even, that, "We high school teachers need cogent and clear facts that counter arguments against evolution."

In contrast, a teacher in Illinois explains, "Comparative embryology supports relationships among organisms that... [are] easy for students to recognize. I have accumulated well over 100 semester hours in the sciences and have no problem teaching big bang theory and evolution." Not surprisingly, she devotes over 22 hours to evolution – 50% more than the national average. Another teacher, from New York, told us that, "Over the years I have had letters/notes from parents condemning my teaching evolution/origin of life." But this teacher, who has a master's degree and over 40 credit hours in biology (including an evolution course), also tells us that, "I have never wavered in teaching evolution, cell theory and the origin of life and the first cells." Indeed, in the last chapter, we reported that teachers varied substantially in how they rated their own expertise in evolution, with about 13% rating themselves exceptional, 48% as "very good" compared with their peers, 37% rating themselves as "typical," and 2% as below average. Not surprisingly, those with the most biology credits, a completed evolution class, and advanced degrees in science rated themselves highest, so self-confidence may well account for the credentials effects we have seen.

A second way that scientific training may be operating is through socialization – by contributing to teachers' identification with the scientific enterprise and its norms and priorities. Griffith and Brem (2004) find that, among the small number of teachers they studied, some are much more likely to see themselves as "scientists" than others. These scientists, all tenured and experienced, expressed "a deep love of science" and "evolutionary theory is to them essential to any biology curriculum" (796). These science-identifying teachers teach evolution more extensively and in more depth. We tried to assess whether this sort of identification exists for our teachers as well and asked all teachers to complete six sentences regarding their own self-concept as science teachers.

I think of myself as

   A. a mentor . . .

      (1) Every day, (2) often, (3) sometimes, (4) rarely, or (5) never

   B. a scientist . . .

      (1) Every day, (2) often, (3) sometimes, (4) rarely, or (5) never

   C. an ecologist . . .

      (1) Every day, (2) often, (3) sometimes, (4) rarely, or (5) never

   D. a role model . . .

      (1) Every day, (2) often, (3) sometimes, (4) rarely, or (5) never

   E. a biologist . . .

      (1) Every day, (2) often, (3) sometimes, (4) rarely, or (5) never

   F. an educator . . .

      (1) Every day, (2) often, (3) sometimes, (4) rarely, or (5) never

A factor analysis revealed a two-factor solution, with a clear dimension of identification as scientist (items B, C, and E) and a secondary dimension of educator (items A and D). We therefore used the responses to the questions concerning "scientist," "ecologist," and "biologist" to construct a scale measuring each teacher's identification with the scientific profession.[2] The scale is scored 0 for respondents who said "never" to all three items and scored 1 for those who said "every day" to all items (it has a mean of 0.61, a standard deviation of 0.28, and a reliability of 0.81).

To see how self-confidence and self-identify influence teaching practice, we added our measure of confidence and our measure of identity to our models; the results are reported in Table 7.2.[3] The results not only show the very large effect of self-rated expertise (hinted at in the previous chapter) but also show that the impacts of degrees and credits

---

[2] The sixth identity, "educator," did not contribute to the scale because of a lack of variance (95% of respondents said they think of themselves as an educator "every day"). The scale was created by averaging responses to these three questions, and then values were squared to reduce skewness (untransformed, the skew was −0.90 but after transformation it was only −0.20).

[3] To produce these results, we used ordinary least squares regressions, rather than multilevel models. As Table 7.1 showed, having accounted for several individual level variables, the residual intraclass correlation is now only 0.03 for the model predicting time spent on evolution and essentially 0 for the model examining teacher emphasis. Indeed, for the NAS emphasis model, the intercept variance becomes impossible to estimate in more complex models. Although the intercept variance retains statistical significance in the former model, the effective clustering is negligible. As a specification check, we estimated all models using both techniques and in no case were the results different.

Table 7.2. Ordinary least squares regression models assessing the impacts of teacher educational credentials, self-identification, and expertise

	Predicting Hours of Evolution (N = 854)			Predicting NAS Endorsement (N = 872)		
	B	SE	t	B	SE	t
Standards Index 2007	.64	.33	1.96	**3.50**	1.04	3.39
Seniority (centered)	−.52	.31	−1.71	−1.03	.98	−1.05
Standards × Seniority	**−.49**	.27	−1.83	.09	.85	.10
Believes there is no test	.61	.71	.86	3.34	2.25	1.48
Standards × Believes no test	−.56	.62	−.91	**−3.78**	1.96	−1.93
Teacher is female	**−.52**	.25	−2.08	**−1.53**	.80	−1.91
Credits earned in biology (0–2)	.57	.50	1.13	−.07	1.60	−.04
Science degrees (0–2)	−.36	.39	−.92	1.60	1.22	1.31
Completed evolution class	**2.56**	.62	4.09	**6.10**	1.98	3.08
Has normal certification	−.43	.72	−.61	−.55	2.28	−.24
Identifies as scientist	1.74	1.10	1.57	2.82	3.48	.81
Self-rated expertise (−1 to +2)	**2.66**	.44	5.99	**11.34**	1.41	8.04
Intercept	9.76	1.16	8.43	42.81	3.68	11.63
Adjusted R²	.11			.13		

Bold entries are significant in expected direction at .05 level.

earned are no longer significantly different from 0. There remains an effect of having taken an evolution course, but the magnitude of this effect is roughly halved in both models. Once we account for self-rated expertise, we see no impact of self-identification as a scientist (although this variable is related to both dependent variables if the self-rating is excluded).

To interpret the estimates in the tables, it is useful to think about particular combinations of background characteristics. For example, consider one teacher who has not completed an evolution class and who rates his knowledge of evolution as "typical of most high school biology teachers" and a second teacher who completed a semester-length class in evolution and rates herself as "very good compared to most high school biology teachers." The first teacher, if at the mean on all other variables, would be expected to teach about 11 hours of evolution, and his emphasis score would be about 44 points. In contrast, the second teacher would teach about 16 hours and score over 60 on the NAS scale. These are substantial effects and would surely create very different classroom experiences for the students of these two teachers.

These results suggest that classroom instruction would shift both in quantity and in how closely instruction adheres to the key goals of the NAS if teacher training and certification rules were changed. From this perspective, encouraging teachers to take more science classes, to major in science, to pursue master's degrees in science, and, most fundamentally, to complete a semester-long course in evolution might well have important consequences. First, teachers would gain confidence in their ability to explain and defend principles of evolutionary biology. Second, as a consequence, they would teach more evolution and teach it better (better from the perspective of major scientific organizations).

THE ROLE OF PERSONAL BELIEFS IN EDUCATIONAL AND CLASSROOM CHOICES

For those who would like to see teachers devote more time to evolution and treat it in a manner that is more consistent with the goals of major scientific organizations, the foregoing analyses suggest a simple policy solution: require all prospective biology teachers to be better trained in science. The comments of one of our teachers from Illinois supports this idea. This teacher wrote that, "after my undergraduate studies my perception of evolution was inaccurate. It wasn't [un]til after I received a master of science that I felt like I had a good and accurate understanding of evolution and how natural selection happens. I would bet that very few high school biology teachers understand evolution enough to teach it." If we interpret the regression estimates as representing causal effects, requiring more science education would have a substantial impact in thousands of high school classrooms.

However, we need to consider a second possible story that is also consistent with the evidence. And this is that attitudes toward evolution are part of teachers' fundamental values and are not easily transformed. It is not that these values are *impossible* to change. Whereas a biology course alone has little effect on fundamental values concerning evolution (Bishop and Anderson 1990; Lawson and Weser 1990), Ingram and Nelson have shown that a stand-alone evolution course has "positively influenced students' acceptance of evolution" (2005, 18). But even Ingram and Nelson find this to be the case mostly for students who did not hold strong views at the start of the class.

Most of our nonscience majors did not take an evolution course. This may be because it is not required for them, but it may well also be that deeply held values toward evolution may encourage some potential teachers to enroll in an evolution class but lead others to avoid evolutionary biology. Teachers from doctrinally conservative faith traditions may have little interest in sitting through a course on evolution, and forcing them to do so might not change their attitudes. Of course, we lack experimental data that might shed light on cause and effect – and it would be both impossible and unethical to randomly assign some education majors to a required evolution course while assigning others to complete their degree without one. Nevertheless, we can get a sense of whether this alternative causal story is possible. In our survey, we asked each teacher the same question about beliefs about human origins that frequently is used in public opinion polls:

Now, regardless of what you do in the classroom, we would like to ask about your own personal views. Which of the following statements comes closest to your views on the origin and development of human beings?

☐ Human beings developed over millions of years from less advanced forms of life, but God guided this process (theistic evolution).

☐ Human beings developed over millions of years from less advanced forms of life, but God had no part in this process (young earth creationism).

☐ God created human beings pretty much in their present form at one time within the last 10,000 years or so (organic evolution).

The responses to this question are summarized in Figure 7.1 and show that only about three-quarters of teachers report a personal belief in the evolution of human beings. The largest number of these teachers, 47% of the total, selected the *theistic evolution* perspective (that evolution occurred and had divine guidance), whereas 31% of the sample selected the option representing what is often called the *organic evolution* perspective. A total of 14% endorsed the *young earth* position that God created human beings recently, and a sizable number of teachers declined to answer this question (in some cases, telling us that their views were too nuanced to place in any of the choices).[4]

---

[4] As an example of these nuanced views, consider a New York teacher who did not answer the question about his beliefs on human origins. He wrote: "I believe life has evolved in

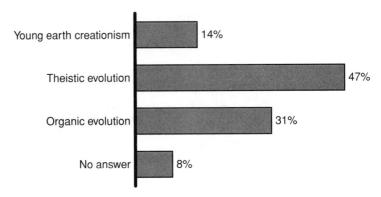

Figure 7.1. Teacher beliefs about human origins (N = 926).

To determine whether self-selection is a possible mechanism, we cross-tabulated the answers to this question with reports concerning the completion of an evolution class; the results are reported in the first column of Table 7.3.

The results show that, of those who express young earth creationist beliefs, 32% completed such a class. This is in contrast to 51% of organic evolutionists.[5] More generally, Table 7.3 shows that teachers who express young earth beliefs completed fewer courses in biology, were slightly less likely to major in a scientific field, and were considerably less likely to hold a graduate degree in a scientific discipline. Of course, it is possible that formal education influenced attitudes rather than the other way around, and it is certain that this happens for many students, in particular those who are initially undecided (Ingram and

the sense that it changes. However, I believe it started in the general forms mentioned in the Bible, not as one cell or organic material cluster. I also believe the impetus for change may occur in accordance with Darwin's theory of Natural Selection, however the mutations that enable survival may be the manifestation of a will to live by adaption and change and not the result of random mutation. This idea resembles Lamark's Theory of Use and Disuse. However, being Biblically minded, I am of the opinion that both the abiotic and biotic environmental changes that seem to lead to changes in living things are the result of the deeds of man. That is, the free will of man ultimately governs how other living things will appear, function and live. This thinking is similar to ideas presented in Jewish Mysticism." However we might classify his views, this teacher teaches relatively little evolution, and what he does teach is not in accordance with NAS expectations (10 hours to evolution, with NAS score of only 17/100 and a procreationist score of 75/100).

5   The table reveals that those who declined to answer this question are nearly identical to young earth creationists in their exposure to evolution instruction at the college level. This hints at the possibility that the results shown in Figure 7.1 may substantially underestimate the number of young earth believers who are teaching general biology at the high school level. See also the teacher in note 4.

Table 7.3. Educational background of teachers, by personal beliefs

Expressed Belief	Percent who completed an evolution course (%)	Percent holding any degree in science (%)	Percent with a graduate degree in science (%)	Percent who earned 40 or more credits in biology (%)	N
Young earth creationism	32	55	13	49	129
No answer	32	53	25	72	75
Theistic evolution	41	63	24	64	438
Organic evolution	51	66	30	71	284
Total	42	62	62	65	926

Note: Entries are the percentage of teachers expressing a particular belief who achieved the criterion.

Nelson 2005). But the tight structuring of evolution beliefs with religion that we demonstrated in Chapter 3 suggests that beliefs about human origins may be especially resistant to change. How much of the association is due to self-selection and how much is due to persuasion and learning effects is impossible to sort out. But self-selection is a clear possibility. This suggests that requiring all science education students to get more training would not change their later choices and priorities as much as implied by our regression models. The overall effect of requiring all science teachers to complete an evolution course is thus difficult to predict. For those open to evolution, it may give them additional confidence to teach it in accord with the expectations of establishment science. For those whose minds are closed to the possibility of either theistic or organic evolution, completing such a class might make no difference at all. However, if such a course were required, it might deter students from some faith traditions from being biology teachers in the first place.

If personal beliefs have the potential to guide course selection while in education school, then it is plausible that these same beliefs will have a direct influence on classroom choices. Brehm and Gates argue that the "very best explanation" for why agents generally do not do as their principals want is that they do not share the same values (1997, 20). Other work on street-level bureaucrats also finds or suggests that they bring their own attitudes and values to bear on how they do their jobs (Keiser 1999, 2010; Keiser and Soss 1998; Meyers and Vorsanger 2003). Of course, some areas of discretion may not be relevant to an employee's most deeply held values. But when they are, we can expect that values will compete with principals' priorities the most (Meier and Bohte 2001). Meier and Bohte (2001) find this to be the case in their study of teachers, where their personal values – stemming, they argue, from their race and ethnicity – guide decisions impacting on racial and ethnic teaching policies, practices, and outcomes.

Such should be the case with instruction in evolution, too, where personal values about evolution and creation can be realized because of the discretion they have in the classroom. And we have already seen in Chapter 6 that standards have only a limited effect in restricting this discretion. Consider in this context the challenge in teaching evolution for one teacher from South Dakota who expressed these strong views: "I have no problem studying evolution as a theory. Nor do I have any problem discussing the Genesis account of creation. I believe the Genesis account. Both I and my students have or will come to the place where we must choose what we believe. The consequences of making the wrong choices are horrible beyond description."

To determine whether personal views and values substantially influence teaching decisions, we added our measure of personal beliefs to our multilevel regression model. The variable is coded so that theistic evolution adherents comprise the contrast category, with dummy variables representing the young earth and organic evolution responses. The results are reported in Table 7.4, and they show extremely large impacts of personal beliefs on teaching.

Looking first at the model predicting hours devoted to evolution, we see that, compared with teachers who believe that God guided evolution, those who express young earth views devote about 2.5 fewer hours to evolution, and those who believe in completely organic or materialistic evolution teach almost 2 hours more. Similarly, the model predicting emphasis in the classroom estimates that young earth believers will score 29 points lower than those who believe in theistic evolution and 39 points lower than materialists. Those who declined to answer resemble the young earth adherents in their emphasis but resemble theistic evolutionists in the time they devote to evolution. Overall, not only do personal beliefs influence instruction, they also have a stronger impact than any other factor we have examined.

Even within the same state, with the same standards and same assessment policies, we see enormous variation in teacher practices.

Table 7.4. OLS regression models assessing the impacts of teacher educational credentials, self-identification, expertise, and personal beliefs about human origins

	Predicting Hours of Evolution (N = 854)			Predicting NAS Endorsement (N = 872)		
	B	SE	t	B	SE	t
Standards Index 2007	.43	.33	1.30	**1.80**	.94	1.92
Seniority (centered)	−.55	.30	−1.80	−1.34	.88	−1.54
Standards × Seniority	−.55	.27	−2.08	−.28	.76	−.36
Believes there is no test	.24	.71	.34	.38	2.03	.19
Standards × Believes no test	−.27	.62	−.44	−1.56	1.76	−.88
Teacher is female	−.45	.25	−1.79	−.92	.72	−1.27
Credits earned in biology (0–2)	.44	.50	.87	−1.15	1.44	−.80
Science degrees (0–2)	−.47	.38	−1.22	.68	1.10	.62
Completed evolution class	**2.44**	.62	3.95	**5.10**	1.77	2.88
Has normal certification	−.44	.71	−.62	−.50	2.05	−.24
Identifies as scientist	1.58	1.09	1.44	.79	3.12	.25
Self-rated expertise (−1 to +2)	**2.32**	.45	5.19	**8.81**	1.29	6.84
Young earth believer	**−2.73**	.88	−3.10	**−28.74**	2.53	−11.35
Organic evolution believer	**1.74**	.67	2.62	**9.91**	1.92	5.16
Did not answer belief question	−.96	1.27	−.76	**−14.46**	3.46	−4.18
Intercept	10.38	1.18	8.79	50.91	3.40	14.95
Adjusted R^2	.13			.30		

Bold entries are significant in expected direction at .05 level.

This variation from teacher to teacher can be seen even within the same school, where we see clearly how practices differ when discretion is linked to personal values: "I enjoy the topic of evolution and have many neat labs and activities for it" wrote one New Jersey teacher; "my students seem to really 'get it' – I've never had problems or questions from parents. There are 3 Bio teachers in my school. One of them shares my feelings on teaching evolution and the other is hard-core religious and has never taught evolution in the 20 years he's been teaching. My curriculum supervisor pretty much leaves it up to us as to what we teach and what we don't." Given comments like this, it is not surprising that the within-state standard deviation (within state sigma, Table 7.1) was an enormous 8.5 hours of instructional time with a correspondingly large standard deviation of 29 points on our NAS emphasis scale. In nearly every state, teachers exhibit a wide range of classroom practices that span virtually the entire range of constitutionally permissible teaching strategies – ranging from teachers who barely mention evolution to those who spend many hours during the school year on evolution by using its framework to help place other topics – such as genetics, ecology, and cell function – in a broader perspective.

CREATIONISM IN THE CLASSROOM

In Chapter 5, we introduced two different ways of identifying teachers who endorse creationism in the classroom. Our low estimate required that a teacher reports at least 1 hour devoted to creationism or intelligent design *and* agrees (or strongly agrees) with at least one statement endorsing creationism as a valid scientific alternative (these questions are described in Table 5.6). Altogether, 14% of our teachers met these combined criteria. Our high estimate of 21% included teachers who reported endorsing creationism but who did not report devoting an hour or more of formal classroom time to the topic.

In this section, we want to explore whether the same personal characteristics that influenced the treatment of evolution also influence the likelihood that teachers will endorse creationism. To do this, we use our "low estimate" classification and give teachers a score of 1 if they meet both criteria and a 0 otherwise. This becomes the dependent variable in a logistic regression model, whose slopes, along with the corresponding odds ratios, are reported in Table 7.5.

The results here are not a precise mirror image of the results for teaching evolution. Indeed, there are some very important differences. One important difference is that the completion of a course devoted to evolution makes no difference at all. That is, completing an evolution course appears to help many teachers do a better job in covering evolution but does not reduce the likelihood, some years later, of explicitly endorsing creationism in the classroom. This is consistent with evidence from other studies that completion of a focused course on evolution has minimal impact on students who do not accept evolution due to strongly held opinions and beliefs.[6]

---

[6] Another difference is the positive interaction between standards and the absence of an aligned assessment test (interaction estimate of 0.62). As standards get more rigorous, the odds of teaching creationism increase sharply. Upon close inspection of the data, however, this interaction appears to be spurious due to the distribution of young earth creationists –

Table 7.5. Models assessing the impacts of teacher educational credentials, self-identification, expertise, and personal beliefs about human origins on the teaching of creationism

	Predicting any creationist teaching (N = 872)			
	Logistic Regression Estimate	Odds ratio	SE	t
Standards Index 2007	−.13	.87	.11	−1.27
Seniority (centered)	.20	1.22	.11	1.86
Standards × Seniority	−.17	.85	.10	−1.70
Believes there is no test	.00	1.00	.24	−.01
Standards × Believes no test	.62	1.85	.24	2.53
Teacher is female	−.29	.75	.14	−2.14
Credits earned in biology (0–2)	.02	1.02	.17	.11
Science degrees (0–2)	.12	1.12	.13	.88
Completed evolution class	−.31	.74	.21	−1.44
Has normal certification	.35	1.41	.26	1.32
Identifies as scientist	.44	1.56	.37	1.20
Self-rated expertise (−1 to +2)	−.15	.86	.15	−.96
Young earth believer	**1.39**	4.01	.24	5.74
Organic evolution believer	**−1.35**	.26	.32	−4.20
Did not answer belief question	**1.02**	2.77	.33	3.11
Intercept	−1.95	11.64	.42	−4.64
Pseudo R^2	.14			

Bold entries are significant in expected direction at .05 level.

In one respect, however, our analysis of teaching creationism is similar to our analysis of teaching evolution: personal beliefs are again the most powerful predictor of teachers' behavior. Compared with teachers who express a belief in theistic evolution, the odds that young earth adherents will teach creationism is about four times as high (odds ratio of 4.01), and the odds of an organic evolutionist mentioning creationism in a positive light is about four times lower (odds ratio of 0.26).

their being over-represented in both states with cursory evolution standards that have assessment tests and states with rigorous standards but without testing. Both conditions would give a license to teachers to teach in ways that undermine rigorous instruction in evolution and do so without sanction. But we are not convinced that the interaction is anything more than an artifact of how teachers are distributed geographically, a topic we take up more generally in the next chapter.

Table 7.6. The association between teaching practices and personal beliefs concerning human origins

Personal belief	Hours devoted to evolution	NAS Endorsement Score	Endorses creationism in the classroom (%)	N
Young earth creationism	9.6	25	40	129
No answer	12.6	35	28	75
Theistic evolution	13.5	57	16	438
Organic evolution	16.5	71	5	284
Total	13.8	55	17	926

PLACING MULTIVARIATE ESTIMATES IN CONTEXT

As the comments and the regression results make clear, personal values and beliefs about evolution are closely linked to how teachers choose to teach it. And we should emphasize that these multiple regression estimates underestimate the true differences because they assume that all other variables are equal. As we have seen (in Table 7.3), these three groups of teachers are certainly not equal in other respects. When we look at the unadjusted data, reported in Table 7.6, we see the profound differences in the classroom experiences of students whose teachers have different personal beliefs about human origins. A typical student who is taught by a teacher with young earth creationist beliefs will receive a little less than 10 hours of evolution instruction, and that instruction will not include much indication that evolution is well established as a fact in the scientific community.

In addition, students taught by a young earth believer will have a 40% chance of being exposed to instruction that endorses creationism as a valid, scientific alternative to establishment evolutionary biology. Among the young earth teachers who endorse creationism in the classroom, they report spending an average of three hours on creationism and intelligent design during the year.

Finally, what are we to make of thirteen teachers who express a belief in organic evolution but also validate creationism or intelligent design in their classrooms? This is a small number, and we might consider chalking this up to measurement error. But most seem to fall into two camps. Some felt strongly about teaching "both sides" of the debate in spite of their own feelings. For example, one teacher from Ohio explained, "I consider myself strongly on the side of evolution, but I do recognize the validity of creationism, and more importantly I recognize that we have an obligation to expose students to both." A Minnesota teacher also teaches "both sides," as a kind of concession to his very religious students: "I have many fundamentalist Christians in my classes and, for many missionary responsibilities. I ask them to listen to the concepts and learn them well. I do not tell them that they have to change their beliefs but I do tell them they are accountable for the information." This teacher strongly disagreed with the notion that creationism is a valid scientific alternative, but, interestingly, agreed that, when he teaches, he emphasizes "that many reputable scientists" view these as legitimate alternatives to Darwinian theory.

A second group consists of those who apparently believe in organic evolution but also in the intervention of an intelligent designer. Six of the thirteen teachers in this group reported that they "have encouraged students to consider how unlikely it is that complex organs (e.g., the eye) or complex processes (blood clotting) could have occurred simply by random mutation and natural selection." None, however, chose to elaborate on this in the open-ended questions, so we lack context to provide a more grounded interpretation.

SUMMARY AND DISCUSSION

In the previous chapter, we showed that state curricular standards have only very small effects on how educators actually teach in their classrooms. Some teachers new to the profession rely on standards to some extent, and high-stakes tests that are aligned with content standards can also influence teachers. But even among those susceptible to influence, state content standards explained only a tiny portion of the cross-teacher variance in instruction.

As street-level bureaucrats, teachers exercise considerable discretion. In this chapter, we showed that this discretion allows them to be guided, first and foremost, by teachers' personal acceptance of evolution. Additional important factors include their educational background and self-confidence concerning the subject matter. Beliefs, of course, exert a stronger influence on some teachers than others. Some young earth believers set their personal views aside and may teach evolution in an acceptable, if not enthusiastic, way. Consider the teacher from Pennsylvania who told us:

> In my opinion, Evolution is one of the greatest "scientific" frauds forced upon us. We are mandated to teach this nonsense to students while all the supposed "evidence" consists of suppositions, guesses, "might-be's," and "imagines." Agreement with evolution is based on faith and amounts to a scientific religion. Teaching evolution does nothing to increase students' understanding of life nor does it "unify" all of Biology. Evolution is only taught to students so that these impressionable youngsters can learn to deny our creator-God.

Although we cannot say that he taught evolution enthusiastically, he devoted 10 hours to the topic and reports spending no time on creationism at all. It is clear that personal beliefs influenced his teaching. But they did not also lead him to cross into areas that are constitutionally questionable.

But for many others, personal beliefs result in outright defiance of state standards and Supreme Court rulings. One Texas teacher, for example, responded this way when we asked if he had anything else to say: "I am an evangelical Christian. Enough said." When we looked at his survey responses, we found that he reported spending about 10 hours on evolution and 16–20 hours on creationism or intelligent design.

On the other side of the ledger, the roughly 33% of teachers who reject a role for God in guiding evolution also exercise discretion and typically *exceed* state expectations concerning evolution. They not only spend more time on evolution but deliberately counter the notion that evolution is a "theory" and therefore unproven. Organic evolutionists were far more likely to "strongly agree" that they emphasize "evolution is a fact" (46%) than teachers that accept evolution but see the hand of God somewhere in the background (29%). Believers in organic evolution are not just meeting state expectations but are taking up the challenges posed by the major scientific organizations that see science threatened by the widespread skepticism about evolution. This is typified by a teacher from Florida, who told us:

> Evolutionary Theory is one of my passions. I leisurely read about evolution (Gould, Wilson, Dawkins, etc.) and incorporate it into my teaching. I start by teaching the students about science and the goals of science in answering questions about the natural world. I then explain that evolution by natural selection is the best possible explanation for the diversity of life and the similarities and differences seen throughout the natural world. I explain that creationism and ID have no scientific merit and are not accepted by the scientific community. They are super-natural explanations which are outside the boundaries of science. With the argument I present, it is very difficult for students to not accept evolution.

Although the typical teacher from Florida devoted about 12 hours to evolution, this teacher spent about 20 hours and clearly was motivated to get students to "accept evolution" and not merely do well on examinations.

We also see evidence that personal beliefs matter for those who identified themselves as theistic evolutionists. They occupy the middle ground in terms of time devoted to evolution and the types of themes that are emphasized. Compared with organic evolution adherents, these teachers were about 33% more likely to strongly agree that "I focus heavily on what students need to know to meet state science standards" and twice as likely to "deliberately avoid making statements that might be deemed offensive by some students or their parents." They accept the findings of evolutionary biology but do not see that it is their mission to persuade their skeptical students to also accept them.

Thus, in ways that are sometimes subtle and sometimes conspicuous and bold, teachers' personal beliefs play a major role – largely unconstrained by the state content standards and textbook selection procedures that provoke such heated political battles. However, this does not mean that teachers are completely unconstrained. Each teacher works in a community with a distinctive cultural mix, and the community may exert far more influence on teacher conduct than documents drafted in the state capital. To examine this, we focus on community context in our next chapter.

8 Teachers in Their Schools and Communities

There are worse things taught in our schools, and I will continue to support local control of education.

New Hampshire Governor Stephen Merrill (1995)[1]

In the previous chapter, we showed how the individual characteristics of teachers help explain their varied approaches to teaching evolution and why some teachers are willing to cross the constitutional line by treating creationism as a scientific alternative to evolutionary biology. To a large extent, the analyses suggest that the type of learning opportunities afforded to each of the nation's public school students is a chance event, based almost entirely on the particular teacher they encounter in their general biology class.

But such an interpretation would not tell the entire story. And that is because teachers are not randomly distributed across classrooms, nor are they as immune to community influences as they are to state content standards. In this sense, it is again useful to think of teachers as street-level bureaucrats who are entrusted to implement state policy while also being afforded substantial autonomy commensurate with their positions as credentialed professionals. In Chapter 6, we assessed the extent to which teachers are responsive to state standards – official policies that are crafted by state policy makers. These policy makers include those directly elected by the people, as well as political appointees and civil servants who will reflect various degrees

---

[1] Merrill was discussing a decision by the school board of Merrimack, New Hampshire to consider adding creationism to the formal curriculum. Quoted in "Town Divided Over Whether to Teach Creationism in Schools," *New York Times*, February 13, 1995; http://www.nytimes.com/1995/02/13/us/town-divided-over-whether-to-teach-creationism-in-schools.html; accessed April 5, 2010.

of responsiveness to public opinion. In this chapter, we shift our focus from this top–down conception of democratic control to a bottom–up model (Meier and O'Toole 2006) and assess their responsiveness to the communities they serve.

Decades of research on street-level bureaucracy have shown how local culture and politics can influence policy implementation (e.g., Percival, Johnson, and Neiman 2009; Soss 2000; Weissert 1994; Whitford 2002; Wilson 1989). This literature spans many domains of public policy, including the administration of anti-poverty and social insurance programs, environmental regulation, and local service delivery. However, although teachers are frequently offered as ideal typical examples of street-level bureaucrats (Meier and Bohte 2001; Weatherley and Lipsky 1978), we know of no empirical studies that seek to explain teacher behavior in terms of the local political or ideological environment. As we will show, however, taking account of the community context enriches our understanding of evolution instruction in the United States.

COMMUNITIES, TEACHERS, AND TEACHING PRACTICES

The characteristics of the local community can be related to classroom instruction in many ways. We will focus on three of these in this chapter: (1) the fostering of shared values between teachers and their community; (2) the emergence of pressures on teachers applied by parents, clergy, or (indirectly) school administrators and local officials; and (3) through *contextual effects* whereby community values influence teaching practices in subtle but measurable ways.

Assortative Hiring

It is widely appreciated that civil servants may share local values and exercise their authority and discretion to implement policy in accord with these shared values (e.g., Fording, Soss, and Schram 2007). The simplest way that teachers' values come to match those of the communities is through the processes of hiring and retention. As Percival, Johnson, and Neiman note, "the staff and leadership of local agencies might ... be recruited in ways that reflect the views of the local legislature [or] ... School Board" (2009, 166). In this way, the policy preferences of the broader community can lead to the hiring of teachers who share the community's values and beliefs. Indeed, research on the geographic preferences of those seeking their first teaching jobs show that, "In seeking their first teaching jobs, prospective teachers appear to search very close to their hometowns and in regions that are similar to those where they grew up" (Boyd et al. 2005, 127). The authors estimate that, "Sixty-one percent of teachers entering public school teaching in New York from 1999 to 2002 first taught in schools located within 15 miles of their hometown" (2005, 117). This would produce similarity between community values and those of newly hired teachers.

Pressure on Teachers

Local environments may influence policy implementation via the presence and strength of local advocacy groups or by increasing the presence of individuals who would seek to directly influence instruction. Organized groups will not merely reflect a diffuse public opinion but are effective when they can apply pressure to elected officials (school boards), supervisors (superintendents and principals), and front-line public employees such as teachers (see e.g., Sabatier, Loomis, and McCarthy 1995; Scholz and Wei 1986).

Contextual Effects

It has long been appreciated that local cultures can indirectly influence public employees. This can occur by influencing how managers and bureaucrats interpret and selectively emphasize certain aspects of written laws, rules, and policies. Or it may be more deliberate, if public employees feel that it is proper for their implementation of policy to reflect local sentiment (Percival et al. 2009). In his influential *Street-Level Bureaucracy*, Lipsky argued that when local communities are indifferent to how a public policy is implemented, street-level bureaucrats generate their own goals and objectives. But when the community is characterized by a strongly held consensus, civil servants will respond to community sentiment (1980, 46). The Minnesota teacher we encountered in the last chapter who accommodated his very religious students illustrates this idea. But whether community opinion has a systematic impact on teaching cannot be discerned from such anecdotes.

WHICH TEACHERS WORK IN WHICH COMMUNITIES?

In Chapter 3, we showed that public opinion concerning evolution reflected the social and religious composition of each state. Indeed, a simple summary index of cosmopolitanism/traditionalism explained 50% of the variation in state public opinion (see Figure 3.2). We can use this summary of local cosmopolitanism/traditionalism to determine whether particular types of communities are characterized by certain types of teachers.

To measure the local political culture (relative cosmopolitanism versus relative traditionalism), we used the same measures as we did earlier, but this time pertaining to the local environment. The congregational census conducted by the Association of Statisticians of American Religious Bodies provides detailed denominational membership data at the level of the county (see Jones et al. 2002), and we again calculated the percentage of the adult population that are adherents of doctrinally conservative Protestant denominations. This was rescaled to range from 0 to 1. The U.S. Census also provides a breakdown of educational attainment at the level of the school district, and we used this to calculate the percentage of each district's adult population that holds an advanced degree. With the latter measure rescaled to run from -1 (the highest observed rate of advanced degrees) to 0 (the lowest rate), we can add our two components to again get an index that runs from -1 (most cosmopolitan) to $+1$ (most traditional).

This index provides a continuous indicator of the relative balance between the two constituencies that comprise the polar ends of the evolution/creationism debate and who are especially influential in shaping overall state public opinion. However, it is useful to begin by classifying school districts into a small number of categories to see how local culture is related to the characteristics of teachers, their beliefs, and their teaching practices. In the tables below, we classify school districts into four categories based on where they fall relative to the 15th, 50th, and 85th percentiles. Table 8.1 shows that biology teachers in the most cosmopolitan districts – the 15% lowest scoring

Table 8.1. Teachers' educational qualifications by level of school district traditionalism

	Percent of teachers (%)	Percent who completed a course in evolution (%)	Percent with graduate degree in science (%)	40 or more credits in biology (%)
Most cosmopolitan districts (N = 136)	10	59	38	75
Somewhat cosmopolitan (N = 350)	43	42	24	65
Somewhat traditional (N = 296)	37	41	29	63
Most traditional districts (N = 139)	10	32	22	55
Total	100%	43	65	65

district environments in our sample – were nearly twice as likely to have completed a course in evolution compared with those teaching in the most traditional districts (59% compared with 32%). The data also reveal meaningful differences in terms of academic credits in biology and whether the teacher holds a graduate degree in a scientific discipline. Thus, in terms of formal training and credentials, teachers in the most cosmopolitan school districts have considerably more formal qualifications than those teaching in districts with large numbers of doctrinally conservative Protestants.

In the last chapter, we saw that the personal beliefs of teachers were the most powerful predictor of classroom teaching practices. Table 8.2 shows that these beliefs are also strongly related to district characteristics. Reading across each row of the cross-tabulation, we

Table 8.2. The distribution of teachers' personal beliefs by level of school district traditionalism

	Young earth creationism (%)	Theistic evolution (%)	Organic evolution (%)	Total
Most cosmopolitan districts (N = 136)	4	39	57	100%
Somewhat cosmopolitan (N = 350)	8	53	39	100%
Somewhat traditional (N = 296)	18	55	27	100%
Most traditional districts (N = 139)	37	53	11	100%
Total	15	52	33	100%

see that, in the most cosmopolitan districts, more than half of the biology teachers express a personal belief in organic evolution of human beings. This is nearly twice the national average and more than five times the prevalence in the most traditional districts. We see a mirror pattern with respect to young earth creationism. In the school districts in which advanced degree owners outnumber doctrinally conservative Protestants, we found almost no teachers who believe that God created human beings in the last 10,000 years. But students in the 15% of districts that are most traditional have nearly a four in ten chance of being taught by a teacher who holds this belief.

Why do we see such a stark pattern? We suggest that the process of hiring teachers is analogous to patterns of assortative mating (in which men and women marry partners who are a lot like themselves). Hiring, like mating, is based on the actions of two parties. On the one hand, there is likely to be substantial self-selection on the part of those applying for teaching positions. Few fans of Richard Dawkins will apply for teaching positions in communities dominated by fundamentalist church culture. And few biblical literalists will apply for teaching positions in Berkeley, Cambridge, or even Austin. In addition, local districts are not keen on controversy either and will steer away from teachers who they believe will not fit in. Indeed, a college transcript indicating that an aspiring science teacher completed a semester-long course in evolution may provide an initial (though imperfect) signal about whether that prospective teacher will share a community's values.[2]

Whatever the mechanisms, however, our main point both here and in the remainder of this section is that traditional districts and cosmopolitan districts tend to hire teachers whose training, beliefs, and teaching practices serve to reinforce or harmonize with the prevailing

---

[2] We wondered if the reason for this was really financial, because the most cosmopolitan districts are more affluent and spend as much as 70% more per pupil than the most traditional communities. This suggests that the most cosmopolitan districts may have the capacity to hire more teachers with graduate degrees and extensive science training, even accounting for the higher cost of living in these communities. But this turns out to not be the case. In supplemental analyses, we found that after accounting for community religious and educational context, the level of per pupil spending was unrelated to any of the indicators of teachers' credentials: the number of credits in biology, highest degree earned, or completing a class in evolution.

Table 8.3. Teaching practices by level of school district traditionalism

	Percent of teachers (%)	Mean hours devoted to evolution	Mean score on NAS support scale	Percent endorsing creationism (%)
Most cosmopolitan districts (N = 136)	10	16.3	63.1	10
Somewhat cosmopolitan (N = 350)	43	14.8	58.5	18
Somewhat traditional (N = 296)	37	13.0	51.8	24
Most traditional districts (N = 139)	10	10.6	44.8	33
Total	100%	13.8	55.0	21

local culture. Of course, hiring practices will not eliminate all mismatches between local and teacher values. But when these occur, balance may be restored by teachers who seek to relocate to a district with a culture more in tune with their own values and background.

If the educational and religious composition of a school district is associated with the credentials and the personal beliefs of the biology teachers who work there, it is a foregone conclusion that we will see differences in teaching practices. Table 8.3, which summarizes our three indicators of teaching by type of district, shows substantial differences. The number of hours devoted to evolution is above 15 hours in districts that are slightly more cosmopolitan, but the time given to evolution drops steadily after that as the number of highly educated citizens falls and the number of conservative Protestants rise. The degree that teachers emphasize the positions of major scientific organizations also falls as the community becomes increasingly traditional. And, most dramatically, the probability that a teacher will devote an hour or more to creationism in a supportive way rises rapidly as religious conservatives increase in numbers. In the 50% of districts that are cosmopolitan, one in every six students will encounter a teacher who endorses creationism in the classroom. But children growing up in the more traditional areas have roughly one chance in four of having a teacher who is sympathetic to creationism and expresses that sympathy in the classroom.

Earlier, we suggested that community context could influence teaching practices via three mechanisms: (1) selective hiring of teachers who share the community's values, (2) pressure on teachers that comes from mobilized interest groups, and (3) a more diffuse effect of community public opinion. The strong linkage between the educational and religious composition of a school district and the personal beliefs of teachers provides compelling evidence for selection and "assortative hiring." Beliefs about human origins, we saw in Chapters 2 and 3, are highly structured by relatively permanent characteristics such as religious affiliation and education.

Our findings here are not unlike those of Kenneth Meier and his colleagues, who study school district teachers and administrators as representative bureaucracies (e.g., Meier 1975, 1993; Meier and Bohte 2001; Meier and O'Toole 2006). Meier and Bohte argue that "bureaucracies are political institutions that are capable of representing the interests of citizens just as legislatures or executives do" (2001, 455). They show that, when teachers and administrators mirror the racial and ethnic profiles of their communities – what political scientists call "passive" or "descriptive" representation – they are more responsive to the publics they serve. The reason lies in similar values rooted in race and ethnicity. These studies are conducted at the *collective level*, meaning they look at the overall percentage of minority teachers and administrators and compare these with their communities; their findings show that bureaucratic discretion "strengthens the relationship between active and passive representation" (Meier and Bohte 2001, 468).

Looking dyadically – meaning individual teachers and the communities in which they teach – we find similar patterns. Although we expect teaching practices to change over the lives of teachers, their personal beliefs about human origins are likely to change more slowly, if at all. So selective hiring and job searching appear to be important mechanisms that link teachers with communities that are *much like themselves* in terms of shared values. Thus, communities get the type of instruction that is most in line with their preferences. We return to this at the end of the chapter, where we consider this finding more broadly in the context of "who decides?" But first we continue in our exploration of the geographic distribution of teachers by considering another mechanism through which local communities might get what they want: through pressure from organized groups of local citizens, outspoken parents, or other groups in the community.

PRESSURE FROM THE COMMUNITY

Several previous studies have shown that teachers report pressure to drop evolution from their classes or to teach creationism from residents, church leaders, administrators, and local school board members (Donnelly and Boone 2007; Moore 2002b). Some fear that "chronic pressure" from creationists "thwart their attempts to teach evolution" because it leads administrators to discourage any teaching that might bring controversy (Griffith and Brem 2004). Prior research, however, has shown little counter pressure to teach evolution (Tatina 1989).

However, if assortative hiring results in frequent matches between teachers' personal sentiments and that of their communities, parents and local groups may not see a need to try to overtly influence the curriculum and classroom practices of teachers. Thus, we need to examine teacher reports of pressure in the context of their local political cultures.

In order to get teachers' perspectives on the pressure they may have experienced from the community, we asked a series of questions asking if they had ever received pressure about teaching evolution (both pressure to teach it *and* pressure not to) and creationism or intelligent design (again, pressure to either teach it or not). For each of these four possibilities, we probed about the source of the pressure, asking specifically about school board members, school administrators, parents, and local religious leaders, along with a residual category for other sources of pressure. The results from this portion of our survey are presented in Table 8.4, which reports the percentage of all teachers who reported a specific kind of pressure from a particular source.

The most striking pattern in teachers' reports is that pressure is infrequent. Only 33% of teachers checked at least one of the twenty options available on the questionnaire, and these are roughly evenly distributed across the pro- and anti-evolution categories. One teacher recounted to us, "I feel lucky to teach in a district where evolution has yet to be a big issue. I also feel lucky that my colleagues in the science department share my convictions about evolution being the key to understanding biology as a whole. Questions have occasionally arisen from students or parents, but we have never had an ongoing debate

Table 8.4. Teacher reports of pressure on what to teach, from specific community sources

	Source of pressure				
Direction of pressure	Administrator (%)	Local religious leader (%)	Parent (%)	School board member (%)	Other (%)
Pro-evolution pressure:					
To teach evolution	5	0	1	2	10
To **not** teach creationism or ID	4	1	3	2	6
Anti-evolution pressure:					
To teach creationism or ID	1	3	9	2	4
To **not** teach evolution	2	3	11	2	4

Note: Entries are the percentage of all teachers surveyed ($N = 926$) who reported a particular kind of pressure from a specific source.

with any group within or outside of the school and community." The data suggest that this teacher's experience is typical of the large majority of teachers nationwide.

The pressures reported by teachers were roughly balanced between those generally in the pro-evolution direction and those generally from individuals hostile to evolution. About 5% of teachers reported that an administrator or school board member encouraged them to teach evolution or not teach intelligent design, presumably trying to keep these teachers' practices consistent with the official curriculum. For example, a Pennsylvania teacher in a predominantly cosmopolitan school district reports to us, "Logically, a scientist looks at both sides of an issue. My principal refused to allow me to introduce intelligent design although there is a state standard that reads about opposing ideas to evolution."[3] And a Tennessee teacher in a district with high numbers of both well educated and conservative Protestant citizens told us, "I have had one student complain about [my teaching] creationism and of course I was paid a visit by one of my administrators to stop what I am doing."

We see also that 10% of teachers report pro-evolution pressures from "other sources." Unfortunately, few teachers specified these

---

[3] This teacher is mistaken about Pennsylvania's standards, which contains no language suggesting that the state encourages the discussion of "opposing views."

"other" sources, but we speculate that these include professional colleagues both in and outside of their school. One teacher from a highly traditional district in Georgia talked about more general pressure, "My personal opinion is that as a science educator, I should teach my students to always investigate, and to research all possible explanations. I do not agree that I am forbidden to discuss Intelligent Design or creation. I should be able to present my students w/facts covering both evolution and intelligent design and then allow my students to reach their own decision. We are pressured by both the state and the textbook to teach evolution as if it is a 'Law' or fact instead of as a theory." Yet this kind of experience represents but a small portion – no more than 20% – of the teachers that either explicitly teach creationism or provide only minimal coverage of evolution.

On the other side, we see that most pressure to either cut back on coverage of evolution or to teach creationism or intelligent design comes from parents rather than from administrators or religious leaders. All told, about 15% of our teachers reported receiving pressure with an anti-evolution or pro-creationism message from parents. One Ohio teacher, currently serving as department head, reports "two phone calls of concern that we were not going to teach intelligent design." And a Nevada teacher recounts, "About 5 years ago a student I had the year before came to talk to me about intelligent design one afternoon. He had a video he wanted me to watch. He also wanted to know if I would show the video to my students. I don't believe ID is a science and so I politely declined. The young man must have contacted the principal because the principal wanted to know why I wouldn't show the video. I had to write him a letter explaining my view on why I teach Evolution through Natural Selection but not by ID." Several teachers reported instances of communication from parents in various forms. A New York educator explains, "Over the years I have had letters/notes from parents condemning my teaching evolution, origin of life." And another teacher from New York: "Though we have some students that do not accept evolution, the teaching of evolution is rarely the subject of parent or community complaint. This year the other teacher did receive, in his school mailbox, an unsigned letter supposedly from some community organization asking him to mend his ways and cease leading youth astray by emphasizing evolution."

Table 8.5. Summary of teacher reports of pressure about teaching evolution or creationism

	Number of teachers	Percent
Teachers who report no pressure of any kind	615	66
Teachers reporting only pro-evolution pressure	111	12
Teachers reporting only anti-evolution pressure	116	13
Teachers reporting pressure in both directions	84	9
Total	926	100

When we combine these results, we can summarize the direction of pressures experienced by teachers. This is shown in Table 8.5.

Given our early analysis based on the traditionalism–cosmopolitanism continuum, we might expect that pro-evolution pressure would be most common in communities with the largest number of highly educated respondents, whereas anti-evolution pressures would be reported most by teachers in communities with large fundamentalist populations. However, this turns out not to be the case. Table 8.6 cross-tabulates our summary of reported pressures by the type of community. Reading down the columns, we can see that teachers in *mixed* communities actually report more instances of being pressured than those in the more homogeneous cosmopolitan or traditional areas.

Table 8.6. The association between community traditionalism and teacher reports of pressure

	Most cosmopolitan districts (N = 136) (%)	Somewhat cosmopolitan (N = 350) (%)	Somewhat traditional (N = 296) (%)	Most traditional districts (N = 139) (%)
Teachers who report no pressure of any kind	74	63	64	74
Teachers reporting only pro-evolution pressure	12	12	13	10
Teachers reporting only anti-evolution pressure	7	14	14	9
Teachers reporting pressure in both directions	7	10	10	6
	100%	100%	100%	100%

This apparent paradox is actually consistent with the literature on street-level bureaucracy. To understand why we do not see more pressure applied in the more extreme communities, we need to appreciate several key points. As we have seen, teachers actively try to assess their classroom environment and respect the sensibilities of their students, while at the same time finding the right combination of teaching in accord with their personal beliefs and the curricular expectations set by others. Second, with some rare exceptions notwithstanding, very few teachers want to deliberately provoke controversy. This makes doing their job difficult and will draw the attention of their principal, superintendent, and school board members – thereby jeopardizing the autonomy they enjoy in the classroom.

Indeed, our open-ended interviews provide many accounts of teachers being cognizant of their environment and eager to avoid controversy. An Illinois teacher tells us that her "students have almost all been raised in tightly knit church groups and I'm afraid if I pushed evolution they wouldn't listen to anything else I try to teach them." A teacher in neighboring Indiana tells us that his students are seemingly "programmed to hate anything that is about 'evolution.' So I teach my same lessons but use careful wording. We have a large Apostolic Christian Community that will not allow discussion on evolution." More typically, a California educator explains that she has "never had a serious problem but I do tread very carefully and respectfully."

Yet, avoiding controversy requires having a good understanding of community sentiment. Lipsky argued that, in the absence of a strong consensus, communities will send ambiguous signals to street-level bureaucrats and administrators, leaving public employees uncertain about how to manage community sentiment. A lack of consensus may reflect indifference, and this is likely to be common on most curricular issues. But evolution is different: a lack of consensus may instead represent a community that is polarized rather than indifferent – making it especially difficult for teachers to avoid practices that provoke elements in the community.

In this view, it is the teachers' actions that generate overt pressures – translating latent public opinion into complaints to supervisors, office visits, angry letters, and confrontations at open houses. To show that this is the case, we report summaries of teaching practices broken down by the kinds of pressures received by teachers. If overt pressures

Table 8.7. Teaching practices by the kinds of pressures reported

	Mean hours devoted to evolution	Mean score on NAS support scale	Percent endorsing creationism (%)
Teachers who report no pressure of any kind (N = 615)	13.2	53.1	19
Teachers reporting only pro-evolution pressure (N = 111)	13.8	49.4	16
Teachers reporting only anti-evolution pressure (N = 116)	15.2	67.5	9
Teachers reporting pressure in both directions (N = 84)	16.1	59.8	15
Total	13.8	55.0	17

influenced teaching, we would see that those reporting pressure to teach evolution would devote more hours to it and those pressured to teach creationism would be more likely to do so. In fact, Table 8.7 shows just the opposite. Those who receive pressure to devote more time to evolution and/or less time to creationism are precisely those teachers who teach less evolution than average, are least likely to teach in accord with the scientific establishment, and most likely to endorse creationism in the classroom. And we see the opposite pattern for those reporting anti-evolution pressure – pressure is received precisely by those who teach evolution more rigorously. We should emphasize that the statistical association is not especially strong and remind readers that pressure is infrequent. Nevertheless, the correlation suggests that teacher decisions stimulate community responses rather than the community based pressures altering teacher behavior.

COMMUNITY SENTIMENT

Taken together, these various analyses suggest that overt pressure on teachers is rare because many teachers' beliefs fit into the prevailing culture of their communities (assortative hiring) and because teachers learn ways of doing their job without provoking controversy, especially when they teach in communities with a strong pro-evolution or anti-evolution consensus.

The answers to our open-ended questions show that one strategy of conflict avoidance is to avoid language that is likely to inflame local passions. A number of teachers explained how they use "change over time" instead of the "E-word," for example. Others addressed potential conflict head on, by devoting the first portion of their class to a discussion of the nature of science, and the different domains of science and religion. Still others, we saw, emphasized that students should be pragmatic and learn the material for the purpose of passing examinations.

But can the nature of the community influence teaching in other, potentially more fundamental, ways? That is, do teachers accommodate local opinion subtly and voluntarily by altering the time devoted to evolution, the themes they emphasize, or in the likelihood of introducing creationist ideas into the classroom? If so, we should expect that the religious and educational composition of the community should influence teaching practices above and beyond any self-selection affects based on credentials, prior training in evolution, and personal beliefs. Certainly teachers are aware of their political environments – often cued by the behavior of their students. For example, one teacher said:

> I've taught in both Illinois and Colorado and seen a big difference in how the teaching of evolution is viewed by students and parents in the two different states. In Illinois I've taught in the suburbs of Chicago where there have been no issues raised in regards to the subject matter. There is the occasional question of how I see creationism fitting in and the questions are presented in an open manner. I taught in a town of 100,000+ in western Colorado. Here I encountered a higher percentage of students who were resistant to even having evolution presented as a theory. I had several students write correct answers to test questions but add Bible quotes to interject their beliefs.

And this teacher from Virginia: "I teach in a very conservative area–Baptist mostly–so it is an interesting tightrope." And, a Tennessee teacher in one of the most evangelical communities in the nation said, "Many semesters I receive 'gifts' from students during the evolution units. i.e. Religious tracts hidden where I will find them. A few Bibles over the years, open to specific passages and highlighted. Invitation to churches and Sunday School. Requests to be placed on prayer lists or visited by local ministers. Written rebuttals by 'knowledgeable' youth pastors and Sunday School teachers."

But does an understanding of local political culture actually influence teaching? Only a few teachers admitted that it did, as in the case of a Tennessee teacher whose instinct was to engage her students but eventually decided to devote less time to the details of evolutionary biology. "I live in Tennessee and we do have many comments like 'I do not come from a monkey.' Parents have not complained about the way we handle evolution and we keep the discussion to a minimum. We ask the students to keep an open mind while studying this topic and they usually do. I am inclined to try and discuss the subject in more detail so kids will quit thinking evolution means we come from monkeys, but apparently that could provoke parental issues." But most teachers did not admit to substantially changing the content of their instruction, but instead used careful and diplomatic language. For instance, the Indiana teacher quoted above who teaches in a community with a large Apostolic Christian population hostile to evolution explains that he uses "'change over time' instead of the word evolution, and surprisingly most are OK with that... So I teach my same lessons but use careful wording."

Beyond these anecdotes, however, the question remains as to whether diffuse community sentiment – absent direct pressure and after accounting for assortative hiring – influences teaching behavior. To answer this question empirically, we return to multivariate models, which can account for other influences we have identified in this chapter. As independent variables, we include all the factors that we employed when modeling teaching practices in the previous chapter, including all factors that may be related to assortative hiring. We then add measures of the religious composition of the county and the educational composition of the school district. The results for models predicting the amount and emphasis of evolution teaching are reported in Table 8.8, and the key variables measuring the characteristics of the local community appear near the bottom of the table.

The models show that local context has a small but statistically significant impact on teaching practices, even after accounting for factors that we have already linked to assortative hiring. The first model

Table 8.8. Ordinary least squares regression models assessing the impact of local religious and educational context on teaching practices

	Predicting hours of evolution (N = 849)			Predicting NAS endorsement (N = 872)		
	B	SE	t	B	SE	t
Standards Index 2007	.20	.34	.59	**1.74**	1.02	1.70
Seniority (centered)	**−.59**	.23	−2.58	**−1.41**	.70	−2.00
Standards × Seniority	**−.52**	.20	−2.62	−.26	.44	−.58
Believes there is no test	.20	.65	.31	1.03	1.63	.63
−Standards × Believes no test	−.21	.69	−.31	−1.66	1.77	−.94
Teacher is female	**−.52**	.16	−3.26	**−1.29**	.74	−1.74
Credits earned in biology (0–2)	.48	.45	1.05	−1.22	1.60	−.76
Science degrees (0–2)	−.49	.39	−1.25	.46	.81	.56
Completed evolution class	**2.36**	.60	3.97	**4.92**	1.66	2.96
Has normal certification	−.41	.77	−.54	−.52	2.37	−.22
Identifies as scientist	1.49	1.27	1.17	1.40	2.88	.49
Self-rated expertise (−1 to +2)	**2.23**	.45	4.97	**8.43**	1.73	4.87
Young earth believer	**−2.26**	.91	−2.48	**−28.50**	2.99	−9.52
Organic evolution believer	**1.34**	.67	2.00	**9.21**	1.89	4.88
Did not answer belief question	−.74	1.29	−.57	**−14.32**	6.14	−2.33
Conservative Protestant proportion	**−5.04**	2.62	−1.93	4.72	6.09	.77
Advanced degree proportion	**10.51**	5.85	1.80	**47.91**	13.62	3.52
Intercept	10.44	1.59	6.58	46.70	3.52	13.27
Adjusted R²	.16			.32		

Bold entries are significant in expected direction at .05 level.

shows that teachers in counties with large numbers of doctrinally conservative Protestants devote fewer class hours to evolution than other teachers. More specifically, the model suggests that teachers in a community with 28% conservative Christians (the 85th percentile) will teach about 1.25 fewer hours than an otherwise similar teacher in a community at the 15th percentile (4% doctrinally conservative Protestants). Similarly, teachers in highly educated school districts (12% holding advanced degrees) will devote roughly an additional hour to evolution compared with districts with lower levels of adult educational attainment (0.9 hours more). It is useful to emphasize that these contextual effects are above and beyond any impacts of teachers' personal beliefs and their credentials.

The second model shows a slightly different pattern. Here, we see no net impacts of the local religious environment and a small, but discernable, impact of the community's educational composition on teaching emphasis. Teachers in the most highly educated communities score about four points higher on our NAS scale than otherwise identical teachers in low education communities.[4]

In Table 8.9, we report our analysis of whether teachers introduce creationism into the classroom in a positive way. Our dependent variable is a simple indicator scored 1 if the teacher reported *both* that they devote an hour or more to creationism and that they endorse this as a valid scientific alternative – either themselves or by referring to "many reputable scientists" – and a 0 for all other teachers. The independent variables are the same as in the previous models, and we estimate effects with logistic regression. The results show *no context effects* for teaching creationism. The substantial geographic variation in teaching creationism that we saw in Table 8.3 appears not to be a result of subtle community influences but largely due to the mechanisms that connect young earth teachers with highly traditional communities. And once in place, teachers motivated to introduce creationism into the classroom seem uninfluenced by the prevailing cultural community in which they work.

---

[4] We should emphasize that high-quality national data on religious composition is only available at the county level. No doubt, we would have identified substantially larger effects of religion if we could have measured at the level of school district. But, even if we have underestimated religion's impact, we have shown that it is quite relevant.

Table 8.9. Logistic regression model assessing the impacts of local religious and educational context on the teaching of creationism

	Predicting any creationist teaching (N = 872)			
	Logistic regression estimate	Odds ratio	SE	t
Standards Index 2007	−.13	.88	.09	−1.42
Seniority (centered)	.19	1.21	.11	1.73
Standards × Seniority	−.17	.84	.08	−2.03
Believes there is no test	.01	1.01	.20	.07
Standards × Believes no test	**.61**	1.84	.17	3.56
Teacher is female	−.29	.75	.18	−1.65
Credits earned in biology (0–2)	.02	1.02	.15	.12
Science degrees (0–2)	.14	1.15	.13	1.08
Completed evolution class	−.32	.73	.25	−1.28
Has normal certification	.38	1.46	.33	1.15
Identifies as scientist	.41	1.50	.40	1.02
Self-rated expertise (−1 to +2)	−.15	.86	.14	−1.06
Young earth believer	**1.37**	3.93	.20	6.94
Organic evolution believer	**−1.33**	.27	.34	−3.85
Did not answer belief question	**.96**	2.61	.37	2.59
Conservative Protestant proportion	.19	1.21	.60	.32
Advanced degree proportion of population	−.41	.66	3.23	−.13
Intercept	−1.98		.54	−3.65
Pseudo R^2	.14			

Bold entries are significant in expected direction at .05 level.

SUMMARY AND DISCUSSION

Frederick Mosher, in the introduction to his book about the public bureaucracy and democracy (1982), argues that the capabilities, orientation, and values of the unelected bureaucrats are shaped by their background, training, and education. He asks whether "a public service so constituted" can be made to operate in a "manner compatible with democracy?"

Principle agent models have addressed this question from a top–down perspective, focusing largely on how principles structure legislation and policy discretion to keep their agents in line. These models address our question of "who decides?" by assessing how teachers, as agents of the state education departments and local school boards, implement curricular decisions made by the state and codified in state standards. Our analysis in Chapter 5 showed that there is a great deal of variation across our teachers; in Chapter 6, we showed that they are not particularly responsive to standards. In line with principle agent models, however, we demonstrate that high-stakes tests can make a difference in some cases, and more generally that some teachers are more responsive to these state-level guidelines than are others.

In Chapter 7, we showed that, when top–down controls do not operate, teachers acting as street-level bureaucrats are strongly influenced by their personal values. Yet we should not conclude too quickly that teachers acting on their own demonstrates a lack of democratic responsiveness. Indeed, Kenneth Meier and his colleagues (e.g., Meier and O'Toole 2006) argue that popular control is most effectively achieved not from the top but from the bottom–up, when bureaucracies are responsive to the clientele and communities they serve.

In this chapter, we find multiple mechanisms of this bottom–up democratic control. We drew upon our understanding of the social bases of the evolution wars, which showed that the major social cleavages are rooted in education and religion. This allowed us to rank communities according to two criteria: (1) by the percentage of adults who are affiliated with doctrinally conservative Protestant churches (often referred to as fundamentalist or evangelical in popular writings), and (2) by the percentage of adults who have earned a graduate or professional degree. As a shorthand, we referred to the most highly educated settings as "cosmopolitan" and those with relatively large conservative Protestant populations as "traditional." This simple classification of communities turned out to be a very powerful way of understanding community context and its implications for the science instruction received by high school students.

We found evidence that teachers are much like the communities they serve. The most traditional communities tend to employ teachers with somewhat less formal training in biology, who are less likely to have majored in a scientific field, and less likely to have completed a university-level class in evolution. The personal beliefs of teachers in the most traditional communities are varied – but tilt heavily in the direction of young earth creationism. This combination of beliefs and formal training creates a very high probability that students in such communities will receive a scientific education that departs substantially from the ideal curriculum envisioned by members of the National Academy of Sciences, National Research Council and other major scientific organizations. The students in such communities are also quite likely to encounter teachers who *emphasize* that creationism is a valid scientific alternative to evolutionary biology.

Most students in the more cosmopolitan communities have quite a different experience. Their biology teachers are far more likely to have extensive coursework in biology and in evolution in particular. The likelihood of being taught by a teacher who personally believes in a young earth is essentially zero. And the likelihood of their teacher legitimizing creationism is low (but, at 10%, still of concern to many).

The bureaucracy, in other words, is in many places representative of the public it serves, at least in terms of the values critical to their exercise of discretion. But this bottom–up control occurs in other ways too. Most educators teach in communities with more diverse populations – where the balance among traditionalists and cosmopolitans is not heavily tipped in one direction or another. These teachers receive more ambiguous cues from the community and report receiving somewhat more pressure to teach one way or the other – sometimes feeling pressure from both sides of the conflict. Yet wherever they teach, educators seem well aware of their community, are sensitive to possible reactions from students, and actively seek to teach in ways that reduce the likelihood of controversy. The teachers decide, we found in Chapter 7, but so too does the local community.

9 The Battle for America's Classrooms

Maybe down the road, when science can answer all questions (which in my opinion will never happen), the "Intelligent Designer" hypothesis will be put to rest and all religious institutions will crumble out of existence.

Florida Teacher (2007)[1]

Every modern discussion of man's future, the population explosion, the struggle for existence, the purpose of man and the universe, and man's place in nature rests on Darwin.

Biologist Ernst Mayr in the preface to Darwin's *Origin of the Species* (1974)

Well did God make man in a breath of holy fire
Or did he crawl on up out of the muck and mire

Bruce Springsteen, *Part Man, Part Monkey* (1998)

THE EVOLUTION–CREATION WARS of the past ninety years are a familiar feature of the political landscape. So familiar that it is easy to think of this conflict as both normal and inevitable. But even the most cursory examination of other nations shows that this political conflict is distinctly American. Its emergence in the 1920s as a salient culture war was a result of the fragmentation of American Protestantism, the professionalization of science, and the rapid expansion of public education.

---

[1] The teacher provided this quotation as part of completing the National Survey of High School Biology Teachers. Ernst Mayr wrote this in his preface to the 1974 edition of the *Origin of Species*. Bruce Springsteen's quotation is from the lyrics to his *Part Man, Part Monkey*, released in the 1998 album "Tracks."

The evolution–creation war of the 1920s remains with us today – changed in some ways but remarkably similar in others. The continuity is a result of several factors. Of great importance is the fact that the earliest political opposition to evolution was transformed into a social movement. Sustained by its own anti-evolution associations and by religious organizations, anti-evolutionism became institutionalized. Over many decades, the movement retained the resources to support speaking tours by its most charismatic orators, built large membership bases that provided financial contributions, and disseminated its ideas via pamphlets, books, broadcasts, internet sites, and research institutes. Associated with specific faith traditions, anti-evolutionism has also been sustained by support from an array of churches and seminaries. Simultaneously, the professionalization and growth of science provided an institutional home for proponents of evolution. Today's scientific organizations have large bureaucracies, public relations offices, and a lobbying presence in the halls of power.

Organizations on both sides of the culture war provided communications apparatuses for spreading new arguments and for motivating core constituencies. Their most visible activities provided symbols that promoted cohesion among otherwise far-flung individuals or congregations. Thus, religious and scientific organizations have institutionalized the conflict. In some cases, the mission to battle one's opponent was passed from generation to generation, creating continuity.

This conflict has been further institutionalized within the American party system. We have noted that three serious Republican candidates for president in 2008 acknowledged that they do not accept evolution. On the other side, antifundamentalism has found a home in the Democratic Party. Thus, as the two major political parties have become increasingly polarized along social, cultural, and religious lines, the issue has mapped comfortably onto this cleavage.

A second factor promoting continuity of the evolution–creation war is the highly decentralized system of public education in the United States. America's federal system places responsibility for public education with each of the fifty states, almost all of which engage in second-order devolution by giving substantial autonomy to the more than 10,000 school districts that directly govern and finance public schools.[2] This fragmentation of governance, combined with the federal courts' role adjudicating claims related to civil rights and civil liberties, creates thousands of potential arenas of conflict – from the fifty state legislatures and their corresponding departments and boards of education, through the thousands of school boards, and on down to individual schools and classrooms. Moreover, federal court decisions typically provide only partial victories to one side or the other – which usually spur innovation by the losing side (usually anti-evolutionists) to reframe their policies so that they achieve similar ends without running afoul of the Constitution.

In addition, public opinion concerning evolution remains remarkably stable. Since the very first opinion polls on evolution in the early 1980s, scientists have published thousands of scientific papers that have fleshed out the details of evolution and have reported fossil discoveries that filled important gaps in the scientific record. The evidence consistent with a very old earth, of diverse contemporary species having common ancestors, and of human origins in earlier primates is much stronger now than a quarter century ago. And yet, U.S. public opinion has hardly changed. As in 1982, more Americans today prefer the teaching of creationism to the teaching of evolution, although the largest numbers of citizens support the inclusion of both approaches.

Taken together, federalism, the devolution of responsibilities to school districts, the strong organizational structures supporting each side in the conflict, the mapping of the issue on one of the fundamental cleavages in the American party system, and the stability of public opinion all suggest that the battle for America's classrooms will continue in the future. These features of the U.S. political landscape have provided the oxygen that has allowed the evolution–creation fires to burn for nearly a century.

The fuel for the fire, however, is the intensity of opinion on both sides, a result of the perceived stakes of winning or losing in the long run. The Florida teacher quoted at the beginning of this chapter exemplifies one element of intensity. At some intellectual level, this teacher acknowledges the possibility that scientific evidence might eventually

---

[2] Only Hawaii does not devolve educational governance to smaller geographic locales.

show that the intelligent design thesis is wrong. But he also fears that, if evolution were decisively proven, "all religious institutions will crumble out of existence." In the end, this creates too much dissonance, and the teacher continues, "But I believe that science will never be able to answer everything, simply because the 'Intelligent Designer' will not allow it."

This teacher illustrates the challenge that scientists face in the popular war of ideas. The anti-evolution movement's birth coincided with – indeed was central to – the development of the fundamentalist religious movement in the United States, and so long as many citizens view acceptance of evolution as a test of their faith in God, public education efforts will have only limited impact. If scientists are not likely to win the battle of ideas among ordinary citizens, they should instead pay close attention to what goes on in the American science classroom.

WHO DECIDES?

This long-standing conflict has become intertwined with American popular culture, politics, and intellectual life. Indeed, even Bruce Springsteen has something to say. At a concert in neighboring New Jersey shortly before the start of the *Kitzmiller v. Dover* intelligent design trial, the rock superstar told the crowd: "Folks in Dover aren't sure about evolution. Here in New Jersey, we're counting on it."[3] As political scientists, we believe we have brought another perspective to this issue, one that focuses on a question central to every court case and nearly every state-level and local controversy: who decides?

This is a central question – perhaps *the* central question – in political science. In a democratic system, the people, at least to some extent, should decide. But democratic theorists recognize as well the need for two counterweights to majority rule. The first is the protection of constitutional rights. Civil liberties are especially important when the rights of minorities are threatened by majoritarian impulses. And

---

[3] Judge John Jones III conveyed this anecdote in a public lecture at Penn State University on December 1, 2009. There are several versions of it; one can be found in an ACLU blog: http://aclupa.blogspot.com/2008/08boss-hearts-dover.htm1 (accessed December 22, 2009).

courts have been clear that alternatives to evolution cannot be separated from efforts to unconstitutionally establish religion in the public schools.

The second counterweight lies in the need for policies to be shaped by informed expertise. Andrew Jackson tried to democratize the public bureaucracy, and the Progressives tried to depoliticize it. Political scientists have therefore paid close attention to the proper role of professional, educated, and at times autonomous public servants in a democratic system – thus, our intense attention to the teachers. We refer to them at points in our text as street-level bureaucrats, but this is certainly not intended to denigrate their professionalism and contributions. Rather, it allows us to focus systematically on their role as public servants, serving what many see as among the most responsive public institutions in American political life – the local public schools.

Throughout this book, we have sought to determine who decides what students will learn. Public opinion, as noted, has been stable and largely antagonistic to the complete omission of evolution alternatives in the classroom. But it also varies across the states and school districts. We see responsiveness to this opinion at two levels: among the state policy makers who write state standards and through assortative hiring, representative bureaucracy, and pressure among teachers at the local level. It is only by looking at responsiveness at these two levels that we can piece together an accurate account of who really decides.

We find considerable responsiveness, but it is not absolute. By separating the policy process into the development of standards and the implementation of curricula in the classroom, we gain insights into what happens when public opinion does not rule. Experts matter a great deal, and we find evidence in our statistical models that their importance is shaping evolution policy at the state level. And courts, of course, have increasingly limited the available policy space within which policy can be responsive to public opinion.

But most importantly, we find that teachers decide. For some, these decisions are shaped by state standards. But we also find considerable evidence that their decisions are based on their own training, confidence, and personal values. Scientists and other proponents of science-based science education are, we believe, well advised to pay more attention to teachers: what they know, what they believe, and what they teach.

TEACHERS: PAST AS PROLOGUE

From the pro-evolution perspective, John Scopes, Don Aguillard, Susan Epperson, and the science teachers in Dover, Pennsylvania, are often portrayed as iconic educators who challenged anti-evolution legislation. From the anti-evolution perspective, teachers who seek to teach creationism, such as John Peloza, Ray Webster, Rodney LeVake, and Roger DeHart, are not so much iconic heroes as they are martyrs in a just cause – educators who suffered consequences for challenging the prevailing scientific orthodoxy. Our data show that these cultural images are quite atypical of the nation's science teachers. Most teach not only without controversy, but without any explicit pressure from school administrators, public officials, parents, or community leaders. Many struggle to balance their state curricular mandates with their personal and professional convictions, sometimes balancing this with a concern for how their students will fare on standardized tests. In this struggle, few teachers court controversy; quite the contrary, the most common theme emerging from teachers' responses was that they are highly attuned to the sensibilities of their students and seek to adapt their teaching goals to their environment.

As in the case of other kinds of street-level civil servants, we found that it is the values of individual teachers that most of all determine the *de facto* public policy in the nation's public schools. Absent consistent monitoring, strong controls, and sanctions, most teachers are free to teach what they believe is best, constrained only by their desire to avoid controversy. The result is an enormous variety of teaching approaches to evolution even when teachers are supposed to be guided by the same standards and assessment tests.

Teachers' approaches to teaching evolution are diverse. About one-fifth see their goal as to not merely teach the standards and textbook material, but to go out of their way to champion the idea that evolution is a scientific fact – in effect, that there is no "controversy" to teach. In stark contrast, nearly one-fifth undermine the conclusions of evolution biology by explicitly telling students that they believe (or "many prominent scientists believe") that creationism or intelligent design is a "valid scientific alternative" to evolution. From a political perspective, this suggests that establishment science and anti-evolution opponents have each managed to control about one in five classrooms in the nation's public schools.

Among the anti-evolution teachers, many appear to be hard-core creationists who are unabashed in their criticism of evolutionary biology. Others may be genuinely ambivalent and troubled by the contradictions between their faith and their knowledge of science and their solution is often to teach "both sides" and let students consider the evidence and make up their own minds.

What these approaches all have in common, however, is the abdication of science as a superior form of reason about the natural world and a rejection of the idea that science and faith speak to distinct and nonoverlapping domains. Unlike many teachers who believe that their faith in God is consistent with the methods, findings, and conclusions of evolutionary biology, other educators who "teach the controversy" are telling students that they may make up their own minds by ignoring scientific evidence and the conclusions of university-based scientists without sacrificing an accurate view of nature and natural history. Indeed, the equation of evolution with a political philosophy – something that can be debated largely in terms of personally held values – seriously undermines the legitimacy of science.

And what of the other 60% of teachers? Among them, we also see evidence of a political stalemate. Some teach a watered-down version of evolution – sometimes because they lack the training in evolution that would give them confidence to deal with skepticism, and sometimes because they deliberately avoid controversy and steer clear of terms and specific topics that they believe might provoke reactions from their students or parents. Some of these teachers avoid discussions of creationism, but nevertheless also undermine the legitimacy of science by placating their students and encouraging them to only learn the material for the purpose of passing a test or being better prepared to debate with their enemies. Students are smart enough to pick up the message underlying such advice.

Whatever the specifics, however, watered-down instruction in evolution could very well contribute to maintaining the status quo and help explain the remarkable stability in public opinion. If teachers have been cautious rather than enthusiastic in their presentation of science, we should not be surprised that rising education levels in the last twenty-five years have not been accompanied by increasing support for teaching evolution in the nation's schools or increasing acceptance of human evolution.

Finally, the characteristics of teachers not only contribute to the stability of public opinion generally but also to the over-time reproduction of the social and geographic divisions that characterize the evolution–creation wars. *Assortative hiring* – the tendency for cosmopolitan districts to hire the most enthusiastic supporters of evolution and for traditional districts to hire teachers who are skeptical about human evolution – means that students are unlikely to be challenged to think about perspectives that are different from those in their prevailing culture. Thus, the distribution of teachers contributes to strengthening the geographic contours of this contemporary culture war.

Throughout our work on this project, skeptics and supporters alike have asked, "but is this just about the south?" Living and writing just a bit more than 100 miles away from Dover, we often chuckle, but we turn to the data as well. Certainly at the state level, opinion toward evolution shows predictable regional patterns; although the strong support for teaching "both sides," even in New England and the coasts, may surprise many. But our data on assortative hiring and the match between teachers' personal values and those of their communities is analyzed at the community level. Traditional communities, like Dover, are found in every state, as are cosmopolitan communities, like State College – home to Penn State. Yet, even in the most cosmopolitan communities, students have a one in ten chance of encountering a biology teacher who endorses creationism.

THE FUTURE OF THE POLITICAL BATTLE

How will the evolution–creation battle unfold in the coming decades? Our research suggests a number of arenas in which we think conflict is likely. It also points to potential strategies that activists might pursue in the coming decades as they continually seek to gain an edge over their opponents.

One important arena of conflict will be the state boards of education. The standards movement that overtook educational policy in the late 1990s is, if anything, accelerating. Most states require that their standards be evaluated, modified, and reapproved every five to ten years. This sets up potential venues of conflict and debate on a regular basis. Moreover, as more and more states implement high-stakes tests for science, the content of the standards will be viewed as increasingly consequential.

We showed that the content of state standards in the year 2000 reflected public opinion. But the nation's major science organizations were successful in encouraging many states to redraft their standards, so that, by 2007, many more reflected the goals and priorities of the scientific establishment. This ebb and flow of majoritarian democracy and guardianship is characteristic of earlier waves in the battle as well: the elimination of evolution from textbooks in the 1920s and 1930s, the Sputnik era reforms of science curriculum, and the grass roots backlash to the NSF-sponsored textbooks in the 1970s. There is no reason to believe that these cycles will not continue in the future, with sustained efforts by both sides to win the upper hand in determining how evolution figures into each state's official curricular goals. But what forms will political conflict take in the coming decades?

We see two emerging trends that may be especially important to the outcomes of these battles. One is the potential role of business and industry in the process of developing science standards. There is at least anecdotal evidence that the business community can play a role in encouraging standards that tilt more toward the scientific establishment than to majority opinion. For example, Jacobs (2006) sees businesses' involvement as having played an important role in the development of "great" standards in three states. The process of globalization may accelerate this trend as increased global competition gives business more leverage to specify the types of training it expects of its workforce. To the extent that a forthright treatment of evolution is seen as promoting an understanding of the nature of science generally, businesses that depend on a scientifically literate workforce may support reforms promoted by the major scientific societies. Likewise, modern corporate executives may not want their home states to be subject to ridicule in the way that Kansas was during the 1990s.

The second trend to watch is specific to the standards movement itself. At this writing, forty-six states have banded together to produce a common set of standards for mathematics and reading (McNeil

2009). If this experiment comes to fruition, it will be logical for many to propose a common science curriculum for the nation as a whole. Such a process, in which the educational bureaucrats from forty or more states negotiate among themselves, could lead to any number of outcomes. On the one hand, such a conference of bureaucrats would be more insulated from public sentiment than their individual state boards of education. This suggests the possibility of standards that are at odds with public preferences. On the other hand, the process of gaining consensus among the representatives of such a diverse range of states could lead to standards that represent the lowest common denominator and the avoidance of anything that might be controversial. And we would expect such a battle to be joined by the two major political parties; indeed, proposed national history standards contributed to mobilization of the Republican Party during the 1994 election. But whatever the outcome, such a process could have a major impact on the standards in the fifty states.

Of course, we demonstrated that standards have only minimal impact on instruction today, and there are a number of reasons to think this will continue. Science may never become a high-stakes subject, such as math or reading, so that its assessment tests may never carry the same consequences for students and schools in much of the nation. Seniority and tenure may continue to protect experienced teachers from sanctions when they depart from proscribed curricula. And the constant churning of standards and assessment – the same feature that ensures regular periods of controversy at boards of education – may continue to promote confusion among teachers about what standards actually include.

On the other hand, we examined teaching practices in a period of enormous flux. Most states with exams had deployed them for only a few years, and in some cases the exams were still being rolled out. And in the initial phase of the standards movement, many state documents underwent radical rewriting. As standards and assessment become more institutionalized, it is possible that revisions will be more incremental, promoting consensus among teachers about what is actually expected of their students. And once assessment tests have been in place for many years, teachers may grow accustomed to "teach to the test." Thus, it is possible that standards in the future will have more bite than they do today. Indeed, with more stable standards, we might later come to see that the impact of seniority was not so much a career stage effect but a generational one. That is, today's younger teachers may continue to teach to standards as they mature.

FUTURE BATTLES FOR THE NATION'S CLASSROOMS: TEACHERS AT THE CENTER?

The crucial role played by teachers suggests that political actors on both sides will focus on teachers as a way to influence how policies are actually implemented in the classroom. This is not unique to the teaching of evolution, of course. For example, efforts to increase the formal education of teachers were central to the No Child Left Behind (NCLB) Law, which would have sanctioned schools if they failed to have a sufficient number of "highly qualified" teachers. NCLB also mandated high-stakes testing as a means of influencing the choices that teachers make, and thereby limiting their discretion as street-level bureaucrats.

Consistent with these past efforts, we can expect that the major scientific organizations will urge states to increase the requirements for new science teachers – encouraging more teachers to complete rigorous courses of study in biology while training to be future educators. Our analyses suggest that the single most important change would be to require all new biology teachers to have completed an evolution course while in college. Although the causal impact of this may be less than suggested by our models, a side effect of such a policy might be to discourage some conservative Protestant undergraduates from pursuing a career of teaching biology altogether – an effect that would change the balance of creationists and evolution believers among the ranks of teachers.

Indeed, one may imagine efforts to implement this not only through public policy – which may be quite difficult – but through lobbying college departments of biology to all require an evolution course for all biology majors. The challenges to such a proposal, however, are formidable. States may be comfortable specifying teacher certification requirements in broad terms (number of credits, amount of in-service teaching, and broad categories of training) but typically leave specific requirements to the individual colleges of education. Among these, many will not want to – or may be unable to afford to – require that all biology majors take a semester-long course in evolutionary biology. Smaller colleges in particular may not have the instructional expertise or scale needed to offer such a specific course. As a result, efforts in this direction are likely to be slow and uneven.

On the anti-evolution side, the emerging political strategy seems to be the emphasis of *academic freedom* for public school teachers. In particular, they seek laws that will protect the jobs, salaries, and working conditions of teachers who expose students to instruction critical of evolution. We saw that pro-evolution and anti-creationism pressure was most likely to come from administrators. Thus, those in the creationist or intelligent design camps would like to eliminate this pressure – allowing teachers to present evidence supporting intelligent design or creationism if, in their professional judgment, that evidence is germane to the curriculum. This strategy would have the effect of balancing any control over teachers that is enhanced by high-stakes testing.

In this, we have an ironic reversal of principals during the last century. In the 1920s, it was John Scopes who symbolized the academic freedom argument, whereas anti-evolutionists like Bryan insisted that teachers should do as they were told by their employer, the state government. This would be a standard argument in the creationist repertoire through 1968, when this approach was dealt a decisive blow by the Supreme Court in *Epperson v. Arkansas*. Today, the roles are inverted. Those advocating a more rigorous approach to evolution in the public schools look to the state – its standards, its assessment tests, and its bureaucratic apparatus – to control teachers and at least nudge them toward more rigorous treatments. In this environment, it is creationist teachers who look to academic freedom as a protection against managerial oversight of their teaching and against potential sanctions. How far these arguments advance – both in state legislatures and in the inevitable challenges in appellate courts – remains to be seen.

The battle to control America's science classrooms, then, is far from over. In the first decade of the twenty-first century, we see that organized science has won almost all the crucial legal cases, but these have translated into a patchwork of mostly vague and cursory content standards across the states. And the few state standards that approach the ideals of the scientific establishment are not implemented consistently in classrooms. It was the rapid rise of educational enrollment that made the teaching of evolution really matter to ordinary citizens in the 1920s. And it is for quite similar reasons that classrooms remain the most crucial arena in the evolution–creationism war. Whether the official curriculum reflects majority wishes or the ideals of the scientific community, control of the nation's classrooms will depend on the training, values, and constraints placed on the nation's biology teachers – they will remain the central figures in the battle to control America's classrooms.

APPENDIX TO CHAPTER 2

A2.1: Documentation for Table 2.1

Sources and question wording:

Virginia Commonwealth University Life Sciences Survey (9/14/2005–9/29/2005) [Data provided directly by Survey and Research Evaluation Laboratory, Virginia Commonwealth University]

Regardless of what you may personally believe about the origin of biological life, which of the following do you believe should be taught in public schools? . . . Evolution only–evolution says that biological life developed over time from simple substances. Creationism only–creationism says that biological life was directly created by God in its present form at one point in time. Intelligent design only–intelligent design says that biological life is so complex that it required a powerful force or intelligent being to help create it. Or some combination of these?

[If "some combination"] *Which approaches do you think should be taught?*

Harris Interactive Poll (6/17/2005–6/21/2005) [Data acquired from the Odum Institute, University of North Carolina]

Regardless of what you may personally believe, which of these do you believe should be taught in public schools? . . . Evolution only: Evolution says that human beings evolved from earlier stages of animals. Creationism: Creationism says that human beings were created directly by God. Intelligent design only: Intelligent design says that human beings are so complex that they required a powerful force or intelligent being to help create them.

CCD/Williamsburg Charter Foundation Survey (12/1/1987–12/15/1987) [Data acquired from the American Religious Data Archive (ARDA), The Pennsylvania State University]

Do you think public schools should only teach the Bible's account of the creation of life on earth, or should they only teach evolution, or should they teach both?

NBC/Associated Press Poll (10/25/81–10/26/1981) [Data acquired from the Roper Center, University of Connecticut]

Do you think public schools should teach only the scientific theory of evolution, only the Biblical theory of creation, or should schools offer both theories?

A2.2: Documentation for Table 2.2 and Table 2.3

Sources and question wording:

University of North Carolina, Southern Focus Poll (2/4/1998–2/24/1998) [Data acquired from the Odum Institute, University of North Carolina]

Would you generally favor or oppose teaching creation along with evolution in public schools?

Gallup Poll (6/25/1999–6/27/1999) [Data acquired from the Roper Center, University of Connecticut]

I'm going to read a variety of proposals concerning religion and public schools. For each one, please tell me whether you would generally favor or oppose it....
   Teaching creation along with evolution in public schools.

CBS/New York Times Poll (11/18/04–11/21/04) [Data acquired from the Roper Center, University of Connecticut]

Newsweek Poll (12/2/04–12/3/04) [Data acquired from the Roper Center, University of Connecticut]

Pew Typology Callback Survey (3/17/05–3/27/05) [Data acquired from the Pew Research Center]

Pew Religion and Public Life Poll (7/7/05–7/17/05) [Data acquired from the Pew Research Center]

Pew Religion and Public Life Poll (7/6/06–7/19/06) [Data acquired from the Pew Research Center]

Would you generally favor or oppose teaching creation along with evolution in public schools?

Would you generally favor or oppose teaching creation instead of evolution in public schools?

A2.3: Method of creating a single measure from paired evolution questions used in Table 2.4 and Table 2.5

Starting in 1999, major polling organizations have employed a two-question format for assessing public opinion concerning the teaching of evolution in public schools. With some modest assumptions, the answers to these two questions can be combined into ordinal scales. Here is the logic for doing so.

The basic questions are:

"instead of" Would you generally favor or oppose teaching creation instead of evolution in public schools? (1 = yes, 2 = no, 9 = dk)

"along with" Would you generally favor or oppose teaching creation along with evolution in public schools? (1 = yes, 2 = no, 9 = dk)

Table A2.1. All response combinations of answers to "along with" and "instead of" questions (Illustration from 2005 Pew Callback poll)

	Number	%
0 Creation only	86	7.9
1 Creation along with <u>and</u> instead of	234	21.5
2 Teach both	344	31.6
3 Evolution only	252	23.1
19 Along with but DK Instead	49	4.5
29 Not along with but DK Instead	16	1.5
91 Instead but DK Along with	17	1.6
92 Not instead by DK Along with	15	1.4
99 DK both	77	7.1
Total	1,090	100.0

With three possible responses, there are nine potential combinations of answers. These are described as follows (the data in this example come from the 2005 Pew Typology Callback survey, though the pattern is similar in other surveys).

Interpreting these is not easy and depends on question order. When the "instead of" question is posed first, respondents who favor the middle ground have a dilemma. They may prefer "teach both" but are forced into giving either a "yes" or "no" answer about *replacing* evolution. Many who want to register their opposition to evolution may select the "instead of" category. They may be surprised that the very next question is asking about "along with" and then may not be sure how to answer. A "yes" would reflect their views, but it would contradict the answer they just gave.

Some survey error is also introduced if the "along with" question is posed first. Staunch anti-evolutionists do not know that, in a few seconds, they will have a chance to say that creationism should replace evolution altogether. When given the chance, they then can register this opinion, too, but they can't go back and then say, "now that I've said 'instead of' can I change my answer to the previous question?" So again, we have the potential for the question format to induce apparently inconsistent answers. Clearly, this contradiction is not salient, as 21.5% answered "yes" to both questions.

Now, the question facing us is whether we can use these two imperfect questions to develop a valid scale. So let us look at the nine possible scores and see if we can combine them into an ordered scale: First, the respondents who answered "no" to both questions belong at one end of the scale. This group is about a quarter of the Pew sample. Next are the individuals who reject "instead of" but are not sure about "along with" (code 92 above). However, this is a tiny group (1.4% in the Pew sample) and is not likely to impact results whether folded in or treated as missing. In general, however, it would be nice to give a score to everyone who answered at least one question rather than throw out information.

After the citizens who are not sure about teaching both are those who affirm their preference for teaching creationism along with evolution but reject the elimination of evolution entirely. And this group would be followed by those who favor teaching both (favor "along with) and are not sure about dropping evolution (code 19). Up until now, the ordering is quite clear. We then come to three categories that

Table A2.2. All response combinations of answers to "along with" and "instead of" questions, ordered for scaling as an ordinal measure

	f	%	New Code
0 Creation only	86	7.9	1
1 Creation Along with and Only	234	21.5	1
91 Instead but DK Along with	17	1.6	1
19 Along with but DK Instead	49	4.5	2
2 Teach both	344	31.6	3
92 Not instead by DK along with	15	1.4	4
3 Evolution only	252	23.1	5
Subtotal		91.5	
Ambiguous:			
29 Not along with but DK Instead	16	1.5	−9
99 DK both	77	7.1	−9
Subtotal		8.5	

Source: See Table A2.1.

may be muddled by question ordering. There are the small number of people who endorse creationism instead of and either reject or are unsure about the equal time proposal (codes 1 and 91, above). There is no doubt that this group lies at the conservative end of the scale. But because of question order, quite a few people in the next group – who said "yes," the most conservative option, to both questions – share their view. Why else would they endorse teaching creationism *instead of* evolution. For our analyses, we will combine these three groups (groups 0, 1, and 91 in the table above). This allows us to classify more than 90% of the respondents in rank order from those most opposed to evolution to those who are most supportive.

The new variable, then, would be as indicated by the numeric scores in the righthand column of Table A2.2.

A2.4: Documentation for Table 2.6

Question wording for items used in analysis of Pew Religion and Public Life data:

a. **Policy preferences:** Teaching scale as described in A2.3.
b. **Beliefs about scientific consensus:**

From what you've heard or read, is there general agreement among scientists that humans evolved over time, or not? [scored yes = 2, no = 1]

A2.5: Documentation for Table 2.7

A. Question wording for items used in analysis of *Newsweek* data:
   a. **Policy preferences:** Teaching scale as described in A2.3
   b. **Beliefs about human origins:**

   Which ONE of the following statements come CLOSEST to your views about the origin and development of human beings (READ 1–3 IN ORDER FOR FORM A; AND IN REVERSE ORDER FOR FORM B): (1) Humans developed over millions of years from less advanced forms of life, but God guided this process [scored 2]; (2) Humans developed over millions of years from less advanced forms of life, but God had NO PART in this process [scored 3]; or (3) God created humans pretty much in the present form at one time within the last 10,000 years or so [scored 1].

   c. **Beliefs about the Bible:**

   Now I have a few questions about the Bible ... Do you believe that every word of the Bible is literally accurate – that the events it describes actually happened, or not? (scored yes = 1, no = 2)

B. Question wording for items used in analysis of VCU Life Sciences data:
   a. **Policy preferences:** Teaching scale as described in A2.1, scored 1–3
   b. **Beliefs about human origins:**

   Which of the following statements comes closest to your views on the origin of biological life: (1) Biological life developed over time from simple substances, but God guided this process [scored 2]; (2) Biological life developed over time from simple substances, but God did not guide this process [scored 3]; (3) God directly created biological life in its present form at one point in time [scored 1].

   c. **Beliefs about the Bible:**

   Which of these statements comes closest to describing your feelings about the Bible: (1) The Bible is the actual word of God [scored 1]; (2) The Bible is the Word of God but not everything in it should be taken literally [scored 2]; or t (3) The

Bible is a book written by men and is not the Word of God [scored 3].

C. Question wording for items used in analysis of Pew Religion and Public Life data:
  a. **Policy preferences:** Teaching scale as described in A2.3.
  b. **Beliefs about human origins** [Pew used a two-question sequence. There were two different versions of the initial, filter question, so that the order of alternatives was randomly assigned]:

  [version 1] Some people think that humans and other living things have evolved over time. Others think that humans and other living things have existed in their present form since the beginning of time [scored 1]. Which of these comes closest to your view?

  [version 2] Some people think that humans and other living things have existed in their present form since the beginning of time [scored 1]. Others think that humans and other living things have evolved over time. Which of these comes closest to your view?

  [Those answering "evolved over time" were then asked the following question, with responses rotated randomly]:

  And do you think that humans and other living things have evolved due to natural processes such as natural selection [scored 3], OR A supreme being guided the evolution of living things for the purpose of creating humans and other life in the form it exists today [scored 2]?

  c. **Beliefs about the Bible:**

  Which of these statements comes closest to describing your feelings about the Bible: (1)The Bible is the actual word of God and is to be taken literally, word for word [scored 1]; (2) The Bible is the word of God, but not everything in it should be taken literally, word for word [scored 2]; or (3) The Bible is a book written by men and is not the word of God [scored 3].

A2.6: Documentation for Table 2.8

Question wording for items used in analysis of CBS/*New York Times* data:

a. **Policy preferences:** Teaching scale as described in A2.3.
b. **Church–state liberalism:** Number of liberal answers given to the following four questions:

> Do you favor or oppose giving federal money to faith-based organizations, such as churches or synagogues, to help them run programs such as drug abuse prevention efforts or childhood development programs? [yes=1, no or DK=0]

> Do you think it is acceptable for a religious organization providing social services with federal funds to try and promote their own religious beliefs at the same time, or is this unacceptable? [yes = 1, no or dk = 0]

> What worries you more – public officials who don't pay enough attention to religion and religious leaders [scored 0], or public officials who are too close to religion and religious leaders [scored 1]?

> Do you think government officials and political appointees who have strong religious beliefs should try to use the political system to turn their religious beliefs into law [scored 0], or shouldn't they do this [scored 1]?

A2.7: Documentation for calculations of opinion purged of random guessing

The gist of this analysis is based on the dual-question format employed by several polling organizations, which allows us to assess the potential impact of completely random guessing. If we assume that the random guessers split 50–50 and then remove this number of respondents from each survey answer, we can then treat the distribution of the remaining answers as the preferences of those with more considered opinions. For example, if 50% of the public were guessing as if flipping a coin and the other 50% had "real," considered opinions, we can easily calculate that 40% of the nonguessers support the *replacement* of evolution with creationism and 88% support the proposal to teach both. Indeed, support for introducing creationism in the schools would necessarily be *greater* among those with considered opinions, and not smaller. This result may seem surprising to some, but it is consistent with what we know about information and policy preferences. Citizens with low levels of education and political knowledge are both more likely to give apparently random answers (Converse 1964) or say they do not know (Berinsky 2002) and, as a result, are less likely to express policy preferences that reflect their values (Althaus 1998). In short, any amount of random guessing will have the effect of suppressing expressed support for creationism in the classroom, not inflating it, leaving our three basic conclusions unchanged.

To get this, we follow the logic of Inglehart (1985). Among the "guessers," we initially subtract the percentage saying "don't know" and then allocate the remainder 50–50 to the "favor" and "oppose" responses. In the July 2005 Pew survey, this leads to 18% of the public supporting the measure by guessing. In the data, there were 38% in favor, so the difference (38 − 18 = 20) must be among the 50% with opinions. Twenty over fifty is 40%.

APPENDIX TO CHAPTER 3

A3.1: Documentation for Table 3.1

Sources and question wording:

University of North Carolina, Southern Focus Poll (2/4/1998–2/24/1998)
[Data acquired from the Odum Institute, University of North Carolina]

Religious tradition was coded by the authors based on the RELTRAD coding scheme developed by Steensland et al. (2000).
Policy preferences are measured by

> Would you generally favor or oppose teaching creation along with evolution in public schools?

A3.2: Documentation for Table 3.2

Sources and question wording:

National Opinion Research Center, General Social Surveys (1993, 1994, 2003, 2004) [Data acquired from the ICPSR, University of Michigan]

Religious tradition was coded by the authors based on the RELTRAD coding scheme developed by Steensland et al. (2000).
Origin beliefs are measured by the GSS variables SCITEST4 (1993, 1994, 2003) and SCITESTY (2004).

For each statement below, just check the box that comes closest to your opinion of how true it is. In your opinion, how true is this?

   d. Human beings developed from earlier species of animals.
1. Definitely true
2. Probably true
3. Probably not true
4. Definitely not true

A3.3: Documentation for Table 3.3

Sources and question wording:

National Opinion Research Center, General Social Surveys (1993, 1994, 2003, 2004) [Data acquired from the ICPSR, University of Michigan]

Verbal cognitive ability is each respondent's score on the Thorndike test of verbal intelligence, GSS variable WORDSUM. This is a composite of ten questions that were preceded by the following introduction:

We would like to know something about how people go about guessing words they do not know. On this card are listed some words–you may know some of them, and you may not know quite a few of them. On each line the first word is in capital letters like BEAST. Then there are five other words. Tell me the number of the word that comes closest to the meaning of the word in capital letters. For example, if the word in capital letters is BEAST, you would say "4" since "animal" comes closer to BEAST than any of the other words. If you wish, I will read the words to you. These words are difficult for almost everyone; just give me your best guess if you are not sure of the answer.

Each question was coded as correct (1) or incorrect (0), and the number of correct answers constitutes the values of WORDSUM.

See A3.2 for question wording for origin beliefs.

A3.4: Documentation for Table 3.4

Sources and question wording:

National Opinion Research Center, General Social Surveys (1993, 1994) [Data acquired from the ICPSR, University of Michigan]

Table A3.1. Percentage of citizens endorsing the teaching of only evolution, estimated by multilevel regression with poststratification

State	Estimate (%)	Margin of Error
Massachusetts	40.6	±7
New York	39.0	±5
Connecticut	39.0	±9
New Jersey	38.5	±6
New Mexico	37.9	±9
Rhode Island	37.7	±11
California	37.4	±4
Iowa	34.9	±7
Colorado	34.8	±7
New Hampshire	34.8	±10
Maine	34.4	±9
Missouri	34.3	±6
Oregon	33.1	±7
Minnesota	33.0	±6
Montana	32.9	±8
Illinois	32.9	±6
Idaho	32.6	±8
Wyoming	32.6	±10
Vermont	32.4	±10
District of Columbia	32.3	±10
Ohio	32.3	±5
Florida	31.8	±4
Washington	31.3	±6
Nevada	30.9	±9
Wisconsin	30.7	±6
Arizona	30.7	±7
Maryland	30.5	±7
Hawaii	29.7	±10
Alaska	29.5	±10
Virginia	29.4	±5
Michigan	29.4	±5
South Dakota	29.3	±9
Arkansas	29.0	±7
Utah	28.6	±8
North Dakota	28.4	±10
Nebraska	28.3	±7
Pennsylvania	28.3	±4
South Carolina	27.8	±7
Georgia	27.6	±5
Texas	27.0	±4
Louisiana	27.0	±6
Delaware	26.9	±9

State	Estimate (%)	Margin of Error
Mississippi	26.3	±7
Kentucky	26.0	±6
Oklahoma	25.7	±6
North Carolina	25.7	±4
West Virginia	25.0	±7
Alabama	24.7	±6
Indiana	24.6	±6
Kansas	24.4	±7
Tennessee	23.3	±5

Scientific literacy is measured as the sum of scores from the following four questions:

For each statement below, just check the box that comes closest to your opinion of how true it is. In your opinion, how true is this?

SCITEST1. All radioactivity is made by humans
SCITEST2. Antibiotics kill bacteria, but not viruses
SCITEST3. Astrology – the study of the star signs – has some scientific truth
SCITEST5. All man-made chemicals cause cancer if you eat enough of them.

The response categories are the same as for SCITEST4, described in section A3.2.
See A3.2 for question wording for origin beliefs.

A3.5: Documentation for Table 3.5

Sources and question wording:

National Opinion Research Center, General Social Surveys (1993, 1994)
[Data acquired from the ICPSR, University of Michigan]

Highest degree earned is based on GSS question DEGREE, a summary based on the following questions:

What is the highest grade in elementary or high school that you finished and got credit for?

If finished 9th–12th grade or dk: Did you ever get a high school diploma or a GED certificate?

Did you complete one or more years of college for credit – not including schooling such as business college, technical, or vocational school?

If YES: How many years did you complete?

Do you have any college degree? (If YES: What degree or degrees?)

See section A3.2 for question wording for origin beliefs.

A3.6 Documentation for Table 3.6

Sources and question wording:

National Opinion Research Center, General Social Surveys (1993, 1994)
[Data acquired from the ICPSR, University of Michigan]

REGION is based on the nine major Census Bureau divisions, using the following classification:

New England: ME, VT, NH, MA, CT, RI
Middle Atlantic: NY, NJ, PA
East North Central: WI, IL, IN, MI, OH
West North Central: MN, IA, MO, ND, SD, NE, KS
South Atlantic: DE, MD, WV, VA, NC, SC, GA, FL, DC
East South Central: KY, TN, AL, MS
West South Central: AR, OK, LA, TX
Mountain: MT, ID, WY, NV, UT, CO, AZ, NM
Pacific: WA, OR, CA, AK, HI

See A3.2 for question wording for origin beliefs.

A3.7 Documentation for Table 3.7

Sources and question wording:

National Opinion Research Center, General Social Surveys (1993, 1994)
[Data acquired from the ICPSR, University of Michigan]
Urban categories based in the GSS variable SRCBELT

> See A3.2 for question wording for origin beliefs.

A3.8 Measuring State Public Opinion

Data sets used for multilevel modeling with imputation and poststratification:

Southern Focus Poll 1998
> $N = 1,257$
> Type of question(s): "Along with" (see Table 2.3)
> Coded 1: Does not favor teaching creationism along with evolution

Gallup Poll 1999
> $N = 1,016$
> Type of question(s): "Along with" and "Instead of" (see Tables 2.2 and 2.3)
> Coded 1: Opposes teaching creationism along with and instead of evolution

CBS/*New York Times* 2004
> $N = 885$
> Type of question(s): "Along with" and "Instead of" (see Tables 2.2 and 2.3)
> Coded 1: Opposes teaching creationism along with and instead of evolution

Newsweek 2004
> $N = 1,099$
> Type of question(s): "Along with" and "Instead of" (see Tables 2.2 and 2.3)

Coded 1: Opposes teaching creationism along with and instead of evolution

Pew Center Typology Callback Poll 2005

$N = 1,090$
Type of question(s): "Along with" and "Instead of" (see Tables 2.2 and 2.3)
Coded 1: Opposes teaching creationism along with and instead of evolution

Pew Center Religion and Public Life Poll 2005

$N = 2,000$
Type of question(s): "Along with" and "Instead of" (see Tables 2.2 and 2.3)
Coded 1: Opposes teaching creationism along with and instead of evolution

Pew Center Religion and Public Life Poll 2006

$N = 996$
Type of question(s): Along with
Values coded 1: Does not favor teaching creationism along with evolution

Harris Interactive Poll 2005

$N = 1,000$
Type of question(s): Single question with multiple options (see Table 2.1)
Values coded 1: Prefers teaching only evolution

Virginia Commonwealth University Life Sciences Survey 2005

$N = 1,002$
Type of question(s): Single question with multiple options (see Table 2.1)
Values coded 1: Prefers teaching only evolution

APPENDIX TO CHAPTER 4

A4.1: Documentation for variables used in Tables 4.1 and 4.2

Rigor of Evolution Standards (source and operationalization are described in the text)

Rigor of General Science Standards (source and operationalization are described in the text)

Administrative capacity of state educational agencies

> This is a composite of two measures derived from the *Digest of Education Statistics 1998*, Table 160 (http://nces.ed.gov/programs/digest/d98/d98t160.asp).
>
> 1. DES_fun_ Admin funds per student (T160)
> 2. DES_fte SEA staff per student

These were standardized and averaged.

Public support for public education

> This is based on Berkman and Plutzer's (2005) measure of "support for public schools." Berkman and Plutzer made small area estimates for public support for increasing spending on public schools for all independent K–12 school districts. We took these estimates and created a weighted average in each state (weighted by the adult population) to generate estimates for each state.

Gross state product per capita 1997

> This is obtained from the State Politics data set maintained by the State Politics and Policy data archive (http://academic.

udayton.edu/SPPQ-TPR/DATASETS/statedata.xls; accessed January 3, 2010).

Public support for teaching evolution only

We describe the construction of this measure in Chapter 3, with additional details in Appendix section A3.8. The actual values can be found in Table A3.1.

APPENDIX TO CHAPTER 5

A5.1: The National Survey of High School Biology Teachers

Sampling methods

The data for this book come from a survey of high school biology teachers conducted between March 5, 2007 and May 1, 2007. More precisely, the data are from two simultaneous studies using identical questionnaires and overlapping sampling frames.

One study was a mail-only study with teachers selected randomly from a database maintained by Quality Education Data. The database contains names and school mailing addresses for more than 80% of public school teachers in the United States. To be eligible for selection, teachers needed to be in a public school that included grades 9 and 10. Each teacher had from one to six job descriptors in the database; to be eligible for selection, at least one descriptor has to be "biology," "life sciences," or "AP biology." This meant that a small number of teachers in our sample identified their primary job function as outside of biology, about 2% identified their primary field as in another science or in science support (e.g., computer lab coordinator), and 12% identified themselves as chair of their high school's science department. Those teachers recruited to teach biology from nonscientific fields were, therefore, eligible for inclusion but comprise a trivial proportion of the sample.

Following the *Tailored Design Method* for mail surveys (Dillman 2000), 500 teachers received a prenotification letter, a survey packet (with a two-dollar bill and postage paid return envelope), a reminder postcard, and a replacement packet. We received 200 completed questionnaires for a return rate of 40%. The second study is based on 1,500 names drawn from a *subset* of the original database based on the availability of a working email address. This allowed us to not only include all features from the first study but also two additional e-mail follow-up reminders. These e-mails included a link to a Web version of the survey, making this survey "multimodal" (Dillman 2000; Mokdad, Stroup, and Giles 2003). A total of 739 respondents completed the multimodal study for a return rate of 49%. Respondents from both surveys are combined in all analyses reported in this paper. After excluding 58 "out of scope" respondents (e.g., bad address, no longer teaching, not a biology teacher), the return rate for the combined data set is 48% (926/1,942).

The response rate is calculated using the formula "RR4" from the American Association for Public Opinion Research's *Standard Definitions: Final Dispositions of Case Codes and Outcome Rates for Surveys, 5th edition* (AAPOR 2008). Based on third-party audits of the reliability of commercially available mailing lists of teachers, we estimate that 5% of the original list of 2,000 (100 mailings) were undeliverable or received by teachers ineligible for the survey. Assuming that all remaining unreturned mailings represent eligible respondents, the overall response rate is estimated as 50%.

Representativeness of the Sample

As noted in the text, the combined data set contains teachers from 49 states (no teachers from Wyoming) and the District of Columbia. For details on weighting, see note 2. All analyses in this book are based on unweighted data.

APPENDIX TO CHAPTER 6

A6.1: Coding state content standards in 2007

Two undergraduates comfortable and familiar with basic biology and evolution were hired to code each state's biology or life sciences standards that applied to grades 9 and 10.[1] On their first pass through the standards, the coders answered four specific questions that were intended to assess the *prominence* of evolution in the curriculum (2 questions), the extent to which evolution served as the or one of several guiding themes, and degree to which standards were sufficiently specific to guide teacher behavior.[2]

On two additional passes through the standards, coders then looked specifically for presence of eleven evolution *benchmarks*. Benchmark analysis identifies "an existing statement of academic content knowledge" (Swanson 2005) and then determines how closely the standards align with that content and we will use these codes to assess the validity of our measure.

Overall Quality

Our coders established the overall prominence of evolution in the life science or biology standards by first looking at whether evolution was mentioned at all in the standards and then the level of detail in its

---

[1] In some states, the standards are for a broader range of grades. In every instance, we coded the most narrow range available that encompassed the ninth or tenth grade general biology class.

[2] After the coders completed their work, one of the principle investigators looked for discrepancies between the two coders. When large discrepancies were found, the PI substituted his independent judgment.

treatment.[3] These codes were then combined into a scale that ranged from a score of 1 for standards that do not mention evolution at all, to a maximum score of 9 for standards that both devote a major, detailed section of the standards to evolution and also mention evolution in other sections of the curriculum (e.g., in sections on ecology or genetics). Intermediate scores reflected coders relative rankings of the level of detail. For example, standards that included a phrase or two, typically in a bullet point, received scores of 2.5, whereas standards that included a short, but stand-alone section on evolution might receive a score of 5. This approach allowed us to distinguish not only between the somewhat easy to code states of New York and Iowa or Illinois, but states like Texas, which also received fairly low scores on this dimension, but not as low as Iowa or Illinois. Texas lists thirteen bullet points of "science concepts"; one of these reads that "the student knows the theory of biological evolution."

Second, the coders evaluated the overall treatment of evolution as the course's unifying theme on a five-point scale. The differences here are quite striking. New York, for example, states clearly that, "The theory is the central unifying theme of biology." New Hampshire introduces its science standards with this statement, different from New York's but still quite strong in its placement of evolution as one of several key topics: "Science theories are not hunches or guesses, but all have been subjected to repeated testing and verification. All scientific theories are subject to change as new evidence comes to be accepted by all scientists. Students should develop an understanding of the basic theories that are foundational in science and which guide scientific understanding." A few current scientific theories are listed: Along with the Cell, the Big Bang, Atomic Theory, and Gravity Theory, we find the Theory of Evolution.

Our coders used a five-point scale to complete the phrase:

Overall, evolution appears to be...

1. The unifying theme for the biology/life sciences curriculum
2. One of several unifying themes for the biology/life sciences curriculum

---

[3] There was high agreement among the coders over whether evolution could be found in the standards at all, and whether it was in its own or in multiple sections ($r = 0.85$); there was somewhat less agreement on the secondary question of whether it could be described as cursory, in a few sentences, or very detailed ($r = 0.53$).

3. A major topic whose treatment is comparable to the cell, heredity, or ecology
4. A smaller topic, given less emphasis than others such as the cell, heredity, or ecology
5. An afterthought or very minor topic

Third, our coders assessed the extent to which the standards left teachers broad discretion to avoid teaching evolution or make it difficult to skip without ignoring the standards altogether. The Iowa standards, for example, certainly do not prohibit a teacher from developing detailed and in-depth lesson plans on evolution. The current standards, in fact, are not far from Iowa's early position as the only state not to develop science standards at all but to leave discretion entirely in the hands of local districts and teachers. Iowa's emphasis is on the scientific process rather than on specific content, which is not at all inconsistent with excellent instruction in all facets of evolutionary theory; in fact, national standards recognize the role evolution can play in teaching what the scientific process is all about. But an Iowa teacher so inclined could also easily skip evolution altogether, and it is this distinction our coders attempted to quantify. For each state they used a 1–4 scale to complete this sentence:

The standards for biology/life sciences as a whole . . .
1. Are sufficiently specific and detailed to ensure that teachers will have to cover evolution
4. Are sufficiently vague that a teacher could choose not to cover evolution at all.

Coders could use the numbers "2" and "3" to introduce intermediate evaluations between these two assessments. Intercoder reliability, as estimated by a simple correlation coefficient, was 0.72.

Overall, the three scores – extent of coverage, treatment as major/unifying theme, specificity in guidance to teachers – are highly correlated, indicating that they are all indicators of the same construct. We created a composite scale that is standardized (mean of 0, standard deviation of 1) and measures the rigor with which evolution is addressed in the state standards. High scores indicate states whose content standards address evolution in detail, identify evolution as a major theme, and provide very specific guidance to teachers on the specific topics that students are expected to learn. The scale has an estimated reliability (Cronbach's alpha) of 0.88.

Scale Validity

Reliability is necessary for a measure to be a valid indicator for the concept of interest, but not all reliable measures are valid (Bohrnstedt 1983). To assess the validity of the scale – to assure that we were capturing the rigor of ninth and tenth grade biology standards – we undertook additional analyses. First, we looked to see if our rankings were positively correlated with Lerner's widely used (2000) ratings. As noted earlier, since Lerner's evaluation, twenty-five states have significantly changed their standards. We defined our measure somewhat differently from Lerner and focus only on a subset of the Lerner's content domain (we focus only on grades 9 and 10, compared with the entire K–12 curriculum, and we do not consult content for the sister disciplines of earth science, physics, and chemistry, focusing only on biology). Nevertheless, a valid measure should share considerable content and should correlate with Lerner's assessments for the twenty-five states in which we are evaluating the same standards document. This is exactly what we find: for the twenty-five states that *did not* change standards between Lerner's coding and ours, the measures correlate at 0.65 (significant at 0.01), whereas the twenty-five states that *did* change are not significantly correlated ($r = 0.24$).[4]

As a second test of our measure's validity, we compare our scores with benchmarks coded by us and independently by other scholars. Benchmark analysis is different – rather than capturing the overall tone, organization, and detail of the standards, it emphasizes particular content that is determined to be important. But the benchmarks are not fully independent of our other coding as it is unlikely any of the standards would be considered especially strong without touching on the content in most benchmark studies.

We identified eleven benchmarks, closely following those used by Swanson (2005) and Skoog and Bilica (2002), both of whom drew

---

[4] Gross (Gross et al. 2005) used a coarse, four-category rating system of standards. In spite of the less precise measurement, the fact that many states had changed their standards, and that our analysis was limited to two grades, we find the two ratings correlated at a level of $r = 0.37$.

heavily on the National Research Council's National Standards for Science Education (1996). Our coders went through all fifty states twice, in random order, and coded a benchmark as "achieved" when either coder determined that the basic benchmark content was present in the standards as something students should learn. The eleven benchmarks are:

1. Species evolve over time
2. Speciation
3. Diversity of organisms from evolution
4. Humans share characteristics with other concurrent living things because of shared ancestors
5. Mutations create the variation that changes an organism's offspring
6. Organisms are classified into a hierarchy of groups and subgroups based on similarities
7. Extinction of species is common
8. Extinction occurs when the environment changes and the adaptive characteristics of a species are insufficient to allow its survival
9. Biological evolution accounts for the diversity of species
10. Behaviors have evolved through natural selection
11. Natural selection and its evolutionary consequences provide a scientific explanation for the fossil record of ancient life forms

Figure A6.1 offers a useful second test of validity by comparing the low, middle, and high thirds of states on our composite measure of rigor with the total number of benchmarks found by our coders, by Swanson, and by Skoog and Bilica. In each case, states ranking higher on our measure also have a larger overall number of benchmarks. We are confident that our measure picks up an important dimension about the quality of standards for students in the ninth and tenth grades.

A6.2: Documentation for Table 6.1

Mean hours devoted to evolution

Teachers selected categories in order to indicate the number of hours devoted to evolution and creationism (see Table 5.1). Using category

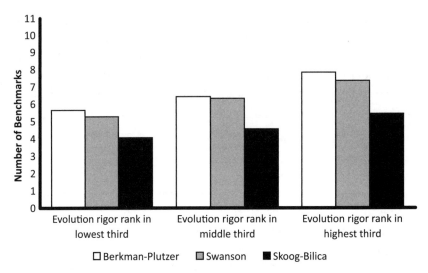

Figure A6.1. Number of evolution benchmarks achieved, by rigor of state evolution standards from lowest to highest third.

midpoints, and assuming a mean of 25 hours for the last category (22 hours and more), we calculated the mean number of hours devoted to each of these three topics.

A6.3: Multilevel Models

A6.3.1 HLM Diagnostics

The top portion of Table A6.1 reports a random intercepts "null model" containing no covariates, and we will begin with the models reported on the left side of the table. The only regression coefficient is the mean intercept, which represents the number of hours of evolution that is taught in the average state, about 14. The bottom portion of Panel A reports the variance components, expressed as standard deviations and identified as σ (the Greek letter "Sigma"). The first describes the variation in state means. A standard deviation of about 2.1 suggests that the states cluster tightly around the national mean, with about two-thirds of the states falling between 12 and 16 hours. We report a significance level for the between state variance component, which is based on a likelihood ratio test of the null hypothesis that σ = 0. If we cannot reject this hypothesis (i.e., if the P value is over 0.05), then multilevel models are not necessary.

Table A6.1. Random intercept, multilevel regression models predicting time devoted to evolution and NAS emphasis scale: null and bivariate models

	Predicting hours of evolution (N = 903)				Predicting NAS endorsement (N = 926)			
	B	SE	t	p	B	SE	t	p
A. Null model								
Intercept	14.00	.45	31.08	.00	54.95	1.24	44.20	.00
Sigma (between states)	2.09	.50		.00	4.60	1.51		.01
Sigma (within states)	8.60	.21			29.04	.69		
Rho (ICC)	.06	.03			.02	.02		
B. Bivariate model								
Standards Index 2007	.89	.41	2.17	.03	2.43	1.12	2.18	.03
Intercept	14.04	.43	32.46	.00	55.09	.01	46.56	.00
Sigma (between states)	1.92	.48		.00	3.99	1.55		.04
Sigma (within states)	8.59	.21			29.03	.69		
Rho (ICC)	.05	.02			.02	.01		

The second variance component describes how teachers vary within each state. We can see that the within state residuals have a standard deviation of about 8.5 hours. The second variance component describes how teachers vary within each state. We can see that the within-state residuals have a standard deviation of about 8.5 hours. The entry labeled ρ (Rho) is the intraclass correlation (usually abbreviated as ICC). This can range from 0 to 1 and tells us the ratio of between-state variance compared to total variance or, in other words, the degree of within state clustering. Although statistically significant, the value of 0.06 is relatively low. In the null model, the value of ρ is analogous to adjusted R^2 in a regression with 49 dummy variables (one representing each state). In other words, the states only account for about 6% of the variance in evolution teaching.

The right of the table reports similar analysis, with the only difference being that the dependent variable is the teacher's score on the NAS emphasis scale. The results appear on the right side of Table A6.1

and do not, however, show a different pattern. The null model shows that almost all of the variation is within-states (SD = 0.29) compared with across-states (SD = 0.05); states account for less than 3% of the total variance across teachers.

A6.3.2 Bivariate HLM models

The model reported immediately below, in Panel B, includes our measure of state standards in 2007 as the only independent variable. The effect of standards is statistically significant but very small in magnitude. The estimated slope of 0.89 tells us that, if states improve their evolution standards enough to go from being the mean state to a state a full standard deviation above average, teachers in that state would be predicted to devote only 1 additional hour to evolution (actually, about 9/10 of an hour). The between state standard deviation has declined from 2.09 to 1.92, and this shows that accounting for state standards only explains a small portion of the interstate difference (in terms of variance, only 16% of the interstate variance is explained by the standards).

The bottom right analysis shows the bivariate multilevel regression of the NAS scale on state standards. It shows that a standard deviation increase in standards would move teachers in the state only 3% up the NAS scale – an effect that is statistically significant but substantively trivial.

A6.3.3 Multivariate multilevel regression models

The results reported in the text of the chapter are based on multilevel regression models. In addition to our measure of standards rigor, these included measures of state testing, teacher seniority, and teacher self-rated expertise. In Table A6.2, we report models that include an objective measure of whether states had an aligned assessment test (derived from Editorial Reports in Education 2007).

Table A6.3 reports otherwise identical models that substitute a teacher's report about his/her state's testing policy in lieu of the objective report. We note that the residual between state variance (3.66) is no longer significantly different from zero in the NAS model ($P = 0.063$). This suggests that accounting for clustering is not necessary

Table A6.2. Random intercept, multilevel regression models assessing the impacts of standards, conditional on teacher seniority and self-rated expertise on hours devoted to evolution

	Predicting hours of evolution (N = 889)			Predicting NAS endorsement (N = 909)		
	B	SE	t	B	SE	t
Standards Index 2007	**.89**	.46	1.91	**3.20**	1.21	2.64
No assessment test	.80	1.03	.78	−.11	2.76	−.04
Standards × No test	−.31	1.39	−.22	−3.02	3.90	−.78
Seniority (centered)	**−.60**	.29	−2.05	−.48	.96	−.50
Standards × Seniority	**−.75**	.26	−2.85	−.92	.86	−1.08
Rate exceptional	**5.50**	.86	6.43	**18.10**	2.83	6.39
Standards × Exceptional	**−1.80**	.81	−2.21	−3.96	2.69	−1.47
Intercept	13.12	.55	23.87	53.82	1.45	37.15
Sigma (between states)	**1.99**	.46		**3.77**	1.54	
Sigma (within states)	8.36	.20		27.98	.67	
Rho (ICC)	.05	.02		.02	.01	

Bold entries are significant in expected direction at .05 level.

Table A6.3. Random intercept, multilevel regression models assessing the impacts of standards, conditional on teacher seniority and self-rated expertise and perceptions of testing

	Predicting hours of evolution (N = 889)			Predicting NAS endorsement (N = 909)		
	B	SE	t	B	SE	t
Standards Index 2007	**1.01**	.49	2.08	**4.46**	1.31	3.40
No assessment test	.99	1.00	.99	−1.03	2.68	−.39
Believes there is no test	−.68	.77	−.88	1.08	2.50	.43
Standards × Believes no test	−.71	.66	−1.08	−4.71	2.10	−2.24
Seniority (centered)	**−.60**	.29	−2.07	−.64	.96	−.67
Standards × Seniority	**−.71**	.27	−2.64	−.45	.88	−.52
Rate exceptional	**5.51**	.86	6.44	**18.07**	2.83	6.40
Standards × Exceptional	**−1.80**	.81	−2.22	−4.03	2.68	−1.51
Intercept	**13.15**	.56	23.50	**53.26**	1.47	36.35
Sigma (between states)	**2.01**	.46		3.66	1.57	
Sigma (within states)	8.35	.20		27.91	.67	
Rho (ICC)	.05	.02		.02	.01	

Bold entries are significant in expected direction at .05 level.

when this particular set of covariates is accounted for in the model. Estimation of the same model by ordinary least squares yields essentially identical conclusions (all estimates have the same sign, same significance, and are all within 0.2 of the MLM estimates) and leads to identical conclusions. For consistency, we use the estimates from the multilevel models throughout this chapter.

REFERENCES

Airasian, Peter. 1988. "Symbolic Validation: The Case of State-Mandated, High-Stakes Testing." *Educational Evaluation and Policy Analysis* 4 (10): 301–313.

Alters, Brian J., and Craig E. Nelson. 2002. "Perspective: Teaching Evolution in Higher Education." *Evolution: International Journal of Organic Evolution* 56 (10): 1891–1901.

Althaus, Scott. 1998. "Information Effects in Collective Preferences." *American Political Science Review* 92 (3): 545–558.

Alwin, Duane F. 1991. "Family of Origin and Cohort Differences in Verbal Ability." *American Sociological Review* 56 (Oct): 625–638.

Alwin, Duane F., and Ryan J. McCammon. 2001. "Aging, Cohorts, and Verbal Ability." *Journal of Gerontology: B Psychological Sciences and Social Sciences* 56 (3): S151–S161.

American Association for the Advancement of Science (AAAS). 1989. "Science for All Americans." http://www.project2061.org/publications/sfaa/online/sfaatoc.htm (accessed February 20, 2008).

American Association for the Advancement of Science (AAAS). 1993. *Benchmarks for Science Literacy*. New York: Oxford University Press.

American Association for Public Opinion Research (AAPOR). "Standard Definitions." http://www.aapor.org/uploads/Standard_Definitions_07_08_Final.pdf (accessed July 2, 2009).

Apple, Michael W., and Anita Oliver. 1996. "Becoming Right: Education and the Formation of Conservative Movements." *Teachers College Record* 97 (3): 419–445.

Archbald, Douglas A., and Andrew C. Porter. 1994. "Curriculum Control and Teachers' Perceptions of Autonomy and Satisfaction." *Educational Evaluation and Policy Analysis* 16 (1): 21–39.

Ayala, Francisco. 2007. *Darwin's Gift to Science and Religion*. Washington, DC: Joseph Henry Press.

Balmer, Randal Herbert. 2002. *Encyclopedia of Evangelicalism*. Louisville, KY: Westminster John Knox Press.

Bandoli, James H. 2008. "Do State Science Standards Matter? Comparing Student Perceptions of the Coverage of Evolution in Indiana and Ohio Public High Schools." *American Biology Teacher* 70 (4): 212–216.

Barber, Benjamin. 1984. *Strong Democracy*. Berkeley: University of California Press.

Barksdale-Ladd, Mary Alice, and Karen F. Thomas. 2000. "What's at Stake in High-Stakes Testing: Teachers and Parents Speak Out." *Journal of Teacher Education* 51 (5): 384–397.

Barrilleaux, Charles. 1999. "Statehouse Bureaucracy: Institutional Consistency in a Changing Environment." In Ronald Weber and Paul Brace, eds. *American State and Local Politics*. New York: Chatham House, pp 97–108.

Barrilleaux, Charles, and Paul Brace. 2007. "Notes from the Laboratories of Democracy: State Government Enactments of Market – and State-Based Health Insurance Reforms in the 1990s." *Journal of Health Politics, Policy and Law* 32 (4): 656–683.

Barrilleaux, Charles, and Mark E. Miller. 1988. "The Political Economy of State Medicaid Policy." *The American Political Science Review* 82 (4): 1089–1107.

Behe, Michael. 1998. *Darwin's Black Box: The Biochemical Challenge to Evolution*. New York: Touchstone.

Behe, Michael William A. Dembski, and Stephen C. Meyer (eds). 2000. *Science and Evidence for Design in the Universe*. San Francisco: Ignatius Press.

Berends, Mark. 2000. "Teacher-reported Effects of New American Schools Design: Exploring Relationships to Teacher Background and School Context." *Education Evaluation and Policy Analysis* 22 (1): 65–82.

Berinsky, Adam. 2002. "Silent Voices: Social Welfare Policy Opinions and Political Equality in America." *American Journal of Political Science* 46 (April): 276–287.

Berkman, Michael B., and Eric Plutzer. 2005. *Ten Thousand Democracies: Politics and Public Opinion in America's School Districts*. Washington, DC: Georgetown University Press.

Berkman, Michael B., and Eric Plutzer. 2009. "Public Opinion and the Teaching of Evolution in the American States." *Perspectives on Politics* 7 (September): 485–500.

Berkman, Michael B., Eric Plutzer, and Julianna Pacheco. 2008. "Evolution and Creationism in America's Classrooms: A National Portrait." *PLoS Biol* 6 (5): e124.

Bianchi, Julie A., and Gregory J. Kelly. 2003. "Challenges of Standards-Based Reform: The Example of California's Science Content and Standards and Textbook Adoption Process." *The entity from which ERIC acquires the content, including journal, organization, and conference names, or by means of online submission from the author. Science Education* 87 (3): 378–389.

Binder, Amy. 2002. *Contentious Curricula: Afrocentrism and Creationism in American Public Schools.* Princeton, NJ: Princeton University Press.

Binder, Amy. 2007. "Gathering Intelligence on Intelligent Design: Where Did It Come From, Where Is It Going, and How Should Progressives Manage It?" *American Journal of Education* 113 (4): 549–576.

Bishop, Beth, and Charles W. Anderson. 1990. "Student Conceptions of Natural Selection and its Role in Evolution." *Journal of Research in Science Teaching Volume* 27 (5): 415–427.

Bishop, George. 2004. *The Illusion of Public Opinion.* Lanham, MD: Rowman and Littlefield.

Bohrnstedt, George W. 1983. "Measurement." In Peter H. Rossi, James D. Wright, and Andy B. Anderson, eds. *Handbook of Survey Research.* New York: Academic Press, pp 69–121, Chapter 3.

Bolce, Louis, and Gerald de Maio. 1999a. "The Anti-Christian Fundamentalist Factor in Contemporary Politics." *Public Opinion Quarterly* 63: 508–542.

Bolce, Louis, and Gerald de Maio. 1999b. "Religious Outlook, Culture War Politics, and Antipathy toward Christian Fundamentalists." *Public Opinion Quarterly* 63: 29–61.

Boyd, Donald, Hamilton Lankford, Susanna Loeb, and James Wykoff. 2005. "The Draw of Home: How Teachers' Preferences for Proximity Disadvantage Urban Schools." *Journal of Policy Analysis and Management* 24 (1): 113–132.

Brace, Paul, Kellie Sims-Butler, Kevin Arceneaux, and Martin Johnson. 2002. "Public Opinion in the American States: New Perspectives Using National Survey Data." *American Journal of Political Science* 46 (Jan): 173–189.

Branch, Glenn, and Eugenie C. Scott. 2009. "The Latest Face of Creationism." *Scientific American* 300 (1): 92–99.

Bray, Gerald. 1996. *Biblical Interpretation: Past and Present.* Leicester: InterVarsity Press.

Brehm, John, and Scott Gates. 1997. *Working, Shirking, and Sabotage: Bureaucratic Response to a Democratic Public.* Ann Arbor: University of Michigan Press.

Bryan, William Jennings. 1924. *Seven Questions in Dispute.* Grand Rapids: Fleming H. Revell.

Budwig, Gilbert. 1930. "Air Regulation." *The Scientific Monthly* 31 (Sept): 241–244.

Campbell, David E. 2006. "Religious 'Threat' in Contemporary Presidential Elections." *Journal of Politics* 68 (1): 104–115.

Carlsen, William S. 1991. "Effects of New Biology Teachers Subject-Matter Knowledge on Curricular Planning." *Science Education* 75 (6): 631–647.

Cohen, David K., and Deborah L. Ball. 1990. "Relations between Policy and Practice: A Commentary." *Educational Evaluation and Policy Analysis* 12 (3): 331–338.

Converse, Philip. 1964. "The Nature of Belief Systems in Mass Publics." In David Apter, ed. *Ideology and Discontent*. New York: Free Press, pp 206–261.

Coyne, J. A. 2006. "Intelligent Design: The Faith That Dare Not Speak Its Name." In J. Brockman, ed. *Intelligent Thought: Science versus the Intelligent Design Movement*. New York: Vintage Books, pp 3–23.

Dahl, Robert A. 1985. *Controlling Nuclear Weapons: Democracy versus Guardianship*. Syracuse, NY: Syracuse University Press.

Dahl, Robert A. 1989. *Democracy and Its Critics*. New Haven: Yale University Press.

Dahl, Robert A. 1990. *After the Revolution: Authority in a Good Society, Revised Edition*. New Haven: Yale University Press.

Dawkins, Richard. "Review of Blueprints: Solving the Mystery of Evolution." *New York Times*, April 9, 1989.

DeLeon, Peter. 1997. *Democracy and the Policy Sciences*. Albany: State University of New York Press.

Delli Carpini, Michael X., and Scott Keeter. 1989. *What Americans Know About Politics and Why It Matters*. New Haven: Yale University Press.

Dennett, Daniel. 2006. "The Hoax of Intelligent Design and How It Was Perpetuated." In J. Brockman, ed. *Intelligent Thought: Science versus The Intelligent Design Movement*. New York: Vintage Books, pp 33–49.

Dillman, Donald. 2000. *Mail and Internet Surveys: The Tailored Design Method*. New York: John Wiley.

Dobzhansky, Theodosius. 1973. "Nothing Makes Sense Except in the Light of Evolution." *American Biology Teacher* 35 (March): 125–129.

Donnelly, Lisa A., and William J. Boone. 2007. "Biology Teachers' Attitudes toward and Use of Indiana's Evolution Standards." *Journal of Research in Science Teaching* 44: 236–257.

Donnelly, Lisa A., and Troy D. Sadler. 2009. "High School Science Teachers' Views of Standards and Accountability." *Science Education Policy* 93: 1050–1075.

Dorit, Robert. 2007. "Biological Complexity." In Andrew J. Petto and Laurie R. Godfrey, eds. *Scientists Confront Intelligent Design and Creationism*. New York: Norton, pp 231–249.

Douglas, Heather. 2005. "Inserting the Public into Science." In Sabine Maasen and Peter Weingart, eds. "Democratization of Expertise? Exploring Novel

Forms of Scientific Advice in Political Decision-Making." *Sociology of the Sciences*, vol. 24. New York: Springer, pp 153–169, Chapter 9.

Dryzek, John S. 1990. *Discursive Democracy*. Cambridge: Cambridge University Press.

Editorial Projects in Education Research Center. 2007. "State of the States." *Quality Counts 2007: From Cradle to Career*. http://www.edweek.org/ew/articles/2007/01/04/17sos.h26.html (accessed July 11, 2007).

Erikson, Robert, Gerald Wright, and John McIver. 1993. *Statehouse Democracy: Public Opinion and Policy in the American States*. Cambridge: Cambridge University Press.

Eve, Raymond, and Francis Harrold. 1991. *The Creationist Movement in Modern America*. Boston: Twayne Publishers.

Finn, Chester E. 2005. "Forward." In Paul R. Gross, with Ursula Goodenough, Susan Haack, Lawrence S. Lerner, Martha Schwartz, and Richard Schwartz. *The State of State Science Standards*. Washington, DC: Thomas B. Fordham Foundation, pp 8–10.

Fischer, Frank. 1993. "Citizen Participation and the Democratization of Policy Expertise: From Theoretical Inquiry to Practical Cases." *Policy Sciences* 26: 165–187.

Fording, Richard C., Joe Soss, and Sanford F. Schram. 2007. "Devolution, Discretion, and the Effect of Local Political Values on TANF Sanctioning." *Social Service Review* 81 (2): 285–316.

Gelman, Andrew, and Thomas C. Little. 1997. "Poststratification into Many Categories Using Hierarchical Logistic Regression." *Survey Methodologist* 23 (Dec): 127–135.

Gieryn, Thomas F. 1983. "Boundary-Work and the Demarcation of Science from Non-Science: Strains and Interests in Professional Ideologies of Scientists." *American Sociological Review* 48 (6): 781–795.

Gieryn, Thomas F., George M. Bevins, and Stephen C. Zehr. 1985. "Professionalization of American Scientists: Public Science in the Creation/Evolution Trials." *American Sociological Review* 50 (3): 392–409.

Ginger, Ray. 1958. *Six Days or Forever: Tennessee v. John Thomas Scopes*. Oxford: Oxford University Press.

Glynn, Carroll J., Susan Herbst, Garrett J. O'Keefe, and Robert Y. Shapiro. 1999. *Public Opinion*. Boulder, CO: Westview Press.

Goldstein, Lisa. 2008. "Kindergarten Teachers Making 'Street-Level' Education Policy in the Wake of No Child Left Behind." *Early Education and Development* 19 (3): 448–478.

Gould, Stephen J. 1981. "Evolution as Fact and Theory." *Discover* 2 (May): 34–37.

Gould, Stephen J. 1997. "Nonoverlapping Magisteria." *Natural History* 106 (March): 16–22.

Gray, Virginia. 1979. "Anti-evolution Sentiment and Behavior: The Case of Arkansas." *Journal of American History* 52: 352–366.

Griffith, Joyce A., and Sara K. Brem. 2004. "Teaching Evolutionary Biology: Pressures, Stress, and Coping." *Journal of Research in Science Teaching* 41 (8): 791–809.

Griffiths, José-Marie, and Donald W. King. 2008. *Interconnections: The IMLS National Study on the Use of Libraries, Museums and the Internet, Museum Survey Results*. Washington, DC: Institute of Museum and Library Services.

Gross, Paul R., Ursula Goodenough, Susan Haack, Lawrence S. Lerner, Martha Schwartz, and Richard Schwartz. 2005. *The State of State Science Standards*. Washington, DC: Thomas B. Fordham Foundation.

Groves, Robert M., Floyd Fowler, Mick P. Couper, James M. Lepkowski, Eleanor Singer, and Roger Tourangeau. 2004. *Survey Methodology*. New York: John Wiley.

Gusfield, Joseph. 1963. *Symbolic Crusade: Status Politics and the American Temperance Movement*. Urbana: University of Illinois Press.

Habermas, Jurgen. 1994. "Three Normative Models of Democracy." *Constellations* 1 (1): 1–10.

Harmon, Amy. "A Teacher on the Front Line as Faith and Science Clash." *New York Times*, August 23, 2008. http://www.nytimes.com/2008/08/24/education/24evolution.html (accessed December 19, 2009).

Higgins, John M. 2000. "Speaking of Dinosaurs: Discovery Channel Ratings Set Season Record." *Broadcasting and Cable*. http://findarticles.com/p/articles/mi_hb5053/is_/ai_n18377535 (accessed October 29, 2008).

Humes, Edward. 2007. *Monkey Girl: Evolution, Education, Religion, and the Battle for America's Soul*. New York: Ecco Press.

Iannaccone, Laurence, and Frank W. Lutz. 1995. "The Crucible of Democracy: The Local Arena." In Jay D. Scribner and Donald H. Layton, eds. *The Study of Educational Politics: The 1994 Commemorative Yearbook of the Politics of Education Association*. Washington, DC: The Falmer Press, pp 39–52.

Illinois State Board of Education. "Science – State Goal 12: Understand the Fundamental Concepts, Principles and Interconnections of the Life, Physical and Earth." http://www.isbe.net/ils/science/pdf/goal12.pdf (accessed December 22, 2009).

Inglehart, Ronald. 1985. "Aggregate Stability and Individual-Level Flux in Mass Belief Systems: The Level of Analysis Paradox." *American Political Science Review* 79 (1): 97–116.

Ingram, Ella L., and Craig E. Nelson. 2006. "Relationship between Achievement and Students' Acceptance of Evolution or Creation in an Upper-Level Evolution Course." *Journal of Research in Science Teaching* 43 (1): 7–24.

Iowa Department of Education. "Core Content Standards and Benchmarks Corresponding to the Iowa Tests." http://www.iowa.gov/educate/index2 .php?option=com_docman&task=doc_view&gid=1098&Itemid= 99999999 (accessed July 5, 2009).

Jacobs, Joanne. 2006. *It Takes a Vision: How Three Great States Created Great Academic Standards*. Washington, DC: Thomas Fordham Foundation. http://www.edexcellence.net/doc/It%20Takes%20a%20Vision.pdf (accessed July 3, 2009).

Jacobs, Lawrence R., and Robert Y. Shapiro. 2000. *Politicians Don't Pander: Political Manipulation and the Loss of Democratic Responsiveness*. Chicago: University of Chicago Press.

Jones, Bryan. 2001. *Politics and the Architecture of Choice*. Chicago: University of Chicago Press.

Jones, Dale E., Sherry Doty, Clifford Grammich, James E. Horsch, Richard Houseal, Mac Lynn, John P. Marcum, Kenneth M. Sanchagrin, and Richard H. Taylor. 2002. *Religious Congregations and Membership in the United States 2000: An Enumeration by Region, State and County Based on Data Reported for 149 Religious Bodies*. Nashville: Glenmary Research Center.

Keiser, Lael R. 1999. "State Bureaucratic Discretion and the Administration of Social Welfare Programs: The Case of Social Security Disability." *Journal of Public Administration Research and Theory* 9 (1): 87–106.

Keiser, Lael. 2010. "Understanding Street-Level Bureaucratic Decision Making: Determining Eligibility in the Social Security Disability Program." *Public Administration Review* 70 (2): 247–257.

Keiser, Lael R., and Joe Soss. 1998. "With Good Cause: Bureaucratic Discretion and the Politics of Child Support Enforcement." *American Journal of Political Science* 42 (4): 1133–1156.

Kish, Leslie. 1965. *Survey Sampling*. New York: John Wiley.

Kvaal, Steven A., Edward J. Wygonik, Aris Spanos, and Sarah A. Landsberger. 2001. "A Revalidation of the Thurstone Test of Mental Alertness as a Brief Measure of Intelligence through Comparison with the Wechsler Adult Intelligence Scale-III." *Psychological Reports* 88 (April): 581–586.

Labov, Jay. 2006. "National and State Standards in Science and Their Potential Influence on Undergraduate Science Education." *CBE Life Sciences Education* 5 (3): 204–209.

Larson, Edward J. 1989. *Trial and Error: The American Controversy over Creation and Evolution, updated edition*. Oxford: Oxford University Press.

Larson, Edward. 1997. *Summer of the Gods: The Scopes Trial America's Continuing Debate Over Science and Religion*. New York: Basic Books.

Larson, Edward J. 2003. *Trial and Error: The American Controversy over Creation and Evolution, 3rd edition*. Oxford: Oxford University Press.

Lawson, Antono E., and John Weser. 1990. "The Rejection of Nonscientific Beliefs about Life: Effects of Instruction and Reasoning Skills." *Journal of Research in Science Teaching* 27 (6): 589–606.

Lax, Jeffrey R., and Justin H. Phillips. 2009. "How Should We Estimate Public Opinion in the States?" *American Journal of Political Science* 53 (1): 107–121.

Layman, Geoffrey C., and Thomas M. Carsey. 2002. "Party Polarization and 'Conflict Extension' in the American Electorate." *American Journal of Political Science* 46 (4): 786–802.

Leichter, Howard. 1996. "State Governments and Their Capacity for Health Reform." In R. F. Rich and W. D. White, eds. *Health Policy, Federalism, and the American States*. Washington, DC: Urban Institute, pp 151–179.

Lerner, Lawrence. 2000a. "Good and Bad Science in US Schools." *Nature* 407: 287–290.

Lerner, Lawrence. 2000b. *Good Science, Bad Science: Teaching Evolution in the States*. Washington, DC: Thomas B. Fordham Foundation.

Lewontin, Richard C. 1981. "Evolution/Creation Debate: A Time for Truth." *Bioscience* 31 (8): 559.

Lienesch, Michael. 2007. *In the Beginning: Fundamentalism, the Scopes Trial, and the Making of the Antievolution Movement*. Chapel Hill: University of North Carolina Press.

Lincoln, C. Eric, and Lawrence H. Mamiya. 1990. *The Black Church in the African American Experience*. Durham, NC: Duke University Press.

Lippmann, Walter. 1927. *Men of Destiny*. New York: MacMillan.

Lipsky, Michael. 1980. *Street-Level Bureaucracy: Dilemmas of the Individual in Public Services*. New York: Russell Sage Foundation.

Lodge, Milton, Marco Steenbergen, and Shawn Brau. 1995. "The Responsive Voter: Campaign Information and the Dynamics of Candidate Evaluation." *American Political Science Review* 89 (June): 309–326.

Lohr, Sharon L. 1999. *Sampling: Design and Analysis*. New York: Duxbury.

Manna, Paul. 2004. "Management, Control, and the Challenge of Leaving No Child Behind." Paper presented at the Annual Meeting of the Midwest Political Science Association, Chicago, IL.

Manna, Paul, and Diane O'Hara. 2005. "State Governance and Educational Outcomes in the United States." Paper presented at the Annual Meeting of the Midwest Political Science Association, Chicago, IL.

Manza, Jeff, and Fay Lomax Cook. 2002. "A Democratic Polity? Three Views of Policy Responsiveness to Public Opinion in the United States." *American Politics Research* 30 (6): 630–667.

Marsden, George M. 1982. *Fundamentalism and American Culture: The Shaping of Twentieth Century Evangelicalism 1870–1925*. Oxford: Oxford University Press.

Maynard-Moody, Steven, and Michael Musheno. 2003. *Cops, Teachers, Counselors*. Ann Arbor: University of Michigan Press.

McCubbins, Mathew D., Roger Noll, and Barry R. Weingast. 1987. "Administrative Procedures as Instruments of Political Control." *Journal of Law, Economics, and Organization* 3 (2): 243–277.

McDermott, Kathryn A. 1999. *Controlling Public Education: Localism versus Equity*. Lawrence: University Press of Kansas.

McNeil, Michele. 2009. "46 States Agree to Common Academic Standards Effort." *Education Week*, June 8, 2009, online edition. http://www.edweek.org/ew/articles/2009/06/01/33standards.h28.html (accessed June 26, 2009).

Meier, Kenneth J. 1975. "Representative Bureaucracy: An Empirical Analysis." *American Political Science Review* 69 (2): 526–542.

Meier, Kenneth J. 1993. "Latinos and Representative Bureaucracy Testing the Thompson and Henderson Hypotheses." *Journal of Public Administration and Theory* 3 (4): 393–414.

Meier, Kenneth J., and John Bohte. 2001. "Structure and Discretion: Missing Links in Representative Bureaucracy." *Journal of Public Administration and Theory* 11 (4): 455–470.

Meier, Kenneth J., and Laurence J. O'Toole, Jr. 2006. *Bureaucracy in a Democratic State: A Governance Perspective*. Baltimore: Johns Hopkins.

Meyers, Marcia K., and Susan Vorsanger. 2003. "Street-Level Bureaucrats and the Implementation of Public Policy." In B. Guy Peters and Jon Pierre, eds. *Handbook of Public Administration*. New York: Sage Publications, pp 245–259.

Miller, Jon D. 1998. "The Measurement of Civic Scientific Literacy." *Public Understanding of Science* 7: 203–223.

Miller, Jon D. 2004. "Public Understanding of, and Attitudes toward, Scientific Research: What We Know and What We Need to Know." *Public Understanding of Science* 13 (3): 273–294.

Miller, Jon D. 2006. "Civic Scientific Literacy in Europe and the United States." Paper presented to the annual meeting of the World Association for Public Opinion Research, Montreal, Canada, May 17, 2006.

Miller, Jon D., Eugenie C. Scott, and Shinji Okamoto. 2006. "Public Acceptance of Evolution." *Science* 313: 765–766.

Miller, Kenneth R. 2000. *Finding Darwin's God: A Scientist's Search for Common Ground between God and Evolution*. New York: Harper.

Miller, Kenneth R. 2008. *Only a Theory: Evolution and the Battle for America's Soul*. New York: Viking.

Miner, John B. 1957. *Intelligence in the United States*. New York: Springer.

Mokdad, Ali, Donna F. Stroup, and Wayne H. Giles. 2003. "Public Health Surveillance for Behavioral Risk Factors in Changing Environment

Recommendations from the Behavioral Risk Factor Surveillance Team." *MMWR Recommendations and Reports* 52 (May): 1–12.

Monastersky, Richard. 2008. "Creationism Persists in American Science Classrooms." *The Chronicle of Higher Education*, May 20, 2008. http://chronicle.com/ (accessed December 20, 2009).

Mooney, Christopher. 1999. "The Politics of Morality Policy: Symposium Editor's Introduction." *Policy Studies Journal* 27 (4): 675–680.

Mooney, Christopher. 2000. "The Decline of Federalism and the Rise of Morality-Policy Conflict in the United States." *Publius* 30 (1–2): 171–188.

Mooney, Christopher, and Mei-Hsien Lee. 2000. "The Influence of Values on Consensus and Contentious Morality Policy: U.S. Death Penalty Reform, 1956–82." *Journal of Politics* 62 (1): 223–239.

Moore, David W. 2008. *The Opinion Makers: An Insider Exposes the Truth about Polls*. Boston: Beacon Press.

Moore, Randy. 2002a. *Evolution in the Courtroom*. Santa Barbara: ABC-CLIO.

Moore, Randy. 2002b. "Teaching Evolution: Do State Standards Matter?" *BioScience* 52 (4): 378–381.

Moore, Randy, and Karen Kraemer. 2005. "The Teaching of Evolution and Creationism in Minnesota." *American Biology Teacher* 67: 457–466.

Mosher, Frederick C. 1982. *Democracy and the Public Service, 2nd edition*. New York: Oxford University Press.

National Academy of Sciences (NAS). 1998. *Teaching About Evolution and the Nature of Science*. Washington, DC: Steering Committee on Science and Creationism, National Academy Press.

National Academy of Sciences (NAS). 1999. *Science and Creationism: A View from the National Academy of Sciences*. Washington, DC: National Academy Press.

National Academy of Sciences (NAS). 2008a. *Science, Evolution and Creationism*. Washington, DC: National Academy Press.

National Academy of Sciences (NAS). 2008b. "Scientific Evidence Supporting Evolution Continues to Grow." Press release issued by National Academy of Sciences and the Institute of Medicine, Washington, DC, January 3, 2008.

National Center for Science Education. 2002. "Ohio's Draft Standards Earn an A from National Science Standards Expert." http://ncseweb.org/news/2002/03/ohios-draft-standards-earn-from-national-science-standards-e-00311 (accessed July 3, 2009).

National Center for Science Education. 2008. "Antievolution Resolutions Spreading Through Northern Florida." http://ncseweb.org/news/antievolution-resolutions-spreading-through-northern-florida (accessed July 3, 2009).

National Research Council. 1996. *National Science Education Standards.* Washington, DC: National Academy Press.

National Science Board. 1982. *Today's Problems: Tomorrow's Crises.* Washington, DC: U.S. Government Printing Office.

National Science Teachers Association. 1992. *Scope, Sequence, and Coordination of Secondary School Science.* Washington, DC: National Science Teachers Association.

National Science Teachers Association. 2003. "NSTA Position Statement: The Teaching of Evolution." http://www.nsta.org/about/positions/evolution.aspx (accessed November 15, 2008).

Nelkin, Dorothy. 1982. *The Creation Controversy: Science or Scripture in the Schools.* New York: Norton.

New York State Education Department. "The Living Environment: Core Curriculum." http://www.emsc.nysed.gov/ciai/mst/pub/livingen.pdf (accessed December 22, 2009).

Norrander, Barbara. 2001. "Measuring State Public Opinion with the Senate National Election Study." *State Politics and Politics Quarterly* 1 (1): 111–125.

Numbers, Ronald. 1992. *The Creationists: The Evolution of Scientific Creationism.* New York: Knopf.

Numbers, Ronald. 2006. *The Creationists: From Scientific Creationism to Intelligent Design (expanded edition).* Cambridge, MA: Harvard University Press.

Ohio Department of Education. "Ohio K-12 Academic Content Standards, Science, 2002." http://www.ode.state.oh.us/GD/DocumentManagement/DocumentDownload.aspx?DocumentID=733 (accessed April 7, 2010).

Olson, Lynn. 1998. "An 'A' or a 'D': State Rankings Differ Widely." *Education Week*, April 15, 1998. http://www.edweek.org/ (accessed December 19, 2009).

Pacheco, Julianna Sandell. 2008. "Dynamic Public Opinion across the States." Paper presented at the annual State Politics and Policy Conference, Philadelphia, PA, May 30–31, 2008.

Page, Benjamin I., and Robert Y. Shapiro. 1992. *The Rational Public: Fifty Years of Trends in Americans' Policy Preferences.* Chicago: University of Chicago Press.

Paley, William. 1986. *Natural Theology: Evidences of the Existence and Attributes of the Deity. Collected from the Appearances of Nature.* Lincoln-Rembrandt Pub., 12th edition (Originally published 1809).

Park, David K., Andrew Gelman, and Joseph Bafumi. 2006. "State-Level Opinions from National Surveys: Poststratification Using Multilevel Logistic Regression." In Jeffrey E. Cohen, ed. *Public Opinion in State Politics.* Stanford, CA: Stanford University Press, pp 209–228.

Peffley, Mark, and Jon Hurwitz. 1985. "A Hierarchical Model of Attitude Constraint." *American Journal of Political Science* 29 (4): 871–890.

People for the American Way (PFAW). 2000. *Evolution and Creationism in Public Education: An In-depth Reading of Public Opinion.* Washington, DC: PFAW.

Percival, Garrick L., Martin Johnson, and Max Neiman. 2009. "Representation and Local Policy: Relating County-Level Public Opinion to Policy Outputs." *Political Research Quarterly* 62 (March): 164–177.

Pew Internet and American Life Project. 2006. *The Internet as a Resource for News and Information about Science.* Washington, DC: Pew Internet and American Life Project.

Placier, Margaret, Michael Walker, and Bill Foster. 2002. "Writing the 'Show-Me' Standards: Teacher Professionalism and Political Control in U.S. State Curriculum Policy." *Curriculum Inquiry* 32 (3): 281–310.

Plutzer, Eric, and Michael B. Berkman. 2008. "Evolution, Creationism, and the Teaching of Human Origins in Schools." *Public Opinion Quarterly* 72 (3): 540–553.

Ravitch, Diane. 1996. "50 States, 50 Standards: The Continuing Need for National Voluntary Standards in Education." The Brookings Institution, http://www.brookings.edu/articles/1996/summer_education_ravitch.aspx?rssid=k+12+education (accessed February 23, 2009).

Reenock, Christopher, and Brian Gerber. 2008. "Information Exchange and Interest Group Enfranchisement through Agency Design." *Journal of Public Administration Research and Theory* 18 (3): 415–440.

Rennie, John. 1999. "A Total Eclipse of Reason." *Scientific American* 281 (Oct): 124.

Ruse, Michael. 2005. *The Evolution-Creation Struggle.* Cambridge: Harvard University Press.

Ruse, Michael, and Joseph Travis. 2009. *Evolution: The First Four Billion Years.* Cambridge: Belknap Press of Harvard University Press.

Rutledge, Michael L., and Melissa A. Mitchell. 2002. "Knowledge Structure, Acceptance and Teaching of Evolution." *American Biology Teacher* 64 (1): 21–28.

Rutledge, Michael L., and Melissa A. Warden. 2000. "Evolutionary Theory, the Nature of Science and High School Biology Teachers: Critical Relationships." *American Biology Teacher* 62 (1): 23–31.

Sabatier, Paul A., John Loomis, and Catherine McCarthy. 1995. "Hierarchical Controls, Professional Norms, Local Constituencies, and Budget Maximization: An Analysis of U.S. Forest Service Planning Decisions." *American Journal of Political Science* 39 (Feb): 204–242.

Sarfati, Jonathan. 2008. *Refuting Evolution.* Atlanta: Creation Book Publishers.

Sarfati, Jonathan, 2009. "Response to the Latest Anticreationist Agitprop from the US National Academy of Sciences (NAS), Science, Evolution and Creationism."Creation Ministries International, http://creationontheweb .com/content/view/5620/ (accessed February 17, 2009).

Scholz, John T., and FengHeng Wei. 1986. "Regulatory Enforcement in a Federalist System." *American Political Science Review* 80 (Dec): 1249–1270.

Scott, Eugenie C. 1994. "The Evolution of Creationism: The Struggle for the Schools." *Natural History* 103 (10): 12–13.

Scott, Eugenie C. 2006. "The Once and Future Intelligent Design." In Eugenie C. Scott and Glenn Branch, eds. *Not in Our Classrooms: Why Intelligent Design Is Wrong for Our Schools*. Boston: Beacon Press, Chapter 1.

Scott, Eugenie. 2009. "American Antievolutionism: Retrospect and Prospect." In Michael Ruse and Joseph Travis, eds. *Evolution: The First Four Billion Years*. Cambridge: Belknap Press of Harvard University Press, pp 370–400.

Sharp, Elaine. 2002. "Culture, Institutions, and Urban Officials' Responses to Morality Issues." *Political Research Quarterly* 55 (4): 861–883.

Skoog, Gerald. 1979. "The Topic of Evolution in Secondary School Biology Textbooks 1900–1977." *Science Education* 63: 621–640.

Skoog, Gerald, and Kimberly Bilica. 2002. "The Emphasis Given to Evolution in State Science Standards: A Lever for Change in Evolution Education?" *Science Education* 86 (4): 445–462.

Smith, Christian. 1998. *American Evangelicalism: Embattled and Thriving*. Chicago: University of Chicago Press.

Smith, Kevin B. 2002. "Typologies, Taxonomies and the Benefits of Policy Classification." *Policy Studies Journal* 30 (3): 379–395.

Smith, Steven Rathgeb. 2003. "Street Level Bureaucracy and Public Policy." In B. Guy Peters and Jon Pierre, eds. *Handbook of Public Administration*. New York: Sage Publications, pp 354–376.

Smith, Tom W. 1990. "Classifying Protestant Denominations." *Review of Religious Research* 31 (3): 224–245.

Soss, Joe. 2000. *Unwanted Claims: The Politics of Participation in the U.S. Welfare System*. Ann Arbor: University of Michigan Press.

Spillane, James P. 1998. "State Policy and the Non-Monolithic Nature of the Local School District: Organizational and Professional Considerations." *American Educational Research Journal* 35 (1): 33–63.

Spillane, James P., and Karen A. Callahan. 2000. "Implementing State Standards for Science Education: What District Policy Makers Make of the Hoopla." *Journal of Research in Science Teaching* 37 (5): 401–425.

Spillane, James P., Brian J. Reiser, and Todd Reimer. 2002. "Policy Implementation and Cognition: Reframing and Refocusing Implementation Research." *Review of Educational Research* 72 (3): 387–431.

Steensland, Brian, Jerry Z. Park, Mark D. Regnerus, Lynn D. Robinson, W. Bradford Wilcox, and Robert D. Woodberry. 2000. "The Measure of American Religion: Toward Improving the State of the Art." *Social Forces* 79 (1): 291–318.

Stodolsky, Susan S. and Pamela L. Grossman 1995. "The Impact of Subject Matter on Curricular Activity: An Analysis of Five Academic Subjects." *American Educational Research Journal* 32 (2): 227–249.

Swanson, Christopher B. 2005. "Evolution in State Science Education Standards." *Education Week Editorial Reports in Education Research Center.* http://www.edweek.org/media/epe_evolution1105.pdf (accessed July 9, 2009).

Tatina, R. 1989. "South Dakota High School Biology Teachers and the Teaching of Evolution and Creationism." *American Biology Teacher* 51 (5): 275–280.

"Texas Two Step." *New York Times*, January 26, 2009, editorial, New York edition. http://www.nytimes.com/2009/01/26/opinion/26mon3.html (accessed February 19, 2009).

Thorndike, Robert L. 1942. "Two Screening Tests of Verbal Intelligence." *Journal of Applied Psychology* 26 (2): 128–135.

Thorndike, Robert L., and George H. Gallup. 1944. "Verbal Intelligence of the American Adult." *Journal of General Psychology* 30 (Jan): 75–85.

Tiebout, Charles. 1956. "A Pure Theory of Local Expenditures." *Journal of Political Economy* 64 (5): 416–424.

Timar, Thomas. 1997. "The Institutional Role of State Education Departments: A Historical Perspective." *American Journal of Education* 105 (3): 231–260.

Travis, Joseph, and David N. Reznik. 2009. "Adaptation." In Michael Ruse and Joseph Travis, eds. *Evolution: The First Four Billion Years*. Cambridge: Harvard University Press, pp 105–131.

Utah State Office of Education. "Utah Science Core Curriculum Earth Systems Science, Biology, Physics and Chemistry." http://www.uen.org/core/ txFile.do?courseNum=3520&fname=Science3520Biology.pdf (accessed December 22, 2009).

Weatherley, Richard, and Michael Lipsky. 1978. "Street-Level Bureaucrats and Institutional Innovation: Implementing Special Education Reform." *Harvard Educational Review* 47 (May): 171–197.

Weissert, Carol S. 1994. "Beyond the Organization: The Influence of Community and Personal Values on Street-Level Bureaucrats' Responsiveness." *Journal of Public Administration Research and Theory* 4 (2): 225–254.

Whitford, Andrew. 2002. "Decentralization and Political Control of the Bureaucracy." *Journal of Theoretical Politics* 14 (2): 167–193.

Wilcox, Clyde. 1986. "Fundamentalists and Politics: An Analysis of the Effects of Differing Operational Definitions." *Journal of Politics* 48 (4): 1041–1051.

Wilson, David Sloan. 2005. "Evolution for Everyone: How to Increase Acceptance of, Interest in, and Knowledge about Evolution." *PLoS Biology* 3 (12): e364: 2058–2064.

Wilson, James Q. 1989. *Bureaucracy: What Government Agencies Do and Why They Do It.* New York: Basic Books.

Wong, Kenneth. 1995. "The Politics of Education: From Political Science to Multidisciplinary Inquiry." In Jay D. Scribner and Donald H. Layton, eds. *The Study of Educational Politics: The 1994 Commemorative Yearbook of the Politics of Education Association.* Washington, DC: The Falmer Press, pp 21–38.

Woodberry, Robert D., and Christian S. Smith. 1998. "Fundamentalism et al.: Conservative Protestants in America." *Annual Review of Sociology* 24: 25–56.

Zaller, John. 1992. *The Nature and Origins of Mass Opinion.* Cambridge: Cambridge University Press.

Zaller, John, and Stanley Feldman. 1992. "A Simple Theory of the Survey Response: Answering Questions versus Revealing Preferences." *American Journal of Political Science* 36 (3): 579–616.

JUDICIAL OPINIONS AND COURT CASES CITED

Edwards v. Aguillard. 1987. 482 U.S. 578.

Epperson v. Arkansas. 1968. 393 U.S. 97.

Kitzmiller v. Dover. 2005. 400 F. Supp. 2d 707 (M.D. Pa 2005).

LeVake v. Independent School District #656. 2001. (625 N.W. 2d 502 Ed. Law Rep. 356).

McLean v. Arkansas Board of Education. 1982. 529 F. Supp. 1255.

Segraves v. The California State Board of Education. 1981. Sacramento Superior Court #278978.

Roe v. Wade. 1973. 410 U.S. 113.

Scopes v. The State. 1927. 152 Tenn. 424.

Tennessee v. Scopes. 1925.

INDEX

Abortion controversy, 98
Academic freedom argument
  creationist use of, 23, 23n, 226
  legitimization of historically, 18
  overview, 7, 13
Aguillard, Edwards v. See Edwards v.
  Aguillard
Alabama
  content standards in, 107n, 155–156
  doctrinally conservative Protestants in,
    88
  percentage of public supporting the
    teaching of evolution in, 85–87,
    240t
Alaska
  budget per student, 107n
  percentage of public supporting the
    teaching of evolution in,
    240t
  student-teacher ratio, 107n
American Association for the Advancement
  of Science, 2, 99–100
Anti-evolutionism. *See also specific cases*
  basis of, 10–11
  Cold War period history, 17–18
  early history of, 16–17
  Federal court rulings on, 19–21,
    25f
  as fundamentalist social movement, 53,
    64–66
Anti-evolutionists
  cognitive ability in, 75, 76t, 77, 239
  formal education in, 78–79, 79t
  scientific literacy, 77–78, 78t, 239–241
    (*See also* Scientific literacy of general
    public)
  stereotypes, 75

Arizona
  content standards in, 155–156
  percentage of public supporting the
    teaching of evolution in, 240t
  testing standards in, 164–165
Arkansas
  anti-evolution legislation in, 16
  balanced treatment textbooks in,
    17–18
  Bill 590, 19–20
  doctrinally conservative Protestants in,
    88
  percentage of public supporting the
    teaching of evolution in, 240t
  public opinion poll data, 80–81
Arkansas, Epperson v. See Epperson v.
  Arkansas
Arkansas, McLean v. See McLean v.
  Arkansas
Assortative hiring, 195–197, 198t, 201,
  222
Atheist-agnostic opinions, poll data, 71,
  72t, 73t, 75
Attitudes, hierarchical, 53

Balanced treatment (equal-time proposals)
  instructional time allocation data, 140,
    231t, 233t
  National Survey of High School Biology
    Teachers data, 137t, 138t, 140,
    190, 190t
  public opinion data, 33, 36–40
  textbooks, rewriting of, 19–20, 23n
Ball, D. L., 166
Bandoli, J. H., 150
Barksdale-Ladd, M.-A., 161
Belief system approach, 143

277